Good
Reasons

Steps to Writing an Argument

The cover of this book makes a visual argument about genetically modified food. Use these steps to develop your own arguments about food or other topics in the book.

Step 1 Find a Topic

Read your assignment and determine what type of argument is called for (see pages 25–26).

Find a topic that interests you by reading, talking, and exploring (see pages 23–34).

Step 2 Make a Claim and Support It with Good Reasons

Make a claim designed to change readers' views or persuade them to take action.

List your main points and think about the order of those points.

Step 3 Think About What's at Stake

What exactly is the problem or issue, what causes it, and who is most affected?

Has anyone tried to do anything about it? If so, why haven't they succeeded?

Step 4 Analyze Your Potential Readers

Who are your readers?

How familiar will they be with what you are arguing?

Which claims are they most likely to accept and which will they disagree with?

Step 5 Write a Draft

Introduction

Set out the issue or problem, and give some background if necessary.

Argue for the seriousness of the issue or problem.

Give your thesis in one sentence.

Body

Present and interpret your evidence and its significance.

Keep your focus narrow and make your structure clear to your readers.

If you are proposing a solution to a problem, state your solution and its benefits.

Take a few minutes to think about other views on your issue or problem.

Conclusion

Leave your readers with something interesting and provocative.

Issue a call to action—if your readers agree with you, they will want to take action.

Step 6 Revise, Edit, Proofread

For detailed instructions, see Chapter 4.

For a checklist to use to evaluate your draft, see pages 48–49.

Why Do You Need This New Edition?

If you're wondering why you should buy this new edition of *Good Reasons*, here are six great reasons!

1. Looking for help with **critical reading** and analyzing arguments? Chapter 2 and 5 have great new material on "mapping" an argument as a way to understand it, on exploring multiple points of view, and on writing an analysis paper.

2. Would you like a clear and simple overview of the steps you should follow when writing an argument? See the revised, at-a-glance design of the **step-by-step writing guides** in Chapter 8–13.

3. Do you like to look at model papers to see how other students tackle an assignment? See the new, updated, and **fully annotated sample papers** in Chapter 2, 5, 6, 7, 8, 9, 10, 12, 13, and 20.

4. Want some help coming up with good ideas for argument papers? New and updated **"Finding Good Reasons"** assignments in Parts 1 and 3 provide topics and short writing tasks that will help kick-start your thinking about your own assignments.

5. Are you being asked to develop visual and multimedia texts in your course? Chapter 14 and 15, on designing and presenting your work, have been completely revised and include **new help with multimedia assignments** and advice for how to best communicate with words, images and graphics.

6. Would it be helpful to see a quick snapshot of each chapter? New **"Quick Take" features** at the beginning of each chapter give you a brief overview of the key points covered in the chapter.

Good Reasons gets even better when used with **Pearson's MyCompLab**—the gateway to a world of online resources and to an **interactive eText version of *Good Reasons*** developed specifically for you!

Good Reasons

Researching and Writing Effective Arguments

FIFTH EDITION

Lester Faigley

University of Texas at Austin

Jack Selzer

The Pennsylvania State University

Longman

Boston   Columbus   Indianapolis   New York   San Francisco   Upper Saddle River
Amsterdam   Cape Town   Dubai   London   Madrid   Milan   Munich   Paris   Montreal   Toronto
Delhi   Mexico City   Sao Paulo   Sydney   Hong Kong   Seoul   Singapore   Taipei   Tokyo

In memory of our teacher and friend, James L. Kinneavy (1920–1999)

Executive Editor: Lynn M. Huddon
Senior Development Editor: Michael Greer
Senior Supplements Editor: Donna Campion
Senior Marketing Manager: Sandra McGuire
Production Manager: Eric Jorgensen
Project Coordination, Text Design, and Electronic Page Makeup: PreMediaGlobal
Cover Design Manager: John Callahan
Cover Designer: Kay Petronio
Cover Illustration/Photo: Ryman Ryman/Photolibrary
Photo Researcher: Poyee Oster
Senior Manufacturing Buyer: Dennis J. Para
Printer and Binder: RR Donnelley & Sons, Inc./Crawfordsville
Cover Printer: Lehigh-Phoenix Color/Hagerstown

For permission to use copyrighted material, grateful acknowledgment is made to the copyright holders on p. 297, which are hereby made part of this copyright page.

Library of Congress Cataloging-in-Publication Data

Faigley, Lester, 1947-
    Good reasons : researching and writing effective arguments / Lester Faigley,
Jack Selzer. — 5th ed.
        p. cm.
    Includes index.
    ISBN 978-0-205-01264-0
    1. English language—Rhetoric. 2. Persuasion (Rhetoric) 3. Report writing.
    I. Selzer, Jack. II. Title.

PE1431.F35 2010
808'.042—dc22

2010046868

2 3 4 5 6 7 8 9 10—DOC—13 12 11

Longman
is an imprint of

www.pearsonhighered.com

ISBN-13: 978-0-205-01264-0
ISBN-10:   0-205-01264-7

Detailed Contents

 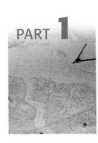

Analyzing Arguments

Writing Arguments

PART **4**

Designing and Presenting Arguments

Researching Arguments

Preface

Nothing students learn in college will prove to be more important to them than the ability to write an effective argument.

Students are aware that campus life is itself filled with arguments. There are hot-button public issues that engage the academic community—binge drinking, for example, or making the university more environmentally sustainable, or how to improve campus housing or study abroad opportunities. Meanwhile, in the classroom and in research programs, you and your academic peers present arguments on current controversies such as climate change and economic policy as well as on scholarly topics such as the workings of evolution, the cultural achievements of ancient Egypt, or the means of determining the material composition of the planet Mercury.

After college, students will particularly need to communicate their ideas and point of view effectively. Their livelihood and their engagement in the community will depend on it. Sometimes as citizens students will be moved to register views on the local school system or local downtown development; or as members of a neighborhood group or a civic organization, they will be suggesting ways of making a positive difference. And certainly in the workplace they will often be making arguments to propose ideas.

Good Reasons gives students a set of rules of thumb that can be used in college and after in order to mount effective arguments. For a number of years we have studied arguments, taught students how to argue, and listened to others talk and write about the art of persuasion. What we have found is that while there is no simple recipe for effective arguments, there are strategies and tactics that writers can rely on in almost any situation to ensure that their ideas are considered seriously.

New to This Edition

- **Four new sample student papers and new annotations on all sample student papers** in the book provide working models students can use to help revise and develop their own work on every type of argument covered in *Good Reasons*.

- **Three new professional readings**, including a definition argument by Michael Pollan and an evaluation argument by P. J. O'Rourke; all professional readings in the book are now fully annotated, to help students recognize and apply features of effective argument writing in their own papers.

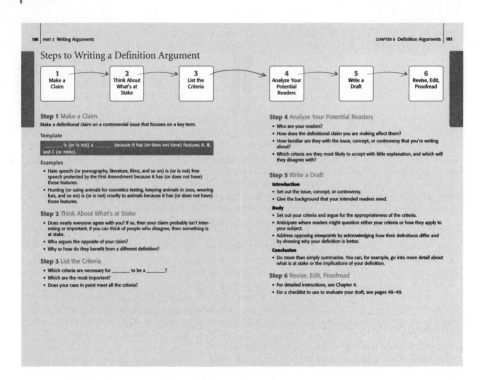

Steps to Writing a Definition Argument

1 Make a Claim	2 Think About What's at Stake	3 List the Criteria	4 Analyze Your Potential Readers	5 Write a Draft	6 Revise, Edit, Proofread

Step 1 Make a Claim

Make a definitional claim on a controversial issue that focuses on a key term.

Template

_____ is (or is not) a _____ because it has (or does not have) features A, B, and C (or more).

Examples

• Hate speech (or pornography, literature, films, and so on) is (or is not) free speech protected by the First Amendment because it has (or does not have) these features.

• Hunting (or using animals for cosmetics testing, keeping animals in zoos, wearing furs, and so on) is (or is not) cruelty to animals because it has (or does not have) these features.

Step 2 Think About What's at Stake

• Does nearly everyone agree with you? If so, then your claim probably isn't interesting or important. If you can think of people who disagree, then something is at stake.

• Who argues the opposite of your claim?

• Why or how do they benefit from a different definition?

Step 3 List the Criteria

• Which criteria are necessary for _____ to be a _____?

• Which are the most important?

• Does your case in point meet all the criteria?

Step 4 Analyze Your Potential Readers

• Who are your readers?

• How does the definitional claim you are making affect them?

• How familiar are they with the issue, concept, or controversy that you're writing about?

• Which criteria are they most likely to accept with little explanation, and which will they disagree with?

Step 5 Write a Draft

Introduction

• Set out the issue, concept, or controversy.

• Give the background that your intended readers need.

Body

• Set out your criteria and argue for the appropriateness of the criteria.

• Anticipate where readers might question either your criteria or how they apply to your subject.

• Address opposing viewpoints by acknowledging how their definitions differ and by showing why your definition is better.

Conclusion

• Do more than simply summarize. You can, for example, go into more detail about what is at stake or the implications of your definition.

Step 6 Revise, Edit, Proofread

• For detailed instructions, see Chapter 4.

• For a checklist to use to evaluate your draft, see pages 48–49.

■ **Redesigned "Steps to Writing" guides** provide a concise, visual overview of the process for drafting, developing, and revising each type of argument covered in *Good Reasons,* helping students to review and apply the concepts and strategies presented in each chapter.

■ **New coverage on designing and presenting multimodal arguments**: Chapter 6 has a new title, "Analyzing Visual and Multimedia Arguments," to reflect its new, broader focus on new media and online texts; Chapter 14 has been similarly updated, expanded, and re-titled to include new coverage of designing multimedia arguments; many of the new examples in the book focus on ways writers are using new forms of digital and multimodal rhetoric to create and deliver arguments to their audiences.

■ Students will find **learning objectives** in the **Quick Take preview** at the beginning of each chapter, reflecting the content that appears in that chapter, and instructions at the end of every chapter for finding supporting resources and assessment activities in MyCompLab.

11

Narrative Arguments

QUICK TAKE

In this chapter, you will learn that

1. Narrative arguments rely on concrete individual stories rather than large-scale statistics (see below)
2. Narrative arguments should allow readers to draw their own conclusions (see page 154)
3. Narrative arguments must strike readers as truthful and representative of larger issues (see page 156)

Charity: water understands the persuasive power of personal stories. Their online campaign features narratives like the story of Louis Mackenzie, a young boy who lost his father in the January 2010 earthquake in Haiti. "I cried and cried and cried when my mom told me he died," the text reads. As many organizations have learned, people often feel more compelled to donate money when they read personal stories like Louis's than when they are barraged with abstract numbers and statistics. Why are such stories effective as arguments? What makes some stories more compelling than others? © 2010 Charitywater.org. Used with permission.

■ **New mini-arguments,** including many visual and multimodal examples, represent every type of argument with an accessible, contemporary example to help students recognize and grasp how different kinds of arguments work today.

Resources for Teachers and Students

Instructor's Manual

The **Instructor's Manual** that accompanies this text was revised by Brian Neff, of The Pennsylvania State University, and is designed to be useful for new and experienced instructors alike. The Instructor's Manual briefly discusses the ins and outs of teaching the material in each chapter. Also provided are in-class exercises, homework assignments, discussion questions for each reading selection, model paper assignments and syllabi, and strategies for integrating the resources in MyCompLab into your course. This revised Instructor's Manual will make your work as a teacher a bit easier. Teaching argumentation and composition becomes a process that has genuine—and often surprising—rewards.

An Interactive Pearson eText in MyCompLab

An e-book version of *Good Reasons* is available in MyCompLab. This dynamic, online version of the text is integrated throughout MyCompLab to create an enriched, interactive learning experience for students.

MyCompLab is an eminently flexible application that empowers student writers and teachers by integrating a composing space and assessment tools with multimedia tutorials, services (such as online tutoring) and exercises for writing, grammar, and research. Students can use MyCompLab on their own, benefiting from self-paced diagnostics and a personal study plan that recommends the instruction and practice each student needs to improve his or her writing skills. Teachers can recommend it to students for self-study, set up courses to track student progress, or leverage the power of administrative features to be more effective and save time. The assignment builder and commenting tools, developed specifically for use in writing courses, bring instructors closer to their student writers, make managing assignments and evaluating papers more efficient, and put powerful assessment within reach. Students receive feedback within the context of their own writing, which encourages critical thinking and revision and helps them to develop skills based on their individual needs. Learn more at www.mycomplab.com.

A CourseSmart eTextbook

Good Reasons is also available as a CourseSmart etextbook. This is an exciting new choice for students, who can subscribe to the same content online and search the text, make notes online, print out reading assignments that incorporate lecture notes, and bookmark important passages for later review. For more information, or to subscribe to the CourseSmart etextbook, visit www.coursesmart.com.

Social Media Resources

Join us to create an online community around your course. For additional teaching tips and other resources and announcements, visit Pearson's Facebook fan page for this book (www.facebook.com/faigleyseries).

Acknowledgments

We are much indebted to the work of many outstanding scholars of argument and to our colleagues who teach argument at Texas and at Penn State. In particular, we thank the following reviewers for sharing their expertise: Kamala Balasubramanian, Grossmont College; Greg Barnhisel, Duquesne University; Jean S. Filetti, Christopher Newport University; Wendy Goodwin, Miami Dade College; Timothy S. Layton, St. Louis Community College at Florissant Valley; Andrea Muldoon, University of Wisconsin-Stout; Amisha Patel, Arizona State University; Jeff Pruchnic, Wayne State University; and Jeff Wylie, Maysville Community and Technical College. We are also grateful to the many students we've taught in our own classes, who have given us opportunities to test these materials in class and who have taught us a great deal about the nature of argument. Special thanks go the students whose work is included in this edition.

We have greatly benefited from working with Lynn Huddon, executive editor, and Michael Greer, development editor, whose talent and creativity continue to impress us and who contribute much to both the vision and the details of *Good Reasons*. They are the best, and we much enjoy working with them on this and other books. Susan "George" Shorn was also a member of the team for this edition and helped us in many ways. Special thanks go to Brian Neff for an outstanding revision of the Instructor's Manual. Lindsay Bethoney at PreMedia Global and Jacqueline Martin and Eric Jorgensen at Pearson Longman did splendid work in preparing our book for publication. We were quite fortunate to again have Elsa van Bergen as our copyeditor, who has no peer in our experience. Finally, we thank our families, who make it all possible.

Lester Faigley

Jack Selzer

Reading and Discovering Arguments

PART

1

1 | Making an Effective Argument

QUICK TAKE

In this chapter, you will learn that

1. Arguments in college writing are different from arguments in casual conversation (see below)
2. People who argue responsibly give evidence for their claims and cite their sources (see page 6)
3. Written arguments are like turns in an ongoing conversation (see page 7)
4. Your readers will take you seriously if you convince them that you are concerned, well informed, fair, and ethical (see page 10)

MadV's *The Message* consists of a series of extremely short videos from YouTube members of words written on hands.

What Exactly Is an Argument?

One of the best-known celebrities on YouTube is an anonymous video director who wears a Guy Fawkes mask and uses the name MadV. In November 2006 he posted a short video in which he held up his hand with the words "One World" written on his palm and invited viewers to take a stand by uploading a video to YouTube. They responded by the thousands, writing short messages written on their palms. MadV then compiled many of the responses in a 4-minute video titled *The Message* and posted it on YouTube.

MadV's project has been praised as a celebration of the values of the YouTube community. The common theme that we all should try to love and better understand other people is one that few oppose. Yet the video also raises the question of how any of the goals might be achieved. One hand reads "Stop Bigotry." We see a great deal of hatred in written responses to many YouTube videos. Slogans like "Open Mind," "Be Colorblind," "Love Is Stronger," "No more racism," and "Yup One World" seem inadequate for the scope of the problem.

Like the ink-on-hand messages, bumper stickers usually consist of unilateral statements ("Be Green," "Save the Whales," or "Share the Road") but provide no supporting evidence or reasons for why anyone should do what they say. People committed to a particular cause or belief often assume that their reasons are self-evident, and that everyone thinks the same way. These writers know they can count on certain words and phrases to produce predictable responses.

In college courses, in public life, and in professional careers, however, written arguments cannot be reduced to signs or slogans. Writers of effective arguments do not assume that everyone thinks the same way or holds the same beliefs. They attempt to change people's minds by convincing them of the validity of new ideas or the superiority of a particular course of action. Writers of such arguments not only offer evidence and reasons to support their position but also examine the assumptions on which an argument is based, address opposing arguments, and anticipate their readers' objections.

Extended written arguments make more demands on their readers than most other kinds of writing. Like bumper stickers, these arguments often appeal to our emotions. But they typically do much more.

- They expand our knowledge with the depth of their analysis.
- They lead us through a complex set of claims by providing networks of logical relationships and appropriate evidence.
- They build on what has been written previously by providing trails of sources.

Finally, they cause us to reflect on what we read, in a process that we will shortly describe as critical reading.

Finding Good Reasons

Who's using up Earth's resources?

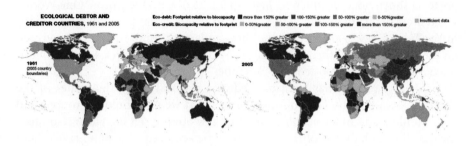

ECOLOGICAL DEBTOR AND CREDITOR COUNTRIES, 1961 and 2005

In the *Living Planet Report* for 2008, the World Wildlife Fund compared the ecological footprints from 1961 and 2005 for each country on Earth. The ecological footprint of a country is determined by its population, the amount of food, timber, and other resources consumed by its average citizen, the area required to produce food, fishing grounds, and the area required to absorb CO_2 emissions minus the amount absorbed by oceans.

Countries fall into four categories: ecological debtor nations (which consume more resources than they can produce), ecological creditor nations (which produce more than they consume), and two categories of ecologically balanced nations, where production and consumption are relatively balanced. In this map you can see that the United States, Mexico, Western Europe, China, India, Pakistan, Japan, and the nations of the Middle East have become ecological debtors with footprints more than 50 percent of their biocapacity—what they are able to produce. Nations such as Canada, Russia, Australia, New Zealand, and most nations in South America are ecological creditors, with footprints less than 50 percent of their biocapacity. In its entirety, the *Living Planet Report* makes the argument that nations should live in balance with what their land, rivers, lakes, and seas can support.

Write about it

1. What might be some of the causes of the differences among the ecological footprints of nations?
2. What is likely to happen in the future when some nations have enough resources (such as clean water and food) and others lack them?
3. Does the map succeed as an argument on its own? Does it contain any of the features of written arguments listed on pages 5–6?

Writing Arguments in College

Writing in college varies considerably from course to course. A lab report for a biology course looks quite different from a paper in your English class, just as a classroom observation in an education course differs from a case study report in an accounting class.

Nevertheless, much of the writing you will do in college will consist of arguments. Some common expectations about arguments in college writing extend across disciplines. For example, you could be assigned to write a proposal for a downtown light-rail system in a number of different classes—civil engineering, urban planning, government, or management. The emphasis of such a proposal would change depending on the course. In all cases, however, the proposal would require a complex argument in which you describe the problem that the light-rail system would improve, make a specific proposal that addresses the problem, explain the benefits of the system, estimate the cost, identify funding sources, assess alternatives to your plan, and anticipate possible opposition. It's a lot to think about.

Setting out a specific proposal or claim supported by reasons and evidence is at the heart of most college writing, no matter what the course. Some expectations of arguments (such as including a thesis statement) may be familiar to you, but others (such as the emphasis on finding alternative ways of thinking about a subject and finding facts that might run counter to your conclusions) may be unfamiliar.

WRITTEN ARGUMENTS . . .	WRITERS ARE EXPECTED TO . . .
State explicit claims	Make a claim that isn't obvious. The main claim is often called a **thesis.** (see pages 40–41)
Support claims with reasons	Express reasons in a **because clause** after the claim (We should do something *because* _____). (see pages 25–26)
Base reasons on evidence	Provide evidence for reasons in the form of facts, statistics, testimony from reliable sources, and direct observations. (see pages 37–38)
Consider opposing positions	Help readers understand why there are disagreements about issues by accurately representing differing views. (see pages 29–31)
Analyze with insight	Provide in-depth analysis of what they read and view. (see Chapters 5 and 6)

(continued)

WRITTEN ARGUMENTS . . .	WRITERS ARE EXPECTED TO . . .
Investigate complexity	Explore the complexity of a subject by asking "Have you thought about this?" or "What if you discard the usual way of thinking about a subject and take the opposite point of view?" (see pages 34–36)
Organize information clearly	Make the main ideas evident to readers and to indicate which parts are subordinate to others. (see pages 44–45)
Signal relationships of parts	Indicate logical relationships clearly so that readers can follow an argument without getting lost. (see page 51)
Document sources carefully	Provide the sources of information so that readers can consult the same sources the writer used. (see Chapters 20 and 21)

How can you argue responsibly?

In Washington, D.C., cars with diplomatic license plates are often parked illegally. Their drivers know they will not be towed or ticketed. People who abuse the diplomatic privilege are announcing, "I'm not playing by the rules."

When you begin an argument by saying "in my opinion," you are making a similar announcement. First, the phrase is redundant. A reader assumes that if you make a claim in writing, you believe that claim. More important, a claim is rarely *only* your opinion. Most beliefs and assumptions are shared by many people. If a claim truly is only your opinion, it can be easily dismissed. If your position is likely to be held by at least a few other people, however, then a responsible reader must consider your position seriously. You argue responsibly when you set out the reasons for making a claim and offer facts to support those reasons. You argue responsibly when you allow readers to examine your evidence by documenting the sources you have consulted. Finally, you argue responsibly when you acknowledge that other people may have positions different from yours.

How can you argue respectfully?

Our culture is competitive, and our goal often is to win. Professional athletes, top trial lawyers, or candidates for president of the United States either win big or lose. But most of us live in a world in which our opponents don't go away when the game is over.

Most of us have to deal with people who disagree with us at times but continue to work and live in our communities. The idea of winning in such situations can only be temporary. Soon enough, we will need the support of those who were on the other side of the most recent issue. You can probably think of times when a friendly argument resulted in a better understanding of all peoples' views. And probably you can think of a time when an argument created hard feelings that lasted for years.

Usually, listeners and readers are more willing to consider your argument seriously if you cast yourself as a respectful partner rather than as a competitor. Put forth your arguments in the spirit of mutual support and negotiation—in the interest of finding the *best* way, not "my way." How can you be the person that your reader will want to join rather than resist? Here are a few suggestions for both your written arguments and for discussing controversial issues.

- **Try to think of yourself as engaged not so much in winning over your audience as in courting your audience's cooperation.** Argue vigorously, but not so vigorously that opposing views are vanquished or silenced. Remember that your goal is to invite a response that creates a dialogue.
- **Show that you understand and genuinely respect your listener's or reader's position even if you think the position is ultimately wrong.** Remember to argue against opponents' positions, not against the opponents themselves. Arguing respectfully often means representing an opponent's position in terms that he or she would accept. Look for ground that you already share with your opponent, and search for even more. See yourself as a mediator. Consider that neither you nor the other person has arrived at a best solution. Then carry on in the hope that dialogue will lead to an even better course of action than the one you now recommend. Expect and assume the best of your listener or reader, and deliver your best.
- **Cultivate a sense of humor and a distinctive voice.** Many textbooks about argument emphasize using a reasonable voice. But a reasonable voice doesn't have to be a dull one. Humor is a legitimate tool of argument. Although playing an issue strictly for laughs risks not being taken seriously, nothing creates a sense of goodwill quite as much as tasteful humor. A sense of humor can be especially welcome when the stakes are high, the sides have been chosen, and tempers are flaring.

Arguments as Turns in a Conversation

Consider your argument as just one move in a larger process that might end up helping you. Most times we argue because we think we have something to offer. In the process of researching what has been said and written on a particular issue, however, often your own view is expanded and you find an opportunity to add your voice to the ongoing conversation.

A Case Study: The Microcredit Debate

Two women financed by microcredit sell scarves in Quito, Ecuador.

World Bank researchers reported in 2009 that 1.4 billion people—over 20 percent of the 6.7 billion people on earth—live below the extreme poverty line of $1.25 a day, with 6 million children starving to death every year. One cause of continuing extreme poverty is the inability of poor people to borrow money because they have no cash income or assets. Banks have seldom made loans to very poor people, who have had to turn to moneylenders that charge high interest rates sometimes exceeding 100 percent a month.

In 1976, Muhammad Yunus observed that poor women in Bangladesh who made bamboo furniture could not profit from their labor because they had to borrow money at high interest rates to buy bamboo. Yunus loaned $27 to forty-two women out of his pocket. They repaid him at an interest rate of two cents per loan. The success of the experiment eventually led to Yunus securing a loan from the government to create a bank to make loans to poor people. The Grameen Bank (Village Bank) became a model for other microfinancing projects in Bangladesh, serving 7 million people, 94 percent of whom are women. For his work with the Grameen initiative, Yunus received the Nobel Peace Prize in 2006.

Microcredit now has many supporters, including Hollywood stars like Natalie Portman and Michael Douglas, companies like Benetton and Sam's Club, and former

President Bill Clinton. But the success in Bangladesh has not been replicated in many other poor countries. Many critics point to the shortcomings of microcredit. This debate can be better understood if you consider the different points of view on microcredit to be different voices in a conversation.

The conversation about microcredit has led others to put new ideas on the table.

Mapping a conversation like the debate about microcredit often can help you identify how you can add to the conversation. What can you add to what's been said?

Some people claim that _____.

Other people respond that _____.

Still others claim that _____.

I agree with X's and Y's points, but I maintain that _____

because _____.

Think About Your Credibility

A few writers begin with instant credibility because of what they have accomplished. If you're a tennis player, likely you will pay attention to advice from Serena Williams. If you're interested in future trends in computers and entertainment, you'll listen to the forecasts of Steve Jobs, the cofounder and CEO of Apple. But if you are like most of the rest of us, you don't have instant credibility.

Think about how you want your readers to see you

To get your readers to take you seriously, you must convince them that they can trust you. You need to get them to see you as

> **Concerned.** Readers want you to be committed to what you are writing about. They also expect you to be concerned with them as readers. After all, if you don't care about them, why should they read what you write?
>
> **Well informed.** Many people ramble on about any subject without knowing anything about it. If they are family members, you have to suffer their opinions, but it is not enjoyable. College writing requires that you do your homework on a subject.
>
> **Fair.** Many writers look at only one side of an issue. Readers respect objectivity and an unbiased approach.
>
> **Ethical.** Many writers use only the facts that support their positions and often distort facts and sources. Critical readers often notice what is being left out. Don't try to conceal what doesn't support your position.

The cover of this book, for example, makes a visual reference to genetically modified (GM) food, which is highly controversial in Japan and Europe and has become increasingly controversial in the United States. The central issue is whether genetically modified food is safe, but the effects on ecosystems, the gene flow into crops that are not genetically engineered, and the control of our food supply by a handful of corporations are also major issues. Because most people in the United States know little about genetically modified food, you will gain credibility by presenting a balanced overview of each of these issues.

Build your credibility

Know what's at stake. What you are writing about should matter to your readers. If its importance is not evident, it's your job to explain why your readers should consider it important.

LESS EFFECTIVE:
We should be concerned about two-thirds of Central and South America's 110 brightly colored harlequin frog species becoming extinct in the last twenty years. (*The loss of any species is unfortunate, but the writer gives us no other reason for concern.*)

MORE EFFECTIVE:
The rapid decline of amphibians worldwide due to global warming may be the advance warning of the loss of cold-weather species such as polar bears, penguins, and reindeer.

Have your readers in mind. If you are writing about a specialized subject that your readers don't know much about, take the time to explain key concepts.

LESS EFFECTIVE:
Reduction in the value of a debt security, especially a bond, results from a rise in interest rates. Conversely, a decline in interest rates results in an increase in the value of a debt security, especially bonds. (*The basic idea is here, but it is not expressed clearly, especially if the reader is not familiar with investing.*)

MORE EFFECTIVE:
Bond prices move inversely to interest rates. When interest rates go up, bond prices go down, and when interest rates go down, bond prices go up.

Think about alternative solutions and points of view. Readers appreciate a writer's ability to see a subject from multiple perspectives.

LESS EFFECTIVE:
We will reduce greenhouse gas and global warming only if we greatly increase wind-generated electricity. (*Wind power is an alternative energy source, but it is expensive and many people don't want windmills in scenic areas. The writer also doesn't mention using energy more efficiently.*)

MORE EFFECTIVE:
If the world is serious about limiting carbon emissions to reduce global warming, then along with increasing efficient energy use, all non-carbon-emitting energy sources must be considered, including nuclear power. Nuclear power now produces about 20 percent of U.S. electricity with no emissions—the equivalent of taking 58 million passenger cars off the road.

Be honest. Readers also appreciate writers who admit what they aren't sure about. Leaving readers with unanswered questions can lead them to think further about your subject.

LESS EFFECTIVE:

The decline in violent crime during the 1990s was due to putting more people in jail with longer sentences.

MORE EFFECTIVE:

Exactly what caused the decline in violent crime during the 1990s remains uncertain. Politicians point to longer sentences for criminals, but the decrease in the population most likely to commit crimes—the 16-to-35 age group—may have been a contributing factor.

Write well. Nothing impresses readers more than graceful, fluent writing that is clear, direct, and forceful. Even if readers don't agree with you in the end, they still will appreciate your writing ability.

LESS EFFECTIVE:

Nobody can live today without taking some risks, even very rich people. After all, we don't know what we're breathing in the air. A lot of food has chemicals and hormones in it. There's a big hole in the ozone, so more people will get skin cancer. And a lot of people have sexually transmitted diseases these days. (The impact of the point is lost with unfocused writing.)

MORE EFFECTIVE:

We live in a world of risks beyond our control to the extent that it difficult to think of anything that is risk free down to the most basic human acts—sex in an era of AIDS, eating in an era of genetically altered food, walking outside in an ozone-depleted atmosphere, drinking water and breathing air laden with chemicals whose effects we do not understand.

For support in learning this chapter's content, follow this path in MyCompLab:
> Resources > Writing > Writing Purposes > Writing to Argue or Persuade.
Review the Instruction and Multimedia resources, then complete the Exercises and click on Gradebook to measure your progress.

2 | Reading Arguments

QUICK TAKE

In this chapter, you will learn that

1. Controversies that are represented in the media as having two sides often involve many nuanced positions (see below)
2. Reading an argument critically involves asking questions before you start reading and rereading it several times (see page 14)
3. Mapping an argument is a good way to understand its structure (see page 17)

Explore Controversies

People in general agree on broad goals for their society: clean water, abundant healthy food, efficient transportation, good schools, full employment, affordable health care, safe cities and neighborhoods, and peace with others near and far. People in general, however, often disagree on how to define and achieve these goals. Controversies surround major issues and causes.

Often controversies are portrayed in the media as pro and con or even take on political labels. But if you read and listen carefully to what people have to say about a particular issue, you usually find a range of different positions on the issue, and you often discover nuances and complexities in the reasons people offer for their positions.

Find controversies

Online subject directories can help you identify the differing views on a large, general topic. Try the subject index of your library's online catalog. You'll likely find subtopics listed under large topics. Also, your library's Web site may have a link to the *Opposing Viewpoints* database.

One of the best Web subject directories for finding arguments is Yahoo's Issues and Causes directory. This directory provides subtopics for major issues and provides links to the Web sites of organizations interested in particular issues.

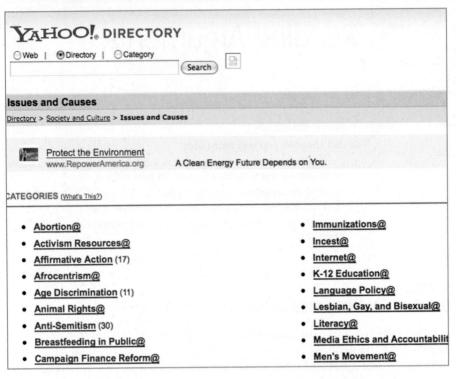

Yahoo! Issues and Causes directory (dir.yahoo.com/Society_and_Culture/Issues_and_Causes/)

Read Critically

After you survey the landscape of a particular issue, turn to careful reading of individual arguments, one at a time.

Before you begin reading, ask these questions

- Where did the argument first appear? Was it published in a book, newspaper, magazine, or electronic source? Many items in library databases and on the Web were published somewhere else first.
- Who wrote this argument? What do you know about the author?
- What does the title suggest argument be about?

Read the argument once without making notes to gain a sense of the content

- When you finish, write one sentence that sums up the argument.

Finding Good Reasons

Has the Internet made everyone writers?

Video blogs, known as vlogs, became a popular genre on YouTube.

Before the Internet was invented, readers had to make some effort to respond to writers by writing to them directly, sending a letter to the editor, or even scribbling or spray-painting a response. The Internet has changed the interaction between writers and readers by allowing readers to respond easily to writers and, in turn, turning readers into writers. Look, for example, at Amazon.com. An incredible amount of writing surrounds any best-selling book—often an author's Web site and blog, newspaper reviews, and over a hundred readers' reviews. Or read a political, sports, culture, fashion, or parenting blog and the comments by readers of those blogs. Think about how the Internet has changed the relationship between readers and writers.

To find a blog that interests you, use a blog search engine such as Bloglines (www. bloglines. com), Google Blog Search (blogsearch.google.com), IceRocket (blogs.icerocket.com), or Technorati (www. technorati. com).

Write about it

1. Using a blog search engine or an online newspaper, find a blog by an author, politician, or news columnist. Answer as many of the questions for critical reading on page 16 as you can.

2. Write a summary of the blog entry.

3. What kinds of reasons do blog writers give for their responses to what they read?

4. How are blogs and online book reviews like or unlike traditional book reviews in print?

Read the argument a second and third time and make notes

- Go back through the text and underline the author's thesis.
- Does your sentence and the author's thesis match? If not, look at the text again and either adjust your sentence or check if you underlined the correct sentence.
- How is the argument organized? How are the major points arranged?
- What reasons or evidence does the writer offer in support of the thesis?
- How does the writer conclude the argument? Does the conclusion follow from the evidence presented?
- Who is the intended audience? What does the writer assume the readers know and believe?
- Do you detect a bias in the writer's position?
- Where do the writer's facts come from? Does the writer give the sources? Are the sources reliable?
- Does the writer acknowledge other views and unfavorable evidence? Does the writer deal fairly with the views of others?
- If there are images or graphics, are they well integrated and clearly labeled?

Annotate what you read

- **Mark major points and key concepts.** Sometimes major points are indicated by headings, but often you will need to locate them.
- **Connect with your experience.** Think about your own experiences and how they match up or don't match up with what you are reading.
- **Connect passages.** Notice how ideas connect to each other. Draw lines and arrows. If an idea connects to something from a few pages earlier, write a note in the margin with the page number.
- **Ask questions.** Note anything that puzzles you, including words you don't know and need to look up.

Map a controversy

Read broadly about an issue and identify three or more sources that offer different points of view on that issue. The sources may approach the issue from different angles or raise different questions instead of simply stating differing positions on the issue. Draw a map that represents the different views. The map on the next page shows some of the different positions on sustainable agriculture.

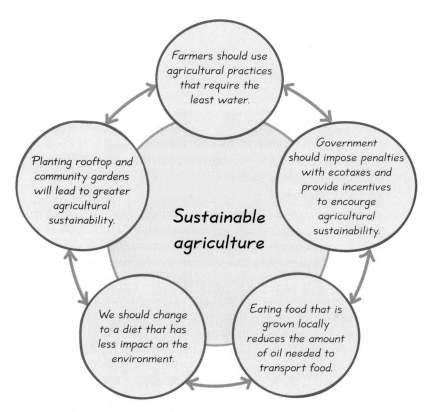

Map of different issues about sustainable agriculture

Recognize Fallacies

Recognizing where good reasons go off track is one of the most important aspects of critical reading. What passes as political discourse is often filled with claims that lack evidence or substitute emotions for evidence. Such faulty reasoning often contains one or more **logical fallacies**. For example, politicians know that the public is outraged when the price of gasoline goes up, and they try to score political points by accusing oil companies of price gouging. It sounds good to angry voters—and it may well be true—but unless the politician defines what *price gouging* means and provides evidence that oil companies are guilty, the argument has no more validity than children calling each other bad names on the playground.

Following are some of the more common fallacies.

Fallacies of logic

■ **Begging the question** Politicians *are inherently dishonest because no honest person would run for public office.* The fallacy of begging the question occurs when the claim is restated and passed off as evidence.

- **Either-or** *Either we eliminate the regulation of businesses or else profits will suffer.* The either-or fallacy suggests that there are only two choices in a complex situation. Rarely, if ever, is this the case. Consider, for example, the case of Enron, which was unregulated but went bankrupt.
- **False analogies** *Japan quit fighting in 1945 when we dropped nuclear bombs on Hiroshima and Nagasaki. We should use nuclear weapons against other countries.* Analogies always depend on the degree of resemblance of one situation to another. In this case, the analogy fails to recognize that circumstances today are very different from those in 1945. Many countries now possess nuclear weapons, and we know their use could harm the entire world.
- **Hasty generalization** *We have been in a drought for three years; that's a sure sign of climate change.* A hasty generalization is a broad claim made on the basis of a few occurrences. Climate cycles occur regularly over spans of a few years. Climate trends, however, must be observed over centuries.
- **Non sequitur** *A university that can raise a billion dollars from alumni should not have to raise tuition.* A non sequitur (a Latin term meaning "it does not follow") ties together two unrelated ideas. In this case, the argument fails to recognize that the money for capital campaigns is often donated for special purposes such as athletic facilities and is not part of a university's general revenue.
- **Oversimplification** *No one would run stop signs if we had a mandatory death penalty for doing it.* This claim may be true, but the argument would be unacceptable to most citizens. More complex, if less definitive, solutions are called for.
- ***Post hoc* fallacy** *The stock market goes down when the AFC wins the Super Bowl in even years.* The *post hoc* fallacy (from the Latin *post hoc, ergo propter hoc,* which means "after this, therefore because of this") assumes that events that follow in time have a causal relationship.
- **Rationalization** *I could have finished my paper on time if my printer had been working.* People frequently come up with excuses and weak explanations for their own and others' behavior. These excuses often avoid actual causes.
- **Slippery slope** We shouldn't grant citizenship to illegal immigrants now living in the United States because no one will want to obey our laws. The slippery slope fallacy maintains that one thing inevitably will cause something else to happen.

Fallacies of emotion and language

- **Bandwagon appeals** *It* doesn't *matter if I copy a paper off the Web because everyone else does.* This argument suggests that everyone is doing it, so why shouldn't you? But on close examination, it may be that everyone really isn't doing it—and in any case, it may not be the right thing to do.

- **Name calling** Name calling is frequent in politics and among competing groups. People level accusations using names such as radical, tax-and-spend liberal, racist, fascist, right-wing ideologue. Unless these terms are carefully defined, they are meaningless.
- **Polarization** *Feminists are all man haters.* Like name calling, polarization exaggerates positions and groups by representing them as extreme and divisive.
- **Straw man** *Environmentalists won't be satisfied until not a single human being is allowed to enter a national park.* A straw man argument is a diversionary tactic that sets up another's position in a way that can be easily rejected. In fact, only a small percentage of environmentalists would make an argument even close to this one.

Note fallacies while you read

Marta Ramos noted a fallacy in James McWilliams's argument against locavorism. You can read her rebuttal argument on pages 180–183.

Consider fruit and vegetable production in New York. The Empire State is naturally equipped to grow a wide variety of fruits, including pears, cherries, strawberries, and some peaches. But none of these compare to its ability to grow apples and grapes, which dominate production (accounting for 94 percent of all fruit grown).

At current levels of fruit production, apples are the only crop that could currently feed New Yorkers at a level that meets the U.S. Recommended Dietary Allowances. Every other fruit that the state produces is not being harvested at a level to provide all New Yorkers with an adequate supply. Other fruits such as bananas and oranges are not produced at all because conditions are unfavorable for growing them.

What does this situation mean in terms of feeding the state with the state's own produce?

In a nutshell, <u>it means citizens would have to give up tropical fruits altogether</u>; rarely indulge in a pear, peach, or basket of strawberries; and gorge on grapes and apples—most of them in processed form (either as juice, in a can, or as concentrate).

McWilliams makes a straw man argument. Locavores prioritize locally produced food but don't argue that it's only what people should eat.

McWilliams, James. "On Locavorism." *New York Times.* New York Times, 26 Aug. 2008. Web. 8 Apr. 2010.

Map and Summarize Arguments

When you finish annotating a reading, you might want to map it.

Draw a map

Marta Ramos drew a map of James McWilliams's argument.

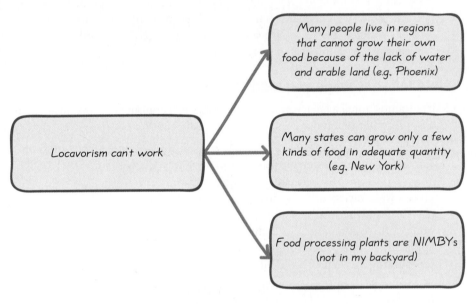

Map of the argument in James McWilliams's "On Locavorism"

Write a summary

A summary should be concise but thorough representation of the source.

- Begin your summary with the writer's name, the title of the argument, and the main point.
- Then report the key ideas. Represent the author's argument in condensed form as accurately as you can, quoting exact words for key points (see pages 253–254 for how to quote and integrate an author's words into your summary).
- Your aim is to give your readers an understanding of what the author is arguing for. Withhold judgment even if you think the author is dead wrong. Do not insert your opinions and comments. Stick to what the author is saying and what position the author is advocating.
- Usually summaries are no longer than 150 words. If your summary is longer than 150 words, delete excess words without eliminating key ideas.

McWilliams, James. "On Locavorism." *New York Times*. New York Times, 26 Aug. 2008. Web. 8 Apr. 2010.

Summary

In "On Locavorism," James McWilliams argues that locavorism—the develop of local food-supply systems—is an impractical goal. He offers three reasons why locavorism is not achievable. First, many people live in regions where they cannot grow their own food because of lack of water and arable land (for example, Phoenix). Second many states can grow only a few kinds of food in adequate quantity (for example, New York), thus restricting food choices and limiting consumption to processed fruits and vegetables for much of the year. Third, many people will not like food processing plants near their homes.

PEARSON
mycomplab

For support in learning this chapter's content, follow this path in MyCompLab:
> Resources > Media Index > Visual Analysis and Rhetoric.
Review the Instruction and Multimedia resources, then complete the Exercises and click on Gradebook to measure your progress.

3 | Finding Arguments

QUICK TAKE

In this chapter, you will learn that

1. Everyday conversations with friends can be rich sources of ideas for written arguments (see page 23)

2. Writing assignments often contain key words that you can use to determine the type of argument you need to write (see page 25)

3. Reading widely about a topic will help you become familiar with the points of view already being debated on an issue (see page 31)

4. Reasons need to be supported with good evidence (see page 37)

Slogans are meant to persuade, but technically they are not arguments because they lack reasons. Nevertheless, you can often supply a reason for a claim made on a sign. What reason might the demonstrator give to support her claim LET US ALL LIVE "THE DREAM"?

Find Arguments in Everyday Conversations

Let's look at an example of a conversation. When the pain in his abdomen didn't go away, Jeff knew he had torn something while carrying his friend's heavy speakers up a flight of stairs. He went to the student health center and called his friend Maria when he returned home.

JEFF: I have good news and bad news. The pain is a minor hernia that can be repaired with day surgery. The bad news is that the fee we pay for the health center doesn't cover hospital visits. We should have health coverage.

MARIA: Jeff, you didn't buy the extra insurance. Why should you get it for nothing?

JEFF: Because health coverage is a right.

MARIA: No it's not. Everyone doesn't have health insurance.

JEFF: Well, in some other countries like Canada, Germany, and Britain, they do.

MARIA: Yes, and people who live in those countries pay a bundle in taxes for the government-provided insurance.

JEFF: It's not fair in this country because some people have health insurance and others don't.

MARIA: Jeff, face the facts. You could have bought the extra insurance. Instead you chose to buy a new car.

JEFF: It would be better if the university provided health insurance because students could graduate in four years. I'm going to have to get a second job and drop out for a semester to pay for the surgery.

MARIA: Neat idea, but who's going to pay for it?

JEFF: OK, all students should be required to pay for health insurance as part of their general fee. Most students are healthy, and it wouldn't cost that much more.

In this discussion, Jeff starts out by making a **claim** that students should have health coverage. Maria immediately asks him why students should not have to pay for health insurance. She wants a **reason** to accept his claim.

Distinguishing arguments from other kinds of persuasion

Scholars who study argument maintain that an argument must have a claim and one or more reasons to support that claim. Something less might be persuasive, but it isn't an argument.

A bumper sticker that says NO TOLL ROADS is a claim, but it is not an argument because the statement lacks a reason. Many reasons support an argument against building toll roads.

- We don't need new roads but should build light-rail instead.
- We should raise the gas tax to pay for new roads.
- We should use gas tax revenue only for roads rather than using it for other purposes.

When a claim has a reason attached, then it becomes an argument.

The basics of arguments

A reason is typically offered in a **because clause**, a statement that begins with the word *because* and that provides a supporting reason for the claim. Jeff's first attempt is to argue that students should have health insurance *because* health insurance is a right.

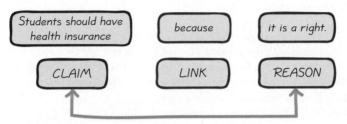

The word *because* signals a link between the reason and the claim. Every argument that is more than a shouting match or a simple assertion has to have one or more reasons. Just having a reason for a claim, however, doesn't mean that the audience will be convinced. When Jeff tells Maria that students have a right to health insurance, Maria replies that students don't have that right. Maria will accept Jeff's claim only if she accepts that his reason supports his claim. Maria challenges Jeff's links and keeps asking "So what?" For her, Jeff's reasons are not good reasons.

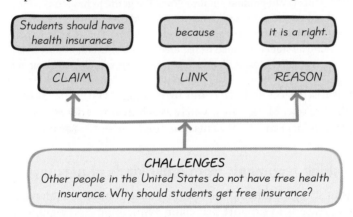

By the end of this short discussion, Jeff has begun to build an argument. He has had to come up with another claim to support his main claim: All students should be required to pay for health insurance as part of their general fee. If he is to convince Maria, he will probably have to provide a series of claims that she will accept as linked to his primary claim. He will also need to find evidence to support these claims.

Benjamin Franklin observed, "So convenient a thing it is to be a rational creature, since it enables us to find or make a reason for every thing one has a mind to do." It is not hard to think of reasons. What *is* difficult is to convince your audience that your reasons are good reasons. In a conversation, you get immediate feedback that tells you whether your listener agrees or disagrees. When you are writing, you usually don't have someone you can question immediately. Consequently, you have to (1) be more specific about what you are claiming, (2) connect with the values you hold in common with your readers, and (3) anticipate what questions and objections your readers might have, if you are going to convince someone who doesn't agree with you or know what you know already.

When you write an argument, imagine a reader like Maria who is going to listen carefully to what you have to say but who is not going to agree with you automatically. Readers like Maria will expect the following.

- A **claim** that is interesting and makes them want to find out more about what you have to say
- At least one **good reason** that makes your claim worth taking seriously
- Some **evidence** that the good reason or reasons are valid
- Some acknowledgment of the **opposing views** and **limitations** of the claim

The remainder of this chapter will guide you through the process of finding a topic, making a claim, finding good reasons and evidence, and anticipating objections to your claim.

Find a Topic

When your instructor gives you a writing assignment, look closely at what you are asked to do. Assignments typically contain a great deal of information, and you have to sort through that information. First, circle all the instructions about the length, the due date, the format, the grading criteria, and anything else about the production and conventions of the assignment. This information is important to you, but it doesn't tell you what the paper is supposed to be about.

Read your assignment carefully

Often your assignment will contain key words such as *analyze, define, evaluate,* or *propose* that will assist you in determining what direction to take. *Analyze* can mean several things. Your instructor might want you to analyze a piece of writing (see Chapter 5), an image (see Chapter 6), or the causes of something (see Chapter 9). *Define* usually means writing a **definition argument**, in which you argue for a definition based on the criteria you set out (see Chapter 8). *Evaluate* indicates an **evaluation argument**, in which you argue that something is good, bad, the best, or the worst in its class according to criteria that you set out (see Chapter 10). An assignment that contains the instructions *Write about an issue using your personal experience* indicates a **narrative argument** (see Chapter 11), while one that says *Take a position in regard to a reading* might lead you to write a **rebuttal argument** (see Chapter 12). *Propose* means that you should identify a particular problem and explain why your solution is the best one in a **proposal argument** (see Chapter 13).

What Is Not Arguable

- **Statements of fact.** Most facts can be verified by doing research. But even simple facts can sometimes be argued. For example, Mount Everest is usually acknowledged to be the highest mountain in the world at 29,028 feet above sea level. But if the total height of a mountain from base to summit is the measure, then the volcano Mauna Loa in Hawaii is the highest mountain in the world. Although the top of Mauna Loa is 13,667 feet above sea level, the summit is 31,784 above the ocean floor. Thus the "fact" that Mount Everest is the highest mountain on the earth depends on a definition of *highest*. You could argue for this definition.

- **Claims of personal taste.** Your favorite food and your favorite color are examples of personal taste. If you hate fresh tomatoes, no one can convince you that you actually like them. But many claims of personal taste turn out to be value judgments using arguable criteria. For example, if you think that *Alien* is the best science-fiction movie ever made, you can argue that claim using evaluative criteria that other people can consider as good reasons (see Chapter 10). Indeed, you might not even like science fiction and still argue that *Alien* is the best science-fiction movie ever.

- **Statements of belief or faith.** If someone accepts a claim as a matter of religious belief, then for that person, the claim is true and cannot be refuted. Of course, people still make arguments about the existence of God and which religion reflects the will of God. Whenever an audience will not consider an idea, it's possible but very difficult to construct an argument. Many people claim to have evidence that UFOs exist, but most people refuse to acknowledge that evidence as even being possibly factual.

If you remain unclear about the purpose of the assignment after reading it carefully, talk with your instructor.

Thinking about what interests you

Your assignment may specify the topic you are to write about. If your assignment gives you a wide range of options and you don't know what to write about, look first at the materials for your course: the readings, your lecture notes, and discussion boards. Think about what subjects came up in class discussion.

If you need to look outside class for a topic, think about what interests you. Subjects we argue about often find us. There are enough of them in daily life. We're late for work or class because the traffic is heavy or the bus doesn't run on time. We can't find a place to park when we get to school or work. We have to negotiate through various bureaucracies for almost anything we do—making an

Finding Good Reasons

Are traffic enforcement cameras invading your privacy?

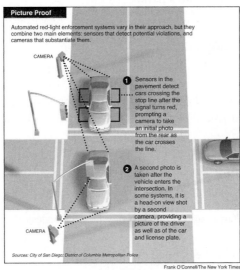

Picture Proof

Automated red-light enforcement systems vary in their approach, but they combine two main elements: sensors that detect potential violations, and cameras that substantiate them.

CAMERA

1 Sensors in the pavement detect cars crossing the stop line after the signal turns red, prompting a camera to take an initial photo from the rear as the car crosses the line.

2 A second photo is taken after the vehicle enters the intersection. In some systems, it is a head-on view shot by a second camera, providing a picture of the driver as well as of the car and license plate.

CAMERA

Sources: City of San Diego; District of Columbia Metropolitan Police

Frank O'Connell/The New York Times

Cameras that photograph the license plates and drivers of vehicles who run red lights, speed, or ride illegally in high-occupancy-vehicle (HOV) and bus lanes are currently in use in many U.S. cities and states. Cameras aimed at catching speeders, already common in Europe, are beginning to be installed in U.S. cities as well. Traffic cameras have become money machines for some communities, but they also have provoked intense public opposition and even vandalism—people have spray painted and shot cameras in attempts to disable them.

Write about it

1. How do you feel about using cameras to catch red-light runners? Speeders? Illegal drivers in HOV and bus lanes? People who don't pay parking tickets? Make a list of as many possible topics as you can think of about the use of cameras to scan license plates.

2. Select one of the possible topics. Write it at the top of a sheet of paper, and then write nonstop for five minutes. Don't worry about correctness. If you get stuck, write the same sentence again.

3. When you finish, read what you have written and circle key ideas.

4. Put each key idea on a sticky note. If you think of other ideas, write them on separate sticky notes. Then look at your sticky notes. Put a star on the central idea. Put the ideas that are related next to each other. You now have the beginning of an idea map.

appointment to see a doctor, getting a course added or dropped, or correcting a mistake on a bill. Most of the time we grumble and let it go at that. But sometimes we stick with a subject. Neighborhood groups in cities and towns have been especially effective in getting something done by writing about it—for example, stopping a new road from being built, getting better police and fire protection, and getting a vacant lot turned into a park.

Listing and analyzing issues

A good way to get started is to list possible issues to write about. Make a list of questions that can be answered "YES, because . . ." or "NO, because . . ." Think about issues that affect your campus, your community, the nation, and the world. Which issues interest you? About which issues could you make a contribution to the larger discussion?

Campus

- Should students be required to pay fees for access to computers on campus?
- Should smoking be banned on campus?
- Should varsity athletes get paid for playing sports that bring in revenue?
- Should admissions decisions be based exclusively on academic achievement?
- Should knowledge of a foreign language be required for all degree plans?
- Should your college or university have a computer literacy requirement?
- Is there any way to curb the dangerous drinking habits of many students on your campus?

Community

- Should people who ride bicycles and motorcycles be required to wear helmets?
- Should high schools be allowed to search students for drugs at any time?
- Should high schools distribute condoms?
- Should bilingual education programs be eliminated?
- Should bike lanes be built throughout your community to encourage more people to ride bicycles?
- Should more tax dollars be shifted from building highways to funding public transportation?

Nation/World

- Should driving while talking on a cell phone be banned?
- Should capital punishment be abolished?
- Should the Internet be censored?
- Should the government be allowed to monitor all phone calls and all e-mail to combat terrorism?
- Should handguns be outlawed?
- Should beef and poultry be free of growth hormones?
- Should a law be passed requiring that the parents of teenagers who have abortions be informed?
- Should people who are terminally ill be allowed to end their lives?
- Should the United States punish nations with poor human rights records?

Narrowing a list

1. Put a check beside the issues that look most interesting to write about or the ones that mean the most to you.
2. Put a question mark beside the issues that you don't know very much about. If you choose one of these issues, you will probably have to do in-depth research—by talking to people, by using the Internet, or by going to the library.
3. Select the two or three issues that look most promising. For each issue, make another list:
   - Who is most interested in this issue?
   - Whom or what does this issue affect?
   - What are the pros and cons of this issue? Make two columns. At the top of the left one, write "YES, because." At the top of the right one, write "NO, because."
   - What has been written about this issue? How can you find out what has been written?

Explore Your Topic

When you identify a potential topic, make a quick exploration of that topic, much as you would walk through a house or an apartment you are thinking about renting for a quick look. One way of exploring is to visualize the topic by making a map.

If you live in a state on the coast that has a high potential for wind energy, you might argue that your state should provide financial incentives for generating more electricity from the wind. Perhaps it seems like a no-brainer to you because wind power consumes no fuel and causes no air pollution. The only energy required is for the manufacture and transportation of the wind turbines and transmission lines. But your state and other coastal states have not exploited potential wind energy for three reasons:

1. **Aesthetics.** Some people think wind turbines are ugly.
2. **Hazard to wildlife.** A few poorly located wind turbines have killed birds and bats.
3. **Cost.** Wind power costs differ, but wind energy is generally more expensive than electricity produced by burning coal.

To convince other people that your proposal is a good one, you will have to answer these objections.

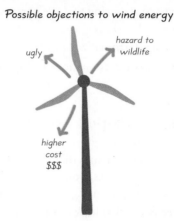

Possible objections to wind energy

The first two objections are relatively easy to address. Locating wind farms 10 kilometers offshore keeps them out of sight of land and away from most migrating birds and all bats. The third objection, higher cost, is more difficult. One strategy is to argue that the overall costs of wind energy and energy produced by burning coal are comparable if environmental costs are included. You can analyze the advantages and disadvantages of each by drawing maps.

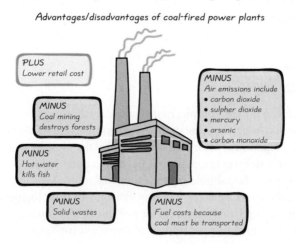

Advantages/disadvantages of coal-fired power plants

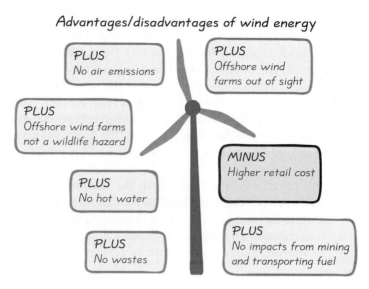

Advantages/disadvantages of wind energy

PLUS
No air emissions

PLUS
Offshore wind
farms out of sight

PLUS
Offshore wind farms
not a wildlife hazard

MINUS
Higher retail cost

PLUS
No hot water

PLUS
No wastes

PLUS
No impacts from mining
and transporting fuel

These maps can help you organize an argument for providing financial incentives for wind energy.

Read About Your Topic

Much college writing draws on and responds to sources—books, articles, reports, and other material written by other people. Every significant issue discussed in today's world has an extensive history of discussion involving many people and various points of view. Before you formulate a claim about a significant issue, you need to become familiar with the conversation that's already happening by reading widely about it.

One of the most controversial and talked-about subjects in recent years is the outsourcing of white-collar and manufacturing jobs to low-wage nations. Since 2000 an estimated 400,000 to 500,000 American jobs each year have gone to cheap overseas labor markets. The Internet has made this migration of jobs possible, allowing companies to outsource not only low-skilled jobs but highly skilled jobs in fields such as software development, data storage, and even examining X-rays and MRI scans.

You may have read about this or another complex and controversial topic in one of your courses. Just as in a conversation with several people who hold different views, you may agree with some people, disagree with some, and with others agree with some of their ideas up to a point but then disagree.

CNN commentator Lou Dobbs has been sharply critical of outsourcing. In *Exporting America: Why Corporate Greed Is Shipping American Jobs Overseas* (2006), Dobbs blames large corporations for putting profits ahead of the good of the nation. He accuses both Republicans and Democrats of ignoring the effects of a massive trade deficit and the largest national debt in American history, which Dobbs claims will eventually destroy the American way of life.

Thomas Friedman, columnist for the *New York Times*, takes a different viewpoint on outsourcing in *The World Is Flat: A Brief History of the Twenty-first Century* (2006). By *flat*, Friedman means that the nations of the world are connected like never before through the Internet and the lowering of trade barriers, putting every nation in direct competition with all the others. Friedman believes that outsourcing is not only unstoppable, but also desirable. He argues that Americans need to adapt to the new reality and rethink our system of education, or else we will be left hopelessly behind.

If you decide to write an argument about the issue of outsourcing, you might use either Dobbs's or Friedman's book as your starting point in making a claim. You could begin by taking on the role of **skeptic,** disagreeing with the author; the role of **contributor,** agreeing with the author and adding another point; or the role of the **analyst,** finding some points to agree with while disagreeing with others.

The skeptic: Disagreeing with a source

It's easy to disagree by simply saying an idea is dumb, but readers expect you to be persuasive about why you disagree and to offer reasons to support your views.

X claims that ————————————, but this view is mistaken because ——————————.

Example claim: Arguing against outsourcing resulting from free trade policies

Thomas Friedman claims that the world is "flat," giving a sense of a level playing field for all, but it is absurd to think that the millions of starving children in the world have opportunities similar to those in affluent countries who pay $100 for basketball shoes made by the starving children.

Example claim: Arguing in favor of outsourcing resulting from free trade policies

Lou Dobbs is a patriotic American who recognizes the suffering of manufacturing workers in industries like steel and automobiles, but he neglects that the major cause of the loss of manufacturing jobs in the United States and China alike is increased productivity—the 40 hours of labor necessary to produce a car just a few years ago has now been reduced to 15.

The contributor: Agreeing with a source with an additional point

Sources should not make your argument for you. With sources that support your position, indicate exactly how they fit into your argument with an additional point.

I agree with _____ and will make the additional point that _____.

Example claim: Arguing against outsourcing resulting from free trade policies

Lou Dobbs's outcry against the outsourcing of American jobs also has a related argument: We are dependent not only on foreign oil, but also on foreign clothing, foreign electronics, foreign tools, foreign toys, foreign cars and trucks—indeed, just about everything—which is quickly eroding the world leadership of the United States.

Example claim: Arguing in favor of outsourcing resulting from free trade policies

Thomas Friedman's claim that the Internet enables everyone to become an entrepreneur is demonstrated by thousands of Americans, including my aunt, who could retire early because she developed an income stream by buying jeans and children's clothes at garage sales and selling them to people around the world on eBay.

The analyst: Agreeing and disagreeing simultaneously with a source

Incorporating sources is not a matter of simply agreeing or disagreeing with them. Often you will agree with a source up to a point, but you will come to a different conclusion. Or you may agree with the conclusions, but not agree with the reasons put forth.

I agree with _____ up to a point, but I disagree with the conclusion _____ because _____.

Example claim: Qualifying the argument against outsourcing resulting from free-trade policies

Lou Dobbs accurately blames our government for giving multinational corporations tax breaks for exporting jobs rather than regulating the loss of millions of jobs, but the real problem lies in the enormous appetite of Americans for inexpensive consumer products like HD televisions that is supported by borrowing money from overseas to the point that our dollar has plummeted in value.

> **Example claim: Qualifying the argument in favor of outsourcing resulting from free-trade policies**
>
> Thomas Friedman's central claim that the world is being "flattened" by globalization and there is not much we can do to stop it is essentially correct, but he neglects the social costs of globalization around the world, where the banner of free trade has been the justification for devastating the environment, destroying workers' rights and the rights of indigenous peoples, and ignoring laws passed by representative governments.

Find Good Reasons

Get in the habit of asking these questions every time you are asked to write an argument.

Can you argue by definition?

Probably the most powerful kind of good reason is an argument from definition. You can think of a definition as a simple statement: _____ *is a* _____. You use these statements all the time. When you need a course to fulfill your social-science requirement, you look at the list of courses that are defined as social-science courses. You find out that the anthropology class you want to take is one of them. It's just as important when _____ *is not a* _____. Suppose you are taking College Algebra, which is a math course taught by the math department, yet it doesn't count for the math requirement. The reason it doesn't count is because College Algebra is not defined as a college-level math class. So you have to enroll next semester in Calculus I.

Many definitions are not nearly as clear-cut as the math requirement. If you want to argue that figure skaters are athletes, you will need to define what an athlete is. You start thinking. An athlete competes in an activity, but that definition alone is too broad, since many competitions do not require physical activity. Thus, an athlete must participate in a competitive physical activity and must train for it. But that definition is still not quite narrow enough, because soldiers also train for competitive physical activity. You decide to add that the activity must be a sport and that it must require special competence and precision. Your because clause turns out as follows: *Figure skaters are athletes because true athletes train for and compete in physical sporting competitions that require special competence and precision.*

If you can get your audience to accept your definitions, you've gone a long way toward convincing them of the validity of your claim. That is why the most controversial issues in our culture—abortion, affirmative action, gay rights, pornography, women's rights, privacy rights, gun control, the death penalty—are argued from definition. Is abortion a crime or a medical procedure? Is pornography protected by the First Amendment, or is it a violation of women's rights? Is the death penalty just or cruel and inhuman? You can see from these examples that definitions often rely on deeply held beliefs.

Because people have strong beliefs about controversial issues, they often don't care about the practical consequences. Arguing that it is much cheaper to execute prisoners who have been convicted of first-degree murder than to keep them in prison for life does not convince those who believe that it is morally wrong to kill. (See Chapter 8.)

Can you argue from value?

A special kind of argument from definition, one that often implies consequences, is the argument from value. You can support your claim with a "because clause" (or several of them) that includes a sense of evaluation. Arguments from value follow from claims like _____ *is a good* _____, or _____ *is not a good* _____.

Evaluation arguments usually proceed from the presentation of certain criteria. These criteria come from the definitions of good and bad, of poor and not so poor, that prevail in a given case. A great burger fulfills certain criteria; so does an outstanding movie, an excellent class, or the best laptop in your price range. Sometimes the criteria are straightforward, as in the burger example. A great burger has to have tasty meat—tender and without gristle, fresh, never frozen—a fresh bun that is the right size, and your favorite condiments.

But if you are buying a laptop computer and want to play the latest games along with your school tasks, you need to do some homework. For realistic graphics the best laptop will have a fast chip, preferably a dual core system. It will be equipped with a wireless modem, so you have access to the Internet at wireless hot spots. The battery life should be at least two hours, the hard drive should be large enough for your needs, the construction should be sturdy, and the warranty should cover the computer for at least three years. The keys for evaluation arguments are finding the appropriate criteria and convincing your readers that those criteria are the right criteria (see Chapter 10).

Can you argue from consequence?

Another powerful source of good reasons comes from considering the possible consequences of your position: Can you sketch out the good things that will follow from your position? Can you establish that certain bad things will be avoided if your position is adopted? If so, you will have other good reasons to use.

Causal arguments take the basic form of _____ *causes* _____ (or _____ *does not cause* _____). Very often, causal arguments are more complicated, taking the form _____ *causes* _____ *which, in turn, causes* _____ *and so on.* In one famous example, environmentalist Rachel Carson in *Silent Spring* makes powerful arguments from consequence. Rachel Carson's primary claim is that *DDT should not be sprayed on a massive scale because it will poison animals and people.* The key to her argument is the causal chain that explains how animals and people are poisoned. Carson describes how nothing exists alone in nature. When a potato field is sprayed with DDT, some of that poison is absorbed by the skin of the potatoes and some washes into the groundwater, where it contaminates drinking water. Other poisonous residue is absorbed into streams, where it is ingested by insect larvae, which in turn are eaten by fish. Fish are eaten by other fish, which are then eaten by waterfowl and people. At each stage, the poisons become more concentrated. (See Chapter 9 for additional examples of causal arguments.)

Proposal arguments are future-oriented arguments from consequence. In a proposal argument, you cannot stop with naming good reasons; you also have to show that these consequences would follow from the idea or course of action that you are arguing. For example, if you are proposing designated lanes for bicycles on the streets of your city, you must argue that they will encourage more people to ride bicycles to work and school, reducing air pollution and traffic congestion for everyone. (See Chapter 13.)

Can you counter objections to your position?

Another good way to find convincing good reasons is to think about possible objections to your position. If you can imagine how your audience might counter or respond to your argument, you will probably include in your argument precisely the points that will address your readers' particular needs and objections. If you are successful, your readers will be convinced that you are right. You've no doubt had the experience of mentally saying to a writer in the course of your reading, "Yeah, but what about this other idea?"—only to have the writer address precisely this objection.

You can impress your readers if you've thought about why anyone would oppose your position and exactly how that opposition would be expressed. If you are writing a proposal argument for a computer literacy requirement for all high school graduates, you might think about why anyone would object, since computers are critical for our jobs and lives. What will the practical objections be? What about philosophical ones? Why hasn't such a requirement been put in place already? By asking such questions in your own arguments, you are likely to develop robust because clauses.

Sometimes, writers pose rhetorical questions. You might say, "But won't paying for computers for all students make my taxes go up?" Stating objections explicitly can be effective if you make the objections as those of a reasonable person with an alternative point of view. But if the objections you state are ridiculous ones, then you risk being accused of setting up a **straw man**—that is, making the position opposing your own so simplistic that no one would likely identify with it. (See Chapter 12.)

Find Evidence to Support Good Reasons

Good reasons are essential ingredients of good arguments, but they don't do the job alone. You must support or verify good reasons with evidence. Evidence consists of hard data, examples, personal experiences, episodes, or tabulations of episodes (known as statistics) that are seen as relevant to the good reasons you are putting forward. Thus, a writer of arguments puts forward not only claims and good reasons but also evidence that those good reasons are true.

How much supporting evidence should you supply? How much evidence is enough? As is usual in the case of rhetoric, the best answer is, "It depends." If a reader is likely to find one of your good reasons hard to believe, then you should be aggressive in offering support. You should present detailed evidence in a patient and painstaking way. As one presenting an argument you have a responsibility not just to *state* a case but to *make* a case with evidence. Arguments that are unsuccessful tend to fail not because of a shortage of good reasons; more often, they fail because the reader doesn't agree that there is enough evidence to support the good reason that is being presented.

If your good reason isn't especially controversial, you probably should not belabor it. Think of your own experiences as a reader. How often do you recall saying to yourself, as you read a passage or listened to a speaker, "OK! OK! I get the point! Don't keep piling up all of this evidence for me because I don't want it or need it." However, such a reaction is rare, isn't it? By contrast, how often do you recall muttering under your breath, "How can you say that? What evidence do you have to back it up?" When in doubt, err on the side of offering too much evidence. It's an error that is seldom made and not often criticized.

When a writer doesn't provide satisfactory evidence to support a because clause, readers might feel that there has been a failure in the reasoning process. In fact, in your previous courses in writing and speaking, you may have learned about various fallacies associated with faulty arguments (pages 17–19).

Strictly speaking, there is nothing false about these so-called logical fallacies. The fallacies most often refer to failures in providing evidence; when you don't provide enough good evidence to convince your audience, you might be accused of committing a fallacy in reasoning. You will usually avoid such accusations if the evidence that you cite is both *relevant* and *sufficient*.

Relevance refers to the appropriateness of the evidence to the case at hand. Some kinds of evidence are seen as more relevant than others for particular audiences. On the one hand, in science and industry, personal testimony is seen as having limited relevance, while experimental procedures and controlled observations have far more credibility. Compare someone who defends the use of a particular piece of computer software because "it worked for me" with someone who defends it because "according to a journal article published last month, 84 percent of the users of the software were satisfied or very satisfied with it." On the other hand, in writing to the general public on controversial issues such as gun control, personal experience is often considered more relevant than other kinds of data.

Sufficiency refers to the amount of evidence cited. Sometimes a single piece of evidence or a single instance will carry the day if it is especially compelling in some way—if it represents the situation well or makes a point that isn't particularly controversial. More often, people expect more than one piece of evidence if they are to be convinced of something. Convincing readers that they should approve a statewide computer literacy requirement for all high school graduates will require much more evidence than the story of a single graduate who succeeded with her computer skills. You will likely need statistical evidence for such a broad proposal.

If you anticipate that your audience might not accept your evidence, face the situation squarely. First, think carefully about the argument you are presenting. If you cannot cite adequate evidence for your assertions, perhaps those assertions must be modified or qualified in some way. If you remain convinced of your assertions, then think about doing more research to come up with additional evidence.

For support in learning this chapter's content, follow this path in MyCompLab:
> Resources > Writing > The Writing Process > Planning.
Review the Instruction and Multimedia resources, then complete the Exercises and click on Gradebook to measure your progress.

4 | Drafting and Revising Arguments

QUICK TAKE

In this chapter, you will learn that

1. Focusing and evaluating your thesis is critical to writing a successful argument (see below)
2. Keeping your readers in mind will help you write your argument (see page 43)
3. Writing an engaging title and introduction will draw your readers into your argument (see page 46)
4. Evaluating your draft using specific strategies will help you identify your goals for revision (see pages 48–49)

People frequently revise things that they own. What objects have you revised?

State and Evaluate Your Thesis

Once you have identified a topic and have a good sense of how to develop it, the next critical step is to write a **working thesis.** Your **thesis** states your main claim. Much writing that you will do in college and later in your career will require an explicit thesis, usually placed near the beginning.

Focusing your thesis

The thesis can make or break your paper. If the thesis is too broad, you cannot do justice to the argument. Who wouldn't wish for fewer traffic accidents, better medical care, more effective schools, or a cleaner environment? Simple solutions for these complex problems are unlikely.

Stating something that is obvious to everyone isn't an arguable thesis. Don't settle for easy answers. When a topic is too broad, a predictable thesis often results. Narrow your focus and concentrate on the areas where you have the most questions. Those are likely the areas where your readers will have the most questions too.

The opposite problem is less common: a thesis that is too narrow. If your thesis simply states a commonly known fact, then it is too narrow. For example, the growth rate of the population in the United States has doubled since 1970 because of increased immigration. The U.S. Census Bureau provides reasonably accurate statistical information, so this claim is not arguable. But the policies that allow increased immigration and the effects of a larger population—more crowding and higher costs of health care, education, and transportation—are arguable.

> **Not arguable:** The population of the United States grew faster in the 1990s than in any previous decade because Congress increased the rate of legal immigration and the government stopped enforcing most laws against illegal immigration in the interior of the country.
>
> **Arguable:** Allowing a high rate of immigration helps the United States deal with the problems of an increasingly aging society and helps provide funding for millions of Social Security recipients.
>
> **Arguable:** The increase in the number of visas to foreign workers in technology industries is the major cause of unemployment in those industries.

Evaluating your thesis

Once you have a working thesis, ask these questions.

- Is it arguable?
- Is it specific?
- Is it manageable given your length and time requirements?
- Is it interesting to your intended readers?

Example 1

Sample thesis

> We should take action to resolve the serious traffic problem in our city.

Is it arguable? The thesis is arguable, but it lacks a focus.

Is it specific? The thesis is too broad.

Is it manageable? Transportation is a complex issue. New highways and rail systems are expensive and take many years to build. Furthermore, citizens don't want new roads running through their neighborhoods.

Is it interesting? The topic has the potential to be interesting if the writer can propose a specific solution to a problem that everyone in the city recognizes.

When a thesis is too broad, it needs to be revised to address a specific aspect of an issue. Make the big topic smaller.

Revised thesis

> The existing freight railway that runs through the center of the city should be converted to a passenger railway because this is the cheapest and quickest way to decrease traffic congestion downtown.

Example 2

Sample thesis

> Over 60 percent of Americans play computer games on a regular basis.

Is it arguable? The thesis states a commonly acknowledged fact. It is not arguable.

Is it specific? The thesis is too narrow.

Is it manageable? A known fact is stated in the thesis, so there is little to research. Several surveys report this finding.

Is it interesting? The popularity of video games is well established. Nearly everyone is aware of the trend.

There's nothing original or interesting about stating that Americans love computer games. Think about what is controversial. One debatable topic is how computer games affect children.

Revised thesis

> Computer games are valuable because they improve children's visual attention skills, literacy skills, and computer literacy skills.

Finding Good Reasons

Should driving while talking be banned?

In a movement to improve driving safety, California, Connecticut, the District of Columbia, New Jersey, New York, Oregon, Utah, and Washington have passed laws banning the use of handheld cell phones while driving except for emergency workers and people making 911 calls. Several other states have banned cell phones while driving for drivers aged 18 and younger.

Proponents of the ban point to a National Highway Traffic Safety Administration study, reporting that approximately 25 to 30 percent of motor vehicle crashes—about 1.2 million accidents each year—are caused by driver distraction. Opponents of the ban argue that anything that distracts the driver—eating potato chips, talking with passengers, spilled coffee—can cause an accident. The answer, they say, is driver education.

Write about it

1. Write a thesis arguing in support of a ban on cell phones while driving, against a ban, or in support of a more limited position such as banning cell-phone use for drivers 18 and under.

2. Think about the audience that would likely oppose your position. For example, if you support a ban on talking while driving, think about the likely responses of high school students, salespeople who spend much of their workdays driving from place to place, and workers who receive assignments by phone. What good reasons would convince readers who hold an opposing view?

3. What reasons would people who oppose your position likely offer in response? What counterarguments could you give to answer these objections?

Think About Your Readers

Thinking about your readers doesn't mean telling them what they might want to hear. Instead, imagine yourself in a dialogue with your readers. What questions will they likely have? How might you address any potential objections?

Understanding what your readers know—and do not know

Your readers' knowledge of your subject is critical to the success of your argument. If they are not familiar with the background information, they probably won't understand your argument fully. If you know that your readers will be unfamiliar with your subject, you have to supply background information before attempting to convince them of your position. A good tactic is to tie your new information to what your readers already know. Comparisons and analogies can be very helpful in linking old and new information.

Understanding your readers' attitudes toward you

To get your readers to take you seriously, you must convince them that they can trust you. You need to get them to see you as

- **Concerned:** Readers want you to be committed to your subject. They also expect you to be concerned about them. After all, if you don't care about them, why should they read what you write?
- **Well informed:** Many people ramble on about any subject without knowing anything about it. College writing requires that you do your homework on a subject.
- **Fair:** Many writers look at only one side of an issue. Readers respect objectivity and an unbiased approach.
- **Ethical:** Many writers use only the facts that support their positions and often distort facts and sources. Critical readers often notice what is being left out. Don't try to conceal what doesn't support your position.

Understanding your readers' attitudes toward your subject

People have prior attitudes about controversial issues. You must take these attitudes into consideration as you write or speak. Imagine, for instance, that you are preparing an argument for a guest editorial in your college newspaper. You are advocating that your state government should provide parents with choices between public and private schools. You plan to argue that the tax dollars that now automatically go to public schools should go to private schools if parents so choose. You have evidence that the sophomore-to-senior dropout rate in private schools is less than half the rate in public schools. Furthermore, students from private schools attend college at nearly twice the rate of public-school graduates. You intend to argue that one of the reasons private schools are more successful is that they spend more money on instruction and less on administration. And you believe that school choice speaks to the American desire for personal freedom.

Not everyone on your campus will agree with your position. How might the faculty at your college or university feel about this issue? How about the administrators, the staff, other students, and interested community members who read the student newspaper? What are their attitudes toward public funding of private schools? How are you going to deal with the objection that many students in private schools do better in school because they come from more affluent families?

Even when you write about a much less controversial subject, you must think carefully about your audience's attitudes toward what you have to say or to write. Sometimes your audience may share your attitudes; other times, your audience may be neutral. At still other times, your audience will have attitudes that differ sharply from your own. Anticipate these various attitudes and act accordingly. If these attitudes are different from yours, you will have to work hard to counter them without insulting your audience.

Organize Your Argument

Asking a series of questions can generate a list of good reasons, but even if you have plenty, you still have to decide which ones to use and in what order to present them. Thinking about your readers' knowledge, attitudes, and values will help you to decide which reasons to present to your audience.

Writing plans often take the form of outlines, either formal outlines or working outlines. A **formal outline** typically begins with the thesis statement, which anchors the entire outline

---

Managing the Risks of Nanotechnology While Reaping the Rewards

THESIS: The revolutionary potential of nanotechnology has arrived in an explosion of consumer products, yet our federal government has yet to recognize the potential risks or to fund research to reduce those risks.

I.   Nanotechnology now is in many consumer products.

    A.   The promise of nanotechnology to revolutionize medicine, energy production, and communication is years in the future, but consumer products are here now.

    B.   Nanotechnology is now in clothing, food, sports equipment, medicines, electronics, and cars.

C.   Experts predict that 15 percent of manufactured products worldwide will contain nanotechnology in 2014.

D.   The question that hasn't been asked: Is nanotechnology safe?

II.   Americans have little awareness of nanotechnology.

A.   Companies have stopped mentioning and advertising nanotechnology.

B.   Companies and the insurance industry paid $250 billion in asbestos claims in the United States alone.

C.   Companies fear exposure to lawsuits if nanotechnology is found to be toxic.

A **working outline** is a sketch of how you will arrange the major sections.

Managing the Risks of Nanotechnology While Reaping the Rewards

SECTION 1: Begin by defining nanotechnology—manipulating particles between 1 and 100 nanometers (nanometer is a billionth of a meter). Describe the rapid spread of nanotechnology in consumer products including clothing, food, sports equipment, medicines, electronics, and cars. State projection of 15 percent of global manufactured goods containing nanotechnology in 2014.

SECTION 2: Most Americans know nothing about nanotechnology. Companies have stopped advertising that their products contain nanotechnology because of fear of potential lawsuits. Asbestos, once thought safe, now is known to be toxic and has cost companies $250 billion in lawsuits in the United States alone.

SECTION 3: Relatively little research has been done on the safety of nanotechnology. No testing is required for new products because the materials are common, but materials behave differently at nano-scale (example—aluminum normally inert but combustible at nano-scale).

SECTION 4: Nanoparticles are highly mobile and can cross the blood-brain barrier and through the placenta. They are toxic in brains of fish and may collect in lungs.

SECTION 5: Urge that the federal government develop a master plan for identifying and reducing potential risks of nanotechnology and provide sufficient funding to carry out the plan.

Write an Engaging Title and Introduction

Many writers don't think much about titles, but they are very important. A good title makes the reader want to see what you have to say. Be specific as you can in your title, and if possible, suggest your stance.

Get off to a fast start in your introduction. Convince your reader to keep reading. Cut to the chase. Think about how you can get your readers interested. Consider using one of the following.

- State your thesis concisely.
- Provide a hard-hitting fact.
- Ask a question.
- Give a vivid description of a problem.
- Discuss a contradiction or paradox.
- Describe a scenario.

Managing the Risks of Nanotechnology While Reaping the Rewards

The revolutionary potential of nanotechnology for medicine, energy production, and communication is now at the research and development stage, but the future has arrived in consumer products. Nanotechnology has given us products we hardly could have imagined just a few years ago: socks that never stink; pants that repel water yet keep you cool; eyeglasses that won't scratch; "smart" foods that add nutrition and reduce cholesterol; DVDs that are incredibly lifelike; bandages that speed healing; tennis balls that last longer; golf balls that fly straighter; pharmaceuticals that selectively deliver drugs; various digital devices like palm pilots, digital cameras, and cell phones that have longer battery lives and more vivid displays; and cars that are lighter, stronger, and more fuel efficient. These miracle products are now possible because scientists have learned how to manipulate nano-scale particles from 1 to 100 nanometers (a nanometer is a billionth of a meter; a human hair is about 100,000 nanometers in width). Experts estimate that 15 percent of all consumer products will contain nanotechnology by 2014. In the rush to create new consumer products, however, one question has not been asked: Is nanotechnology safe for those who use the products and the workers who are exposed to nanoparticles daily?

Write a Strong Conclusion

Restating your thesis usually isn't the best way to finish a paper. Conclusions that offer only a summary bore readers. The worst endings say something like "in my paper I've said this." Effective conclusions are interesting and provocative, leaving readers with something to think about. Give your readers something to take away besides a straight summary. Try one of these approaches.

- Issue a call to action.
- Discuss the implications.
- Make recommendations.
- Project into the future.
- Tell an anecdote that illustrates a key point.

> The potential risks of nanotechnology are reasonably well known. Among the more obvious research questions are the following:
>
> - How hazardous are nanoparticles for workers who have daily exposure?
> - What happens to nanoparticles when they are poured down the drain and eventually enter streams, lakes, and oceans?
> - How readily do nanoparticles penetrate the skin?
> - What happens when nanoparticles enter the brain?
> - What effect do airborne nanoparticles have on the lungs?
>
> Nanotechnology promises untold benefits beyond consumer goods in the fields of medicine, energy production, and communication, but these benefits can be realized only if nanotechnology is safe. The federal National Nanotechnology Initiative spent over $1.7 billion in 2009 on nanotechnology science and engineering research, but it budgeted only $74 million on environmental, health, and safety research in 2009. The federal government needs to create a master plan for risk research and to increase spending at least tenfold to ensure sufficient funding to carry out the plan.

When you finish your conclusion, read your introduction again. The main claim in your conclusion should be closely related to the main subject, question, or claim in your introduction. If they do not match, revise the subject, question, or claim in the introduction to match the conclusion. Your thinking evolves and develops as you write, and often your introduction needs some adjusting if you wrote it first.

Evaluate Your Draft

To review and evaluate your draft, pretend you are someone who is either uninformed about your subject or informed but likely to disagree with you. If possible, think of an actual person and imagine yourself as that person.

Read your draft aloud all the way through. When you read aloud, you often hear clunky phrases and catch errors, but just put checks in the margins so you can return to them later. You don't want to get bogged down with the little stuff. What you are after in this stage is an overall sense of how well you accomplished what you set out to do.

Use the questions in the box on the next two pages to evaluate your draft. Note any places where you might make improvements. When you finish, make a list of your goals for the revision. You may have to write another draft before you move to the next stage.

Checklist for evaluating your draft

Does your paper or project meet the assignment?

- Look again at your assignment, especially at key words such as *define, analyze causes, evaluate,* and *propose.* Does your paper or project do what the assignment requires? If not, how can you change it?

- Look again at the assignment for specific guidelines including length, format, and amount of research. Does your work meet these guidelines?

Can you better focus your thesis and your supporting reasons?

- You may have started out with a large topic and ended up writing about one aspect of it. Can you make your thesis even more precise?

- Can you find the exact location where you link each reason to your thesis?

Are your main points adequately developed?

- Can you explain your reasons in more detail?

- Can you add evidence to better support your main points?

- Do you provide enough background on your topic?

Is your organization effective?

- Is the order of your main points clear? (You may want to make a quick outline of your draft if you have not done so already.)

- Are there any abrupt shifts or gaps?

- Are there sections or paragraphs that should be rearranged?

Are your key terms adequately defined?

- What are your key terms?

- Can you define these terms more precisely?

Do you consider other points of view?

- Where do you acknowledge views besides your own? If you don't acknowledge other views, where can you add them?

- How can you make your discussion of opposing views more acceptable to readers who hold those views?

Do you represent yourself effectively?

- Forget for the moment that you wrote what you are reading. What is your impression of the writer?

- Is the tone of the writing appropriate for the subject?

Can you improve your title and introduction?

- Can you make your title more specific and indicate your stance?

- Can you think of a way to start faster and to get your readers interested in what you have to say?

Can you improve your conclusion?

- Can you think of an example that sums up your position?

- Can you discuss an implication of your argument that will make your readers think more about the subject?

- If you are writing a proposal, can you end with a call for action?

Can you improve your visual presentation?

- Is the type style easy to read and consistent?

- Would headings and subheadings help to mark the major sections of your argument?

- If you have statistical data, do you use charts?

- Would illustrations, maps, or other graphics help to explain your main points?

Respond to the Writing of Others

Your instructor may ask you to respond to the drafts of your classmates. Responding to other people's writing requires the same careful attention you give to your own draft. To write a helpful response, you should go through the draft more than once.

First reading

Read at your normal rate the first time through without stopping. When you finish you should have a clear sense of what the writer is trying to accomplish. Try writing the following:

- **Main idea and purpose:** Write a sentence that summarizes what you think is the writer's main idea in the draft.
- **Purpose:** Write a sentence that states what you think the writer is trying to accomplish in the draft.

Second reading

In your second reading, you should be most concerned with the content, organization, and completeness of the draft. Make notes in pencil as you read.

- **Introduction:** Does the writer's first paragraph effectively introduce the topic and engage your interest?
- **Thesis:** What exactly is the writer's thesis? Is it clear? Note in the margin where you think the thesis is located.
- **Focus:** Does the writer maintain focus on the thesis? Note any places where the writer seems to wander off to another topic.
- **Organization:** Are the sections and paragraphs arranged effectively? Do any paragraphs seem to be out of place? Can you suggest a better order for the paragraphs?
- **Completeness:** Are there sections or paragraphs that lack key information or adequate development? Where do you want to know more?
- **Sources:** Are outside sources cited accurately? Are quotations used correctly and worked into the fabric of the draft?

Third reading

In your third reading, turn your attention to matters of audience, style, and tone.

- **Audience:** Who are the writer's intended readers? What does the writer assume the audience knows and believes?

- **Style:** Is the writer's style engaging? How would you describe the writer's voice?
- **Tone:** Is the tone appropriate for the writer's purpose and audience? Is the tone consistent throughout the draft? Are there places where another word or phrase might work better?

When you have finished the third reading, write a short paragraph on each bulleted item above. Refer to specific paragraphs in the draft by number. Then end by answering these two questions:

- What does the writer do especially well in the draft?
- What one or two things would most improve the draft in a revision?

Edit and Proofread Carefully

When you finish revising, you are ready for one final careful reading with the goals of improving your style and eliminating errors.

Edit for style

- **Check connections between sentences and paragraphs.** Notice how your sentences flow within each paragraph and from paragraph to paragraph. If you need to signal the relationship from one sentence or paragraph to the next, use a transitional word or phrase (e.g., *in addition, moreover, similarly, however, nevertheless*).
- **Check your sentences.** Often you will pick up problems with individual sentences by reading aloud. If you notice that a sentence doesn't sound right, think about how you might rephrase it. If a sentence seems too long, consider breaking it into two or more sentences. If you notice a string of short sentences that sound choppy, consider combining them.
- **Eliminate wordiness.** Look for wordy expressions such as *because of the fact that* and *at this point in time*, which can easily be shortened to *because* and *now*. Reduce unnecessary repetition such as *attractive in appearance* or *visible to the eye* to *attractive* and *visible*. Remove unnecessary words like *very, really,* and *totally*. See how many words you can remove without losing the meaning.
- **Use active verbs.** Make your style more lively by replacing forms of *be* (*is, are, was, were*) or verbs ending in *–ing* with active verbs. Sentences that begin with *There is (are)* and *It is* can often be rewritten with active verbs.

Proofread carefully

In your final pass through your text, eliminate as many errors as you can. To become
an effective proofreader, you have to learn
to slow down. Some writers find that moving from word to word with a pencil slows
them down enough to find errors. Others
read backwards to force them to concentrate on each word.

- **Know what your spelling
  checker can and can't do.**
  Spelling checkers are the greatest
  invention since peanut butter.
  They turn up many typos and
  misspellings that are hard to
  catch. But spelling checkers do
  not catch wrong words (*to much*
  for *too much*), missing endings
  (*three dog*), and other similar errors.

  You can get one-on-one help in developing your ideas, focusing your topic, and
  revising your paper or project at your
  writing center.

- **Check for grammar and punctu-
  ation.** Nothing hurts your credibility more than leaving errors in what
  you write. Many job application letters get tossed in the reject pile because of a single, glaring error. Readers probably shouldn't make such
  harsh judgments when they find errors, but often they do. Keep a grammar handbook beside your computer, and use it when you are uncertain
  about what is correct.

For support in learning this chapter's content, follow this path in MyCompLab:
> Resources > Writing > The Writing Process > Drafting and > Revising.
Review the Instruction and Multimedia resources, then complete the Exercises and
click on Gradebook to measure your progress.

Analyzing Arguments

PART

2

5 | Analyzing Written Arguments

QUICK TAKE

In this chapter, you will learn that

1. A rhetorical analysis aims to understand how people attempt to persuade through language and other actions (see below)
2. A rhetorical analysis examines how a text is structured, including choices of language, subject matter, organization, and appeals to the audience (see pages 55–59)
3. A rhetorical analysis considers the broader context, including how a particular text takes part in a larger conversation going on at the time (see pages 59–63)

What Is Rhetorical Analysis?

To many people, the term *rhetoric* means speech or writing that is highly ornamental or deceptive or manipulative. You might hear someone say, "That politician is just using a bunch of rhetoric" or "The rhetoric of that advertisement is very deceptive." But the term *rhetoric* is also used in a positive or neutral sense to describe human communication; for instance, *Silent Spring* is one of the most influential pieces of environmental rhetoric ever written. As a subject of study, rhetoric is usually associated with effective communication, following Aristotle's classic definition of rhetoric as "the art of finding in any given case the available means of persuasion."

Rhetoric is not just a means of *producing* effective communication but also a way of *understanding* communication. The two aspects mutually support one another: becoming a better writer makes you a better interpreter, and becoming a better interpreter makes you a better writer.

Rhetorical analysis can be defined as an effort to understand how people attempt to influence others through language and more broadly every kind of important symbolic action—not only speeches, articles, and books, but also architecture, movies, television shows, memorials, Web sites, advertisements, photos and other images, dance, and popular songs. It might be helpful to think of rhetorical analysis as the kind of critical reading discussed in Chapter 2. Critical reading—rhetorical analysis, that is—involves studying carefully any kind of persuasive action in order to understand it better and to appreciate the tactics involved.

Build a Rhetorical Analysis

Rhetorical analysis examines how an idea is shaped and presented to an audience in a particular form for a specific purpose. There are many approaches to rhetorical analysis and there is no one "correct" way to do it. Generally, though, approaches to rhetorical analysis can be placed between two broad extremes—not mutually exclusive categories but extremes at the ends of a continuum.

At one end of the continuum are analyses that concentrate more on texts than on contexts. They typically use rhetorical concepts to analyze the features of texts. Let's call this approach **textual analysis.** At the other extreme are approaches that emphasize **context** over text. These focus on reconstructing the cultural environment, or context, that existed when a particular rhetorical event took place. That reconstruction provides clues about the persuasive tactics and appeals. Those who undertake **contextual analysis**—as we'll call this second approach—regard particular rhetorical acts as parts of larger communicative chains, or "conversations."

Now let's examine these two approaches in detail.

Analyze the Rhetorical Features

Just as expert teachers in every field of endeavor—from baseball to biology—devise vocabularies to facilitate specialized study, rhetoricians too have developed a set of key concepts to describe rhetorical activities. A fundamental concept in rhetoric is audience. But there are many others. Classical rhetoricians in the tradition of Aristotle, Quintilian, and Cicero developed a range of terms around what they called the canons of rhetoric in order to describe some of the actions of communicators: *inventio* (invention—the finding or creation of information for persuasive acts, and the planning of strategies), *dispostio* (arrangement), *elocutio* (style), *memoria* (the recollection of rhetorical resources that one might call upon, as well as the memorization of what has been invented and arranged), and *pronuntiatio* (delivery). These five canons generally describe the actions of any persuader, from preliminary planning to final delivery.

Over the years, as written discourse gained in prestige against oral discourse, four canons (excepting *memoria*) led to the development of concepts and terms useful for rhetorical analysis. Terms like *ethos, pathos,* and *logos,* all associated with invention, account for features of texts related to the trustworthiness and credibility of the writer or speaker (ethos), for the persuasive good reasons in an argument that derive from a community's mostly deeply held values (pathos), and for the good reasons that emerge from intellectual reasoning (logos). Fundamental to the classical approach to rhetoric is the concept of *decorum,* or "appropriateness": Everything within a persuasive act can be understood as reflecting a central rhetorical goal that governs consistent choices according to occasion and audience.

An example will make textual rhetorical analysis clearer. If you have not done so already, read "The Border Patrol State" by Leslie Marmon Silko in Chapter 11 (pp. 160–166). In the pages that follow, we use the concepts of classical rhetoric to better understand this essay.

Silko's purpose and argument

What is the purpose of Silko's essay? She wrote the essay well over a decade ago, but you probably find it to be interesting and readable still because it concerns the perennial American issue of civil rights. Silko's essay is especially relevant in light of recent debates concerning the Arizona immigration bill and surrounding controversies about the enforcement of state and federal immigration laws. In this case, Silko takes issue with practices associated with the Border Patrol of the Immigration and Naturalization Service (INS). She feels they are reenacting

The statue of Castor stands at the entrance of the Piazza del Campidoglio in Rome. A textual analysis focuses on the statue itself. The size and realism of the statue makes it a masterpiece of classical Roman sculpture.

the long subjugation of native peoples by the white majority. Silko proposes that the power of the Border Patrol be sharply reduced so that the exploitation of her people might be curtailed, and she supports that thesis with an essay that describes and condemns the Border Patrol's tactics.

Essentially Silko's argument comes down to two good reasons: the Border Patrol must be reformed because "the Immigration and Naturalization Service and Border Patrol have implemented policies that interfere with the rights of U.S. citizens to travel freely within our borders" (para. 8), and because efforts to restrict immigration are ineffective and doomed to fail ("It is no use; borders haven't worked, and they won't work," para. 16). Silko's essay amounts to an evaluation of the Border Patrol's activities, an evaluation that finds those activities lacking on ethical and practical grounds.

Silko's use of logos, pathos, and ethos
Logos

When Silko condemns the unethical actions of the Border Patrol early in the essay, she combines ample evidence with other appeals, including our sense of what is legal, constitutional, fair, and honorable. When she explains the futility of trying to

A contextual analysis focuses on the surroundings and history of the statue. According to legend, Castor (left of staircase) and his twin brother Pollux (right of staircase), the mythical sons of Leda, assisted Romans in an early battle. Romans built a large temple in the Forum to honor them. The statues were discovered in the sixteenth century and in 1583 were brought to stand at the top of the Cordonata, a staircase designed by Michelangelo as part of a renovation of the Piazza del Campidoglio commissioned by Pope Paul III Farnese in 1536.

stop immigration, she appeals again to her readers' reasonableness: Constructing walls across the border with Mexico is foolish because "border entrepreneurs have already used blowtorches to cut passageways through the fence" (para. 15), because "a mass migration is already under way" (para. 16), and because "The Americas are Indian country, and the 'Indian problem' is not about to go away" (para. 17).

The bulk of "The Border Patrol State" amounts to an argument by example. The single case—Silko's personal experience, as a Native American, with the border police—stands for many such cases. This case study persuades as other case studies and narratives do—by serving as a representative example that stands for the treatment of many Native Americans.

Pathos

The logical appeals in Silko's essay are reinforced by her emotional appeals.

- The Border Patrol is constructing an "Iron Curtain" that is as destructive of human rights as the Iron Curtain that the Soviet Union constructed around Eastern Europe after World War II (para. 15).

- "Proud" and "patriotic" Native Americans are being harassed: "old Bill Pratt used to ride his horse 300 miles overland . . . every summer to work as a fire lookout" (para. 1).
- Border police terrify American citizens in a way that is chillingly reminiscent of "the report of Argentine police and military officers who became addicted to interrogation, torture, and murder" (paras. 3–5).

The essay's most emotional moment may be when Silko describes how the Border Patrol dog, trained to find illegal drugs and other contraband, including human contraband, seems to sympathize with her and those she is championing: "I saw immediately from the expression in her eyes that the dog hated them" (para. 6); "The dog refused to accuse us: She had an innate dignity that did not permit her to serve the murderous impulses of those men" (para. 7). Clearly the good reasons in "The Border Patrol State" appeal in a mutually supportive way to both the reason and the emotions of Silko's audience. She appeals to the whole person.

Ethos

Why do we take Silko's word about the stories she tells? It is because she establishes her *ethos*, or trustworthiness, early in the essay. Silko reminds her readers that she is a respected, published author who has been on a book tour to publicize her novel *Almanac of the Dead* (para. 3). She buttresses her trustworthiness in other ways too:

- She quotes widely, if unobtrusively, from books and reports to establish that she has studied the issues thoroughly. Note how much she displays her knowledge of INS policies in paragraph 9, for instance.
- She tells not only of her own encounters with the border police (experiences that are a source of great credibility), but also of the encounters of others whom she lists, name after careful name, in order that we might trust her account.
- She demonstrates knowledge of history and geography.
- She connects herself to America generally by linking herself to traditional American values such as freedom (para. 1), ethnic pride, tolerance, and even a love of dogs.

This essay, because of its anti-authoritarian strain, might seem to display politically progressive attitudes at times, but overall, Silko comes off as hard-working, honest, educated, even patriotic. And definitely credible.

Silko's arrangement

Silko arranges her essay appropriately as well. In general the essay follows a traditional pattern. She begins with a long concrete introductory story that hooks the reader and leads to her thesis in paragraph 8. Next, in the body of her essay, she supports her thesis by evaluating the unethical nature of INS policies. She cites their violation of constitutional protections, their similarity to tactics used in nations that are notorious for violating the rights of citizens, and their fundamental immorality. She also emphasizes how those policies are racist in nature (paras. 11–13).

After completing her moral evaluation of INS policy, she turns to the practical difficulties of halting immigration in paragraph 14. The North American Free Trade Agreement (NAFTA) permits the free flow of goods, and even drugs are impossible to stop, so how can people be stopped from crossing borders? Efforts to seal borders are "pathetic" in their ineffectiveness (para. 15). These points lay the groundwork for Silko's surprising and stirring conclusions: "The great human migration within the Americas cannot be stopped; human beings are natural forces of the earth, just as rivers and winds are natural forces" (para. 16); "the Americas are Indian country, and the 'Indian problem' is not about to go away" (para. 17). The mythic "return of the Aztlan" is on display in the box cars that go by as the essay closes. In short, this essay unfolds in a conventional way: it has a standard beginning, middle, and end.

Silko's style

What about Silko's style? How is it appropriate to her purposes? Take a look at paragraphs 3 and 4. You will notice that nearly all of the fourteen sentences in these paragraphs are simple in structure. There are only five sentences that use any form of subordination (clauses that begin with *when, that,* or *if*). Many of the sentences consist either of one clause or of two clauses joined by simple coordination (connection with conjunctions such as *and* or *but* or a semicolon). Several of the sentences and clauses are unusually short. Furthermore, in these paragraphs Silko never uses metaphors or other sorts of poetic language. Her choice of words is as simple as her sentences. It all reminds you of the daily newspaper, doesn't it? Silko chooses a style similar to one used in newspaper reporting—simple, straightforward, unadorned—because she wants her readers to accept her narrative as credible and trustworthy. Her tone and voice reinforce her ethos.

There is more to say about the rhetorical choices that Silko made in crafting "The Border Patrol State," but this analysis is enough to illustrate our main point. Textual rhetorical analysis employs rhetorical terminology—in this case, terms borrowed from classical rhetoric such as ethos, pathos, logos, arrangement, style, and tone—as a way of helping us to understand how a writer makes choices to achieve certain effects. And textual analysis cooperates with contextual analysis.

Analyze the Rhetorical Context
Communication as conversation

Notice that in the previous discussion the fact that Leslie Marmon Silko's "The Border Patrol State" was originally published in the magazine *The Nation* did not matter too much. Nor did it matter when the essay was published (October 17, 1994), who exactly read it, what their reaction was, or what other people were saying at the time. Textual analysis can proceed as if the item under consideration "speaks for all time," as if it is a museum piece unaffected by time and space. There's nothing wrong with museums, of course; they permit people to observe and appreciate objects in an important way. But museums often fail to reproduce an artwork's original context and cultural meaning. In that sense museums can diminish understanding as much as they contribute to it. Contextual rhetorical analysis is an attempt to understand communications through the lens of their environments, examining the setting or scene out of which any communication emerges.

Similar to textual analysis, contextual analysis may be conducted in any number of ways. But contextual rhetorical analysis always proceeds from a description of the **rhetorical situation** that motivated the event in question. It demands an appreciation of the social circumstances that call rhetorical events into being and that orchestrate the course of those events. It regards communications as anything but self-contained:

- Each communication is considered as a response to other communications and to other social practices.
- Communications, and social practices more generally, are considered to reflect the attitudes and values of the communities that sustain them.
- Analysts seek evidence of how those other communications and social practices are reflected in texts.

Rhetorical analysis from a contextualist perspective understands individual pieces as parts of ongoing conversations.

The challenge is to reconstruct the conversation surrounding a specific piece of writing or speaking. Sometimes it is easy to do so. You may have appropriate background information on the topic, as well as a feel for what is behind what people are writing or saying about it. People who have strong feelings about the environment, stem cell research, same-sex marriage, or any number of other current issues are well informed about the arguments that are converging around those topics.

But other times it takes some research to reconstruct the conversations and social practices related to a particular issue. If the issue is current, you need to see how the debate is conducted in current magazines, newspapers, talk shows, movies and TV shows, Web sites, and so forth. If the issue is from an earlier time, you must do archival research into historical collections of newspapers, magazines, books, letters, and other documentary sources. Archival research usually involves libraries, special research collections, or film and television archives where it is possible to learn quite a bit about context.

An example will clarify how contextual analysis works to open up an argument to analysis. Let's return to a discussion of Silko's "The Border Patrol State" on pages 160–166. It will take a bit of research to reconstruct some of the "conversations" that Silko is participating in, but the result will be an enhanced understanding of the essay as well as an appreciation for how you might do a contextual rhetorical analysis.

Silko's life and works

You can begin by learning more about Silko herself. The essay provides some facts about her (e.g., that she is a Native American writer of note who is from the Southwest). The headnote on page 160 gives additional information (that her writing usually develops out of Native American traditions and tales). You can learn more about Silko using the Internet and your library's Web site. Silko's credibility, her ethos, is established not just by her textual decisions but also by her prior reputation, especially for readers of *The Nation* who would recognize and appreciate her accomplishments.

Perhaps the most relevant information on the Web is about *Almanac of the Dead*, the novel Silko refers to in paragraph 3. The novel, set mainly in Tucson, involves a Native American woman psychic who is in the process of transcribing the lost histories of her dead ancestors into "an almanac of the dead"—a history of her people. This history is written from the point of view of the conquered, not the conqueror. "The Border Patrol State," it seems, is an essay version of *Almanac of the Dead* in that Silko protests what has been lost—and what is still being lost—in the clash between white and Native American cultures. It is a protest against the tactics of the border police. Or is it?

The context of publication

Through a consideration of the conversations swirling around it, contextual analysis actually suggests that "The Border Patrol State" is just as much about immigration policy as it is about the civil rights of Native Americans. The article first appeared in *The Nation*, a respected, politically progressive magazine that has been appearing weekly for decades. Published in New York City, it is a magazine of public opinion that covers theater, film, music, fiction, and other arts; politics and public affairs; and contemporary culture. If you want to know what left-leaning people are thinking about an issue, *The Nation* is a good magazine to consult. You can imagine that Silko's essay therefore reached an audience of sympathetic readers—people who would be receptive to her message. They would be inclined to sympathize with Silko's complaints and to heed her call for a less repressive Border Patrol.

What is more interesting is that Silko's essay appeared on October 17, 1994, in a special issue of *The Nation* devoted to "The Immigration Wars," a phrase prominent on the magazine's cover. Silko's essay was one of several articles that appeared under that banner, an indication that Silko's argument is not just about the violation of the civil rights of Native Americans but also about the larger issue of immigration policy. "The Border Patrol State" appeared after David Cole's "Five Myths about Immigration," Elizabeth Kadetsky's "Bashing Illegals in California," Peter Kwong's "China's Human Traffickers," two editorials about immigration policy, and short columns on immigration by *Nation* regulars Katha Pollitt, Aryeh Neier, and Christopher Hitchens. Together the articles in this issue of *The Nation* mounted a sustained argument in favor of a liberal immigration policy.

The larger conversation

Why did *The Nation* entitle its issue "The Immigration Wars"? Immigration was a huge controversy in October 1994, just before the 1994 elections. When the 1965 Immigration Act was amended in 1990, the already strong flow of immigrants to the United States became a flood. While many previous immigrants came to the United States from Europe, most recent immigrants have come from Asia, Latin America, the Caribbean islands, and Africa. While earlier immigrants typically passed through Ellis Island and past the Statue of Liberty that welcomed them, most recent immigrants in 1994 were coming to Florida, Texas, and California. The arrival of all those new immigrants revived old fears that have been in the air for decades (that they take away jobs from native-born Americans, that they undermine national values by resisting assimilation and clinging to their own cultures, that they reduce standards of living by putting stress on education and social-welfare budgets). Many people countered those fears by pointing out that immigrants create jobs and wealth, enhance the vitality of American culture, become among the proudest of Americans, and contribute to the tax base of their communities. But those counterarguments were undermined when a tide of illegal immigrants—up to 500,000 per year—was arriving at the time Silko was writing.

The Immigration Wars were verbal wars. In the 1994 election, Republicans had united under the banner of a "Contract with America." Some 300 Republican congressional candidates, drawn together by conservative leader Newt Gingrich, agreed to run on a common platform in an ultimately successful effort to gain control of the House of Representatives. Among a number of initiatives, the Contract with America proposed changes in laws in order to curtail immigration, to reduce illegal immigration, and to deny benefits such as health care, social services, and education to illegal residents.

The Contract with America offered support for California's Proposition 187, another important 1994 proposal. This so-called "Save Our State" initiative was designed to "prevent California's estimated 1.7 million undocumented immigrants from partaking of every form of public welfare including nonemergency medical care, prenatal clinics and public schools," as Kadetsky explained in her essay in *The Nation*. The Republican Contract with America and California's Proposition 187 together constituted the nation's leading domestic issue in October 1994. The war of words about the issue was evident in the magazines, books, newspapers, talk shows, barber shops, and hair salons of America—much as it is today.

Silko's political goals

In this context, it is easy to see that Silko's essay is against more than the Border Patrol. It is an argument in favor of relatively unrestricted immigration, especially for Mexicans and Native Americans. Moreover, it is a direct refutation of the Contract with America and Proposition 187. Proposition 187 states "that [the People of California] have suffered and are suffering economic hardship caused by the presence of illegal aliens in this state, that they have suffered and are suffering personal injury and damage caused by the criminal conduct of illegal aliens, [and] that they have a right to the protection of their government from any person or persons entering this country illegally."

Silko turns the claim around. It is the Border Patrol that is behaving illegally. It is the Border Patrol that is creating economic hardship. It is the border police that are inflicting personal injury and damage through criminal conduct. Finally, it is the U.S. government that is acting illegally by ignoring the treaty of Guadalupe Hidalgo, which "recognizes the right of the Tohano O'Odom (Papago) people to move freely across the U.S.-Mexico border without documents," as Silko writes in a footnote. Writing just before the election of 1994 and in the midst of a spirited national debate, Silko had specific political goals in mind. A contextual analysis of "The Border Patrol State" reveals that the essay is, at least in part, an eloquent refutation of the Contract with America and Proposition 187—two items that are not even named explicitly in the essay!

We could do more contextual analysis here. There is no need to belabor the point, however; our purpose has been simply to illustrate that contextual analysis of a piece of rhetoric can enrich our understanding.

Write a Rhetorical Analysis

Effective rhetorical analysis, as we have seen, can be textual or contextual in nature. But we should emphasize again that these two approaches to rhetorical analysis are not mutually exclusive. Indeed, many if not most analysts operate between these two extremes; they consider the details of the text, but they also attend to the particulars of context. Textual analysis and contextual analysis inevitably complement each other. Getting at what is at stake in "The Border Patrol State" or any other sophisticated argument takes patience and intelligence. Rhetorical analysis, as a way of understanding how people argue, is both enlightening and challenging.

Try to use elements of both kinds of analysis whenever you want to understand a rhetorical event more completely. Rhetoric is "inside" texts, but it is also "outside" them. Specific rhetorical performances are an irreducible mixture of text and context, and so interpretation and analysis of those performances must account for both as well. Remember, however, the limitations of your analysis. Realize that your analysis will always be somewhat partial and incomplete, ready to be deepened, corrected, modified, and extended by the insights of others. Rhetorical analysis can itself be part of an unending conversation—a way of learning and teaching within a community.

Steps to Writing a Rhetorical Analysis

Step 1 Select an Argument to Analyze

Find an argument to analyze—a speech or sermon, an op-ed in a newspaper, an ad in a magazine designed for a particular audience, or a commentary on a talk show.

Examples

- Editorial pages of newspapers (but not letters to the editor unless you can find a long and detailed letter)

- Opinion features in magazines such as *Time, Newsweek*, and *U.S. News & World Report*

- Magazines that take political positions such as *National Review, Mother Jones, New Republic, Nation*, and *Slate*

- Web sites of activist organizations (but not blog or newsgroup postings unless they are long and detailed)

Step 2 Analyze the context

Who is the author?

Through research in the library or on the Web, learn all you can about the author.

- How does the argument you are analyzing repeat arguments previously made by the author?

- What motivated the author to write? What is the author's purpose for writing this argument?

Who is the audience?

Through research, learn all you can about the publication and the audience.

- Who is the anticipated audience?
- How do the occasion and forum for writing affect the argument?

What is the larger conversation?

Through research, find out what else was being said about the subject of your selection. Track down any references made in the text you are examining.

- When did the argument appear?
- What other concurrent pieces of "cultural conversation" (e.g., TV shows, other articles, speeches, Web sites) does the item you are analyzing respond to or "answer"?

Step 3 Analyze the text

Summarize the argument

- What is the main claim?

- What reasons are given in support of the claim?
- How is the argument organized? What are the components, and why are they presented in that order?

What is the medium and genre?

- What is the medium? A newspaper? a scholarly journal? a Web site?
- What is the genre? An editorial? an essay? a speech? an advertisment? What expectations does the audience have about this genre?

What appeals are used?

- Analyze the ethos. How does the writer represent himself or herself? Does the writer have any credentials as an authority on the topic? Do you trust the writer?
- Analyze the logos. Where do you find facts and evidence in the argument? What kinds of facts and evidence does the writer present? Direct observation? statistics? interviews? surveys? quotations from authorities?
- Analyze the pathos. Does the writer attempt to invoke an emotional response? Where do you find appeals to shared values?

How would you characterize the style?

- Is the style formal, informal, satirical, or something else?
- Are any metaphors used?

Step 4 Write a draft

Introduction

- Describe briefly the argument you are analyzing, including where it was published, how long it is, and who wrote it.
- If the argument is about an issue unfamiliar to your readers, supply the necessary background.

Body

- Analyze the context, following Step 2.
- Analyze the text, following Step 3.

Conclusion

- Do more than simply summarize what you have said. You might, for example, end with an example that typifies the argument.
- You don't have to end by either agreeing or disagreeing with the writer. Your task in this assignment is to analyze the strategies the writer uses.

Step 5 Revise, edit, proofread

For detailed instructions, see Chapter 4.
For a checklist to evaluate your draft, see pages 48–49.

Barbara Jordan

Statement on the Articles of Impeachment

Barbara Jordan (1936–1996) grew up in Houston and received a law degree from Boston University in 1959. Working on John F. Kennedy's 1960 presidential campaign stirred an interest in politics, and Jordon became the first African American woman elected to the Texas State Senate in 1966. In 1972 she was elected to the United States House of Representatives and thus became the first African American woman from the South ever to serve in Congress. Jordan was appointed to the House Judiciary Committee. Soon she was in the national spotlight when that committee considered articles of impeachment against President Richard Nixon, who had illegally covered up a burglary of Democratic Party headquarters during the 1972 election. When Nixon's criminal acts reached to the Judiciary Committee, Jordan's opening speech on July 24, 1974, set the tone for the debate and established her reputation as a moral beacon for the nation. Nixon resigned as president on August 9, 1974, when it was evident that he would be impeached.

Thank you, Mr. Chairman.

Mr. Chairman, I join my colleague Mr. Rangel in thanking you for giving the junior members of this committee the glorious opportunity of sharing the pain of this inquiry. Mr. Chairman, you are a strong man and it has not been easy, but we have tried as best we can to give you as much assistance as possible.

2   Earlier today, we heard the beginning of the Preamble to the Constitution of the United States: "We, the people." It's a very eloquent beginning. But when that document was completed on the seventeenth of September in 1787, I was not included in that "We, the people." I felt somehow for many years that George Washington and Alexander Hamilton just left me out by mistake. But through the process of amendment, interpretation, and court decision, I have finally been included in "We, the people."

3   Today I am an inquisitor. Any hyperbole would not be fictional and would not overstate the solemnness that I feel right now. My faith in the Constitution is whole; it is complete; it is total. And I am not going to sit here and be an idle spectator to the diminution, the subversion, the destruction, of the Constitution.

4   "Who can so properly be the inquisitors for the nation as the representatives of the nation themselves?" "The subjects of its jurisdiction are those offenses which proceed from the misconduct of public men." And that's what we're talking about. In other words, [the jurisdiction comes] from the abuse or violation of some public trust.

5   It is wrong, I suggest, it is a misreading of the Constitution for any member here to assert that for a member to vote for an article of impeachment means that that member must be convinced that the President should be removed from office. The Constitution doesn't say that. The powers relating to impeachment are an essential check in the hands of the body of the legislature against and upon the encroachments of the executive. [By creating] the division between the two branches of the legislature, the House and the Senate, assigning to the one the right to accuse and to the other the right to judge, the framers of this Constitution were very astute. They did not make the accusers and the judgers the same person.

6   We know the nature of impeachment. We've been talking about it awhile now. It is chiefly designed for the President and his high ministers to somehow be called into account. It is designed to "bridle" the executive if he engages in excesses. "It is designed as a method of national inquest into the conduct of public men." The framers confided in the Congress the power, if need be, to remove the President in order to strike a delicate balance between a President swollen with power and grown tyrannical, and preservation of the independence of the executive.

7   The nature of impeachment: [it is] a narrowly channeled exception to the separation-of-powers maxim. The Federal Convention of 1787 said that. It limited impeachment to high crimes and misdemeanors and discounted and opposed the term *maladministration*. "It is to be used only for great misdemeanors," so it was said in the North Carolina ratification convention. And in the Virginia ratification convention: "We do not trust our liberty to a particular branch. We need one branch to check the other."

8   "No one need be afraid"—the North Carolina ratification convention—"No one need be afraid that officers who commit oppression will pass with immunity." "Prosecutions of impeachments will seldom fail to agitate the passions of the whole community," said Hamilton in the Federalist Papers, number 65. "We divide into parties more or less friendly or inimical to the accused." I do not mean political parties in that sense.

9   The drawing of political lines goes to the motivation behind impeachment; but impeachment must proceed within the confines of the constitutional term "high crime[s] and misdemeanors." Of the impeachment process, it was Woodrow Wilson who said that "Nothing short of the grossest offenses against the plain law of the land will suffice to give them speed and effectiveness. Indignation so great as to overgrow party interest may secure a conviction; but nothing else can."

10   Common sense would be revolted if we engaged upon this process for petty reasons. Congress has a lot to do: Appropriations, Tax Reform, Health Insurance, Campaign Finance Reform, Housing, Environmental Protection, Energy Sufficiency, Mass Transportation. Pettiness cannot be allowed to stand in the face of such overwhelming problems. So today we are not being petty. We are trying to be big, because the task we have before us is a big one.

11   This morning, in a discussion of the evidence, we were told that the evidence which purports to support the allegations of misuse of the CIA by the President is thin.

We're told that that evidence is insufficient. What that recital of the evidence this morning did not include is what the President did know on June the 23rd, 1972.

12   The President did know that it was Republican money, that it was money from the Committee for the Re-Election of the President, which was found in the possession of one of the burglars arrested on June the 17th. What the President did know on the 23rd of June was the prior activities of E. Howard Hunt, which included his participation in the break-in of Daniel Ellsberg's psychiatrist, which included Howard Hunt's participation in the Dita Beard ITT affair, which included Howard Hunt's fabrication of cables designed to discredit the Kennedy Administration.

13   We were further cautioned today that perhaps these proceedings ought to be delayed because certainly there would be new evidence forthcoming from the President of the United States. There has not even been an obfuscated indication that this committee would receive any additional materials from the President. The committee subpoena is outstanding, and if the President wants to supply that material, the committee sits here. The fact is that only yesterday, the American people waited with great anxiety for eight hours, not knowing whether their President would obey an order of the Supreme Court of the United States.

14   At this point, I would like to juxtapose a few of the impeachment criteria with some of the actions the President has engaged in. Impeachment criteria: James Madison, from the Virginia ratification convention: "If the President be connected in any suspicious manner with any person and there be grounds to believe that he will shelter him, he may be impeached."

15   We have heard time and time again that the evidence reflects the payment to defendants' money. The President had knowledge that these funds were being paid and these were funds collected for the 1972 presidential campaign. We know that the President met with Mr. Henry Petersen 27 times to discuss matters related to Watergate, and immediately thereafter met with the very persons who were implicated in the information Mr. Petersen was receiving. The words are: "If the President is connected in any suspicious manner with any person and there be grounds to believe that he will shelter that person, he may be impeached."

16   Justice Story: "Impeachment is intended for occasional and extraordinary cases where a superior power acting for the whole people is put into operation to protect their rights and rescue their liberties from violations." We know about the Huston plan. We know about the break-in of the psychiatrist's office. We know that there was absolute complete direction on September 3rd when the President indicated that a surreptitious entry had been made in Dr. Fielding's office, after having met with Mr. Ehrlichman and Mr. Young. "Protect their rights." "Rescue their liberties from violation."

17   The Carolina ratification convention impeachment criteria: those are impeachable "who behave amiss or betray their public trust." Beginning shortly after the Watergate break-in and continuing to the present time, the President has engaged in a series of public statements and actions designed to thwart the lawful investigation by government prosecutors. Moreover, the President has made public announcements and assertions bearing on the Watergate case, which the evidence will show he knew to be false. These assertions, false assertions, impeachable, those who misbehave. Those who "behave amiss or betray the public trust."

18   James Madison again at the Constitutional Convention: "A President is impeachable if he attempts to subvert the Constitution." The Constitution charges the President with the task of taking care that the laws be faithfully executed, and yet the President has counseled his aides to commit perjury, willfully disregard the secrecy of grand jury proceedings, conceal surreptitious entry, attempt to compromise a federal judge, while publicly displaying his cooperation with the processes of criminal justice. "A President is impeachable if he attempts to subvert the Constitution."

19   If the impeachment provision in the Constitution of the United States will not reach the offenses charged here, then perhaps that 18th-century Constitution should be abandoned to a 20th-century paper shredder.

20   Has the President committed offenses, and planned, and directed, and acquiesced in a course of conduct which the Constitution will not tolerate? That's the question. We know that. We know the question. We should now forthwith proceed to answer the question. It is reason, and not passion, which must guide our deliberations, guide our debate, and guide our decision.

21   I yield back the balance of my time, Mr. Chairman.

Sample Student Rhetorical Analysis

T. Jonathan Jackson

Dr. Netaji

English 1102

11 October 2010

An Argument of Reason and Passion: Barbara Jordan's

"Statement on the Articles of Impeachment"

Barbara Jordan's July 24, 1974 speech before the U.S. House Judiciary Committee helped convince the House of Representatives, and the American public, that President Richard Nixon should be impeached. Nixon was under investigation for his role in the cover-up of the Watergate scandal. He knew about the burglary of Democratic Party headquarters, but denied having any knowledge of it and illegally shielded those responsible. Jordan used her speech to argue that the president should be impeached because his actions threatened the Constitution and the people of the United States; however, Jordan never explicitly states this position in her speech. Instead, she establishes her credibility and then uses logic to set out the evidence against the president.

> Jonathan Jackson provides background information in the first paragraph and his thesis at the end.

In one sense, the audience of Jordan's speech consisted of the other 34 members of the House Judiciary Committee, gathered together to decide whether or not to recommend impeachment. And yet Jordan was not speaking just to a committee meeting; her speech was very public. The Senate Watergate hearings had been televised during the months before her speech, and millions of Americans watched sensational testimony by a host of witnesses. The Senate hearings produced charges that Nixon authorized break-ins at Democratic campaign headquarters in Washington during the 1972 election and that the White House was involved in many political dirty tricks and improprieties.

But the accusations remained only accusations—and Americans remained deeply divided about them—until it was discovered that Nixon had himself collected possible hard evidence: he had taped many conversations in the Oval Office, tapes that could support or refute the charges against the president. Nixon engaged in a protracted legal battle to keep the tapes from being disclosed, on the grounds that they were private

Jackson 2

conversations protected under "executive privilege," and he released only partial and edited transcripts. Finally on July 24, 1974, the courts ruled that Nixon had to turn all his remaining tapes over. That same day, knowing that hard evidence was now at hand, the House Judiciary Committee immediately went into session to vote whether to impeach Nixon. Each member of the committee was given fifteen minutes for an opening statement.

Nixon was a Republican and Jordan, like the majority of the committee, was a Democrat. Jordan had to convince her audience she was not biased against the president simply because of her party affiliation. Jordan was also new to Congress, relatively unknown outside of Texas, and a low-ranking member of the committee. Consequently, she had to establish her ethos to the committee as well as to the television audience. She had to present herself as fair, knowledgeable, and intellectually mature.

> Jackson observes that Jordan had a formidable assignment in establishing her ethos in a short speech.

At the heart of Jordan's argument is her faith in the Constitution. She begins her speech from a personal perspective, pointing out that the Constitution is not perfect because it originally excluded African Americans like her. But now that the Constitution recognizes her as a citizen, Jordan says, her faith in it "is whole, it is complete, it is total." She even implies that, as a citizen, she has a moral duty to protect the Constitution, saying, "I am not going to sit here and be an idle spectator to the diminution, the subversion, the destruction of the Constitution." Jordan's emotional connection to the Constitution shows the audience that she is motivated by a love of her country, not by party loyalty. She establishes herself as someone fighting to defend and protect American values.

> Jackson analyzes how Jordan's fervent allegiance to the Constitution made her appear unbiased.

Jordan describes the Constitution as the accepted authority on the laws related to impeachment. She shows the audience how the Constitution gives her the authority to act as an "inquisitor," or judge. She depicts the Constitution and the American people as potential victims, and the president as the potential criminal. She warns of the need to remove "a President swollen with power and grown tyrannical."

Jackson 3

The appeals to pathos and ethos in the opening of the speech establishes Jordan's motivations and credibility, allowing her to next lay out her logical arguments. Jordan proceeds to explain how the Constitution defines impeachment, and fleshes out this brief definition with evidence from several state Constitutional Conventions. She also quotes Supreme Court Justice Joseph Story. Using evidence from the North Carolina and Virginia Constitutional Conventions, Jordan shows that impeachment was intended only for "great misdemeanors," and that the branches of government were intended to act as a check upon one another.

Next Jordan uses quotations from James Madison, Justice Story, and others to define impeachable offenses. For each offense, Jordan provides an example of an act that President Nixon was known to have committed, and she shows how his actions meet the definition of impeachable offenses. She compares Nixon's meetings with Watergate suspects to Madison's statement that "if the President is connected in any suspicious manner with any person and there be grounds to believe that he will shelter that person, he may be impeached." She pairs Justice Story's statement that impeachment should "protect [citizens'] rights and rescue their liberties from violation" with Nixon's knowledge of the burglary of a private psychiatrist's office. She links Nixon's attempts to bribe a judge and thwart grand jury proceedings with Madison's statement that "a President is impeachable if he attempts to subvert the Constitution."

Jordan uses quotations from respected figures in American history to apply to Nixon's misdeeds.

Jordan had to confront a legal issue: Were the actions of President Nixon serious enough to justify impeachment?

Throughout this section, Jordan repeats the historical quotes before and after her descriptions of the president's acts. This repetition makes the connections stronger and more memorable for the audience. Jordan also contrasts the formal, high-toned language of the Founders and the Constitution with descriptions that make President Nixon's actions sound sordid and petty: He knew about money "found in the possession of one of the burglars arrested on June the 17th," about "the break-in of Daniel Ellsberg's psychiatrist," about "the fabrication of cables designed to discredit the Kennedy Administration." Words like "burglars," "arrested," "break-in," and "fabrication," sound like evidence in a criminal trial. These words are not the kind of language Americans want to hear describing the actions of their president.

Jackson 4

Jordan then adds another emotional appeal, implying that the Constitution is literally under attack. "If the impeachment provisions will not reach the offenses charged here," she says, "then perhaps that 18th-century Constitution should be abandoned to a 20th-century paper shredder." This dramatic image encourages the audience to imagine President Nixon shredding the Constitution just as he had destroyed other evidence implicating him in the Watergate scandal. It implies that if the president is not stopped, he will commit further abuses of power. Jordan also makes the American people responsible for this possible outcome, saying that "we" may as well shred the Constitution if it cannot be used to impeach Nixon. This emotional appeal has the effect of shaming those say they can't or shouldn't vote for impeachment.

> Jackson notes that the metaphor of the paper shredder adds emotional force.

Jordan concludes her speech not by calling for impeachment, but by calling for an answer to the question, "Has the President committed offenses, and planned, and directed, and acquiesced in a course of conduct which the Constitution will not tolerate?" It almost seems like Jordan is being humble and trying not to judge by not stating her position outright. However, the reverse is true: Jordan doesn't state her position because she doesn't need to. The evidence she presented led Congress and the American public inescapably to one conclusion: That President Nixon had committed impeachable offenses. Just two week later, Nixon resigned from office. Jordan had made her point.

> In his conclusion Jackson points out how Jordan shifts the focus to her audience in her conclusion.

Jackson 5

Works Cited

Jordan, Barbara. "Statement on the Articles of Impeachment." *American Rhetoric: Top 100 Speeches*. American Rhetoric, 25 July 1974. Web. 25 Sept. 2010.

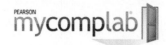

For support in learning this chapter's content, follow this path in MyCompLab:
> Resources > Writing > Writing Purposes > Writing to Analyze.
Review the Instruction and Multimedia resources, then complete the Exercises and click on Gradebook to measure your progress.

6 | Analyzing Visual and Multimedia Arguments

QUICK TAKE

In this chapter, you will learn that

1. Visual arguments have similarities and differences with verbal arguments (see below)

2. Photos and videos used as evidence in visual arguments need to be evaluated critically (see pages 79–81)

3. Visual arguments can be analyzed using strategies similar to those used to analyze a written argument (see pages 81–82)

4. An effective visual analysis takes into account the context of the image as well as its visual elements and any surrounding text (see pages 83–86)

What Is a Visual Argument?

We live in a world flooded with images. They pull on us, compete for our attention, push us to do things. But how often do we think about how they work?

Can there be an argument without words?

Arguments in written language are visual in one sense: we use our eyes to read the words on the page. But without words, can there be a visual argument? Certainly some visual symbols take on conventional meanings. Signs in airports or other public places, for example, are designed to communicate with speakers of many languages.

Some visual symbols even make explicit claims. A one-way street sign says that drivers should travel only in the one direction. But are such signs arguments? In Chapter 3 we point out that scholars of argument do not believe that everything *is* an argument. Most scholars define an argument as a claim supported by one or more reasons. A one-way sign has a claim: all drivers should go in the same direction. But is there a reason? We all know an unstated reason the sign carries: drivers who go the wrong way violate the law and risk a substantial fine (plus they risk a head-on collision with other drivers).

Visual arguments require viewer participation

The *Deepwater Horizon* oil spill (also known as the BP oil spill) was the largest off-shore oil spill in the history of the United States. Caused by an explosion on April 20, 2010, the spill dumped millions of gallons of oil every day for months in spite of efforts to contain it. People around the world were reminded of the spill when they turned on their televisions and saw video of the oil gushing from the well, and nearly everyone was outraged.

People interpreted the oil flowing from the pipe quite differently, inferring multiple because clauses. Citizens were angry for different reasons.

The *Deepwater Horizon* oil spill was a disaster because

- eleven workers were killed and seventeen were injured.
- enormous harm was done to Gulf wetlands, birds, fish, turtles, marine mammals, and other animals.
- the tourism industry suffered another major blow just five years after Hurricane Katrina.
- the fishing and shrimping industries suffered huge losses.

The main oil leak from the *Deepwater Horizon* wellhead. © BP p.l.c.

Photograph of a booth at the Taste of Chicago that was sent on Twitter and enraged people in New Orleans.

- President Obama declared a moratorium on deep-water drilling, threatening the loss of jobs.
- BP and its partners were negligent in drilling the well.
- the spill was an unfortunate act of God like Hurricane Katrina.

Differing interpretations of visual arguments extended beyond the spill itself. A news producer in Chicago took the photo below at the Taste of Chicago festival, sent it to a friend in New Orleans, who sent it to a food writer, who posted it on Twitter. The mayor of New Orleans called it "disgraceful."

Talks shows in both Chicago and New Orleans ranted for a few days about the other city. One comment was perhaps telling about the source of the rage: a menu disclaimer would have been acceptable, but a prominent visual argument, even in text form, was hitting below the belt.

What Is a Multimedia Argument?

Multimedia describes the use of multiple content forms including text, voice and music audio, video, still images, animation, and interactivity. Multimedia goes far back in human history (texts and images were combined at the beginnings of writing), but digital technologies and the Web have made multimedia the fabric of our daily lives. But what exactly are multimedia arguments?

For example, games provide intense multimedia experiences, but are they arguments? Game designers such as Jane McGonigal believe they are arguments. McGonigal maintains that games make people more powerful because they connect them into larger wholes.

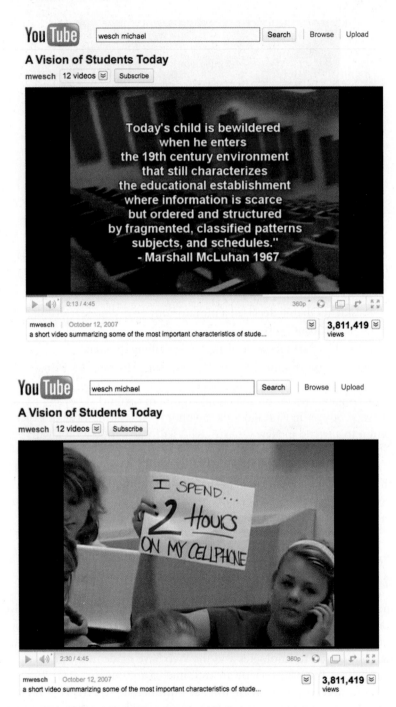

Images from Michael Wesch's *A Vision of Students Today*

Thousands of multimedia arguments have been posted on YouTube. One frequently viewed video is Michael Wesch's *A Vision of Students Today*, posted in October 2007. Wesch's point is that today's education is ill-suited for most students. He enlisted his students to make the point with text and video.

Analyze Visual Evidence

Videos without narration, images, and graphics seldom make arguments on their own, but they are frequently used to support arguments.

Evaluate photographs and videos as evidence

Almost from the beginnings of photography, negatives were manipulated but realistic results required a high skill level. In the digital era anyone can alter photographs. Perhaps there's nothing wrong with using Photoshop to add absent relatives to family photographs or remove ex-boyfriends and ex-girlfriends. But where do you draw the line? Not only do many videos on YouTube use outright deception, but newsmagazines and networks have also been found guilty of these practices.

Ask questions about what you view.

- Who created the image or video? What bias might the creator have?
- Who published the image or video? What bias might the publisher have?
- Who is the intended audience? For example, political videos often assume that the viewers hold the same political views as the creators.
- What is being shown, and what is not being shown? For example, a video ad promoting tourism for the Gulf of Mexico will look very different from a video showing sources of pollution.
- Who is being represented, and who is not being represented? Who gets left out is as important as who gets included.

The ease of cropping digital photographs reveals an important truth about photography: a photograph represents reality from a particular viewpoint. A high-resolution picture of a crowd can be divided into many smaller images that each say something different about the event. The act of pointing the camera in one direction and not in another shapes how photographic evidence will be interpreted. (See the examples on page 80.)

Evaluate charts and graphs

Statistical information is frequently used as evidence in arguments. The problem with giving many statistics in sentence form, however, is that readers shortly lose track of the numbers. Charts and graphs present statistics visually, allowing readers to take in trends and relationships at a glance.

A photographer's choices about who and what to photograph shapes how we see an event.

However, charts and graphs can also be misleading. For example, a chart that compares the amounts of calories in competing brands of cereal might list one with 70 calories and another with 80 calories. If the chart begins at zero, the difference looks small. But if the chart starts at 60, the brand with 80 calories appears to have twice the calories of the brand with 70. Furthermore, the chart is worthless if the data is inaccurate or comes from an unreliable source. Creators of charts and graphs have an ethical obligation to present data as fairly and accurately as possible and to provide the sources of the data.

Ask these questions when you are analyzing charts and graphs

- Is the type of chart appropriate for the information presented?

Bar and column charts make comparisons in particular categories. If two or more charts are compared, the scales should be consistent.

Line graphs plot variables on a vertical and a horizontal axis. They are useful for showing proportional trends over time.

Pie charts show the proportion of parts in terms of the whole. Segments must add up to 100 percent of the whole.

- Does the chart have a clear purpose?

- Does the title indicate the purpose?

- What do the units represent (dollars, people, voters, percentages, and so on)?

- What is the source of the data?

- Is there any distortion of information?

Evaluate informational graphics

Informational graphics more sophisticated than standard pie and bar charts have become a popular means of conveying information. Many are interactive, allowing viewers of a Web site to select the information they want displayed. These information graphics are a form of narrative argument, and the stories they tell have a rhetorical purpose. (See the examples on page 82.)

Build a Visual Analysis

It's one thing to construct a visual argument yourself; it's another thing to analyze visual arguments that are made by someone else. Fortunately, analyzing arguments made up of images and graphics is largely a matter of following the same strategies for rhetorical analysis that are outlined in Chapter 5—except that you must analyze images instead of (or in addition to) words. To put it another way, when you analyze

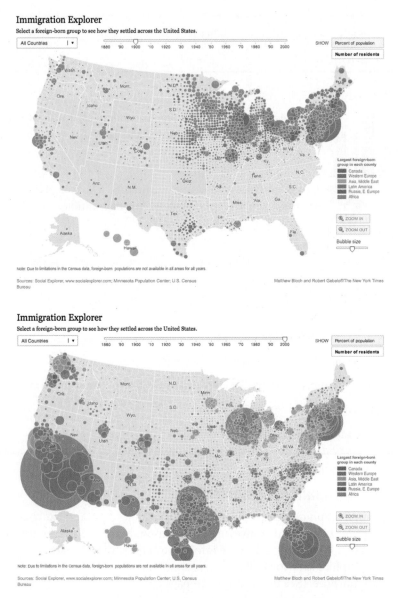

This set of information graphics on immigration tells a story. In 1900 the great majority of immigrants were from Western and Eastern Europe and Russia, and the majority settled in the Northeast and Midwest. In 2000 most immigrants came from Latin America, and they settled in Florida, Texas, and the West Coast along with the metropolitan areas of Chicago and New York City.

a visual argument, think about the image itself as well as its relationship to other images (and discourses). The arguments implied by visual images, like the arguments made through text alone, are carried both by the context and by the image.

Determination and hard work, at any age, can lead to being the best.
Hofstra University, just 50 years old, is already among the
top ten percent of American colleges and universities in
almost all academic criteria and resources.
Professionally accredited programs in such major areas as business,
engineering, law, psychology and education.
A library with over 1.1 million volumes *on campus*—a collection
larger than that of 95% of American universities.
Record enrollments with students from 31 states and 59 countries—
with a student-faculty ratio of only 17 to 1.
The largest, most sophisticated non-commercial television facility
in the East. A high technology undergraduate teaching
resource with broadcast-quality production capability.
A ranking in *Barron's Guide to the Most Prestigious Colleges*—one of
only 262 colleges and universities chosen from almost 4,000.
At Hofstra, determination, inspiration and hard work are qualities
our faculty demands in itself and instills in our students.
These qualities are what it takes to be the best. In anything.

HOFSTRA UNIVERSITY
WE TEACH SUCCESS.

50th Anniversary
Hempstead, L.I., New York 11550

Ad for Hofstra University, 1989

Analyze context

A critical analysis of a visual image, like the analyses of written arguments that we discuss in the previous chapter, must include a consideration of context. Consider, for example, the above advertisement for Hofstra University. The context for the ad is not difficult to uncover through a bit of research. The ad appeared in 1989 and 1990 when Hofstra, located on Long Island 25 miles from New York City, was celebrating its fiftieth anniversary and hoping to use the occasion to enhance its esteem. At the time, Hofstra enjoyed a good reputation for its professional programs, particularly in education and business (which one-third of the 7,500 students were majoring in). However, it was not as highly regarded in the core science and humanities disciplines that are often associated with institutional prestige. In addition, Hofstra was quite well known in the New York metropolitan area—half its students were commuting to school rather than living in dormitories—but it was not attracting many students from outside the region, and its campus life was consequently regarded as mediocre. Its student body was generally well prepared, hardworking, and capable, but its most outstanding applicants were too often choosing other universities.

Feeling that its performance was exceeding its reputation and that it was capable of attracting a more diverse and talented student body, Hofstra developed a national ad campaign designed to change the opinions of prospective students and their parents, as well as the general public. It placed the ads—the ad reproduced here is one of a series—in several magazines and newspapers in order to persuade people that Hofstra was an outstanding university not just in the professions but in all fields, and that the opportunities available to its students were varied and valuable.

Analyze visual and textual elements

Ads make arguments, and the message of the Hofstra ad is something like this: "Hofstra is a prestigious, high-quality institution that brings out the best in students because of its facilities, its academic reputation, its student body, and the strength of its faculty and academic programs." The text of the Hofstra ad expresses that argument specifically: "The best" and "we teach success" are prominently displayed; the size of the print visually reinforces the message; and the fine print supports the main thesis by mentioning Hofstra's facilities (the large library with "a collection [of volumes] larger than that of 95% of American universities," the "television facility . . . with broadcast quality production capability"); its reputation (its ranking in *Barron's Guide to the Most Prestigious Colleges* and its "professionally accredited programs"); and its faculty and students. The ad works by offering good reasons and supporting arguments that are based on logical reasoning and evidence, as well as appeals to our most fervently held values. By placing the ad in prestigious publications, Hofstra enhanced its credibility even further.

In this chapter, however, we are emphasizing visuals in arguments. What kind of argument is made and supported by the image of the young girl with the flute? The photo of the girl is black and white, so that it can be printed easily and inexpensively in newspapers and magazines. But the black and white format also contributes a sense of reality and truthfulness, in the manner of black and white photos or documentary films. (Color images, on the other hand, can imply flashiness or commercialism.) Even in black and white, the image is quite arresting. In the context of an ad for Hofstra, the image is particularly intriguing. The girl is young—does she seem about ten or twelve years of age?—and her readiness for distinguished performance suggests that she is a prodigy, a genius—in other words, the kind of person that Hofstra attracts and sustains. The ad implies that you might encounter her on the Hofstra campus sometime: if she is not a student at Hofstra now, she soon will be. Come to Hofstra, and you too can acquire the traits associated with excellence and success.

The girl is dressed up for some kind of musical performance, and the details of her costume imply that the performance is of a high order: it is not just any costume, but one associated with professional performances of the most rarefied kind, a concert that calls for only the best musicians. The delicacy and refinement of the girl are implied by the posture of her fingers, the highly polished flute that she holds with an upright carriage, and the meticulousness of her tie, shirt, and coat. The girl's expression suggests that she is serious, sober, disciplined, but comfortable—the kind of student (and faculty member) that Hofstra features. (The layout and consistent print style used in the ad reinforce that impression: by offering a balanced and harmonious placement of elements and by sticking to the same type style throughout, the ad stands for the values of balance, harmony, consistency, and order.) The girl is modest and unpretentious in expression, yet she looks directly at the viewer with supreme self-confidence. Her age suggests innocence, yet her face proclaims ambition; her age and the quasi-masculine costume (note that she wears neither a ring nor earrings) give her a sexual innocence that is in keeping with the contemplative life. Come to Hofstra, the image proclaims, and you will meet people who are sober and graceful, self-disciplined and confident, ambitious without being arrogant. The ad is supporting its thesis with good reasons implied by its central image—good reasons that we identified with logos and pathos in the previous chapter.

Speaking of pathos, what do you make of the fact that the girl is Asian? On one hand, the Asian girl's demeanor reinforces cultural stereotypes. Delicate, small, sober, controlled, even humorless, she embodies characteristics that recall other Asian American icons (particularly women), especially icons of success through discipline and hard work. On the other hand, the girl speaks to the Asian community. It is as if she is on the verge of saying, "Come and join me at Hofstra, where you too can reach the highest achievement. And read the copy below me to learn more about what Hofstra has to offer." In this way the girl participates in Hofstra's ambition to attract highly qualified, highly motivated, and high-performing minority students—as well as any other high-performing student, regardless of ethnicity or gender, who values hard work, academic distinction, and the postponement of sensual gratification in return for long-term success.

If she is Asian, the girl is also thoroughly American. She appears not to be an international student but an American of immigrant stock. Her costume, her controlled black hair, and her unmarked face and fingers identify her as achieving the American dream of material success, physical health and well being, and class advancement. If her parents or grandparents came to New York or California as immigrants, they (and she) are now naturalized—100 percent American, completely successful. The social class element to the image is unmistakable: the entire ad speaks of Hofstra's ambition to be among the best, to achieve an elite status. When the ad appeared in 1989, Hofstra was attracting few of the nation's elite students. The girl signals a change. She displays the university's aspiration to become among the nation's elite—those who enjoy material success as well as the leisure, education, and sophistication to appreciate the finest music. That ambition is reinforced by the university's emblem in the lower right-hand corner of the ad. It resembles a coat of arms and is associated with royalty. Hofstra may be a community that is strong in the professions, but it also values the arts.

No doubt there are other aspects of the image that work to articulate and to support the complex argument of the ad. There is more to be said about this ad, and you may disagree with some of the points we have offered. But consider this: By 2009, twenty years after the ad was run, Hofstra's total enrollment had climbed above 12,000, with 7,500 undergraduates. Its admissions were more selective, its student body was more diverse and less regional in character, its graduation rate had improved, its sports teams had achieved national visibility, and its minority student population had grown. Many factors contributed to the university's advancement, but it seems likely that this ad was one of them.

Write a Visual Analysis

Like rhetorical analysis, effective visual analysis takes into account the context of the image as well as its visual elements and any surrounding text. When you analyze a visual image, look carefully at its details and thoroughly consider its context. What visual elements grab your attention first, and how do other details reinforce that impression—what is most important and less important? How do color and style influence impressions? How does the image direct the viewer's eyes and reinforce what is important? What is the relationship between the image and any text that might accompany it? Consider the shapes, colors, and details of the image, as well as how the elements of the image connect with different arguments and audiences.

Consider also what you know or can learn about the context of an image and the design and text that surround it. Try to determine why and when it was created, who created it, where it appeared, and the target audience. Think about how the context of its creation and publication affected its intended audience. What elements have you seen before? Which elements remind you of other visuals?

Sample Student Visual Analysis

Discussion board posts are a frequent assignment in writing classes. Usually they are short essays, no more than 300 words. Sources of any information still need to be cited.

The assignment for this post was to find and analyze an example of a visual metaphor.

Thread: "Use Only What You Need" : The Denver Water Conservation
Campaign
Author: Chrissy Yao
Posted Date: March 1, 2010 1:12 PM

Partial bus bench from Denver Water's conservation campaign

In 2006, Denver Water, the city's oldest water utility, launched a
water ten-year conservation plan based on using water efficiently
("Conservation"). Denver Water teamed up with the Sukle Advertising
firm and produced the "Use Only What You Need Campaign" to help
alleviate the water crisis that the city was enduring (Samuel). The
campaign uses billboard advertising, magazine ads, and even stripped-
down cars to impart messages of water conservation and efficiency.

> Yao describes the ad campaign which uses the partial bus bench.

Clever visual metaphors are at the heart of the campaign. One
example is a park bench with available seating only for one individual.
The words, "USE ONLY WHAT YOU NEED," are stenciled in on the back of
the bench. The bench, which can actually be used for sitting, conveys the
idea that if only one person were using the bench, that would only need
a small area to sit on, not the whole thing. The bench makes concrete
the concept of water conservation.

> Yao analyzes the visual metaphor.

The innovative ad campaign that uses objects in addition to
traditional advertising has proven successful. The simplicity and minimal-
ist style of the ads made a convincing argument about using resources
sparingly. The average water consumption of Denver dropped between
18% and 21% annually from 2006 to 2009.

Works Cited

"Conservation." *Denver Water*. Denver Water, 2010. Web. 23 Feb. 2010.

Samuel, Frederick. "Denver Water." *Ad Goodness*. N.p., 16 Nov. 2006.
  Web. 24 Feb. 2010.

For support in learning this chapter's content, follow this path in MyCompLab:
> Resources   > Media Index   > Visual Analysis and Rhetoric.

Review the Instruction and Multimedia resources, then complete the Exercises and click on Gradebook to measure your progress.

Writing Arguments

PART

3

7 | Putting Good Reasons into Action

QUICK TAKE

In this chapter, you will learn that

1. Most arguments use multiple approaches to achieve a specific purpose (see below)
2. Thinking explicitly about the structure of arguments can help identify different ways to approach your topic (see below)
3. Using different kinds of arguments can help you get started writing about a complex topic (see page 92)

Find a Purpose for Writing an Argument

Imagine that you bought a new car in June and you are taking some of your friends to your favorite lake over the Fourth of July weekend. You have a great time until, as you are heading home, a drunk driver—a repeat offender—swerves into your lane and totals your new car. You and your friends are lucky not to be hurt, but you're outraged because you believe that repeat offenders should be prevented from driving, even if that means putting them in jail. You also remember going to another state that had sobriety checkpoints on holiday weekends. If such a checkpoint had been at the lake, you might still be driving your new car. You live in a town that encourages citizens to contribute to the local newspaper, and you think you could get a guest editorial published. The question is, how do you want to write the editorial?

- You could tell your story about how a repeat drunk driver endangered the lives of you and your friends.
- You could define driving while intoxicated (DWI) as a more legally culpable crime.
- You could compare the treatment of drunk drivers in your state with the treatment of drunk drivers in another state.
- You could cite statistics that alcohol-related accidents killed 13,846 people in 2008.
- You could evaluate the present drunk-driving laws as insufficiently just or less than totally successful.

- You could propose taking vehicles away from repeat drunk drivers and forcing them to serve mandatory sentences.
- You could argue that your community should have sobriety checkpoints at times when drunk drivers are likely to be on the road.
- You could do several of the above.

Finding Good Reasons

What do we mean by diversity?

Colleges and universities talk a great deal about diversity nowadays, but what exactly do they mean by *diversity*? If diversity is connected with people, do they mean diversity of races and ethnicities? Is it diversity of nations and cultures represented among the students? Should the numbers of students of different races, ethnicities, or family income levels be roughly equal to the population of the state where the school is located? Is a campus diverse if about 60 percent of the students are women and 40 percent men, as many campuses now are? Or if diversity is connected with ideas, what makes for a diverse intellectual experience on a college campus?

Write about it

1. Formulate your own definition of what diversity means on a college campus (see Chapter 8).

2. Evaluate diversity on your campus according to your definition. Is your campus good or bad in its diversity (see Chapter 10)?

3. What are the effects of having a diverse campus, however you define diversity (see Chapter 9)? What happens if a campus isn't diverse?

4. If you consider diversity desirable, write a proposal that would increase diversity on your campus, whether it's interacting with people of different backgrounds or encountering a variety of ideas (see Chapter 13). Or if you think too much emphasis is being placed on diversity, write a rebuttal argument against proponents of diversity (see Chapter 12).

Get Started Writing About Complex Issues

You're not going to have much space in the newspaper, so you decide to argue for sobriety checkpoints. You know that they are controversial. One of your friends who was in the car with you said that the checkpoints are unconstitutional because they involve search without cause. However, after doing some research to find out whether checkpoints are defined as legal or illegal, you learn that on June 14, 1990, the U.S. Supreme Court upheld the constitutionality of using checkpoints as a deterrent and enforcement tool against drunk drivers.

But you still want to know whether most people would agree with your friend that sobriety checkpoints are an invasion of privacy. You find opinion polls and surveys going back to the 1980s that show that 70 to 80 percent of those polled support sobriety checkpoints. You also realize that you can argue by analogy that security checkpoints for alcohol are similar in many ways to airport security checkpoints that protect passengers. You decide you will finish by making an argument from consequence. If people who go to the lake with plans to drink know in advance that there will be checkpoints, they will find a designated driver or some other means of safe transportation, and everyone else will also be a lot safer.

The point of this example is that people very rarely set out to define something in an argument for the sake of definition, to compare for the sake of comparison, or to adopt any of the other ways of structuring an argument. Instead, they have a purpose in mind, and they use the kinds of arguments that are discussed in Chapters 8–13—most often in combination—as means to an end. Most arguments use multiple approaches and multiple sources of good reasons.

For support in learning this chapter's content, follow this path in MyCompLab:
> Resources > Writing > The Writing Process > Planning.
Review the Instruction and Multimedia resources, then complete the Exercises and click on Gradebook to measure your progress.

8 | Definition Arguments

QUICK TAKE

In this chapter, you will learn that

1. Definition arguments set out criteria and argue that something meets or doesn't meet those criteria (see page 94)
2. Definitions work by classification and example (see page 95)
3. Because definition arguments are the most powerful arguments, they are often at the center of the most important debates in American history (see page 96)

Graffiti dates back to the ancient Egyptian, Greek, Roman, and Mayan civilizations. Is graffiti vandalism? Or is it art? The debate has gone on for three decades. In the 1980s New York City's subways were covered with graffiti. Many New Yorkers believe that removing graffiti from subway cars was a first step toward the much-celebrated social and economic recovery of the city. For them graffiti was a sign that the subways were not safe. But at the same time, Martha Cooper and Henry Chalfant released a book titled *Subway* Art—a picture book—that celebrated graffiti-covered subways as an art form. Should we appreciate graffiti as the people's art or should graffiti be removed as quickly as possible, which many cities advocate?

Understand How Definition Arguments Work

Definition arguments set out criteria and then argue that whatever is being defined meets or does not meet those criteria.

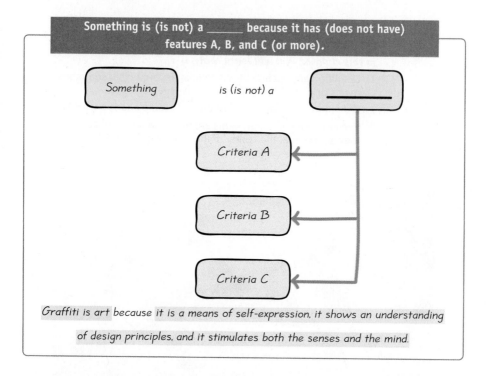

Something is (is not) a _____ because it has (does not have) features A, B, and C (or more).

Something   is (is not) a   _____

Criteria A

Criteria B

Criteria C

Graffiti is art because it is a means of self-expression, it shows an understanding of design principles, and it stimulates both the senses and the mind.

Recognize Kinds of Definitions

Rarely do you get far into an argument without having to define something. Imagine that you are writing an argument about the decades-old and largely ineffective "war on drugs" in the United States. We all know that the war on drugs is being waged against drugs that are illegal, like cocaine and marijuana, and not against the legal drugs produced by the multibillion-dollar drug industry. Our society classifies drugs into two categories: "good" drugs, which are legal, and "bad" drugs, which are illegal.

How exactly does our society arrive at these definitions? Drugs would be relatively easy to define as good or bad if the difference could be defined at the molecular level. Bad drugs would contain certain molecules that define them as bad. The history of drug use in the United States, however, tells us that it is not so simple. In the twentieth century alcohol was on the list of illegal drugs for over a decade, while opium was considered a good drug and was distributed in many patent medicines by pharmaceutical companies. Similarly, LSD and MDMA (methylenedioxymethamphetamine, known better by its street name *ecstasy*) were developed by the pharmaceutical industry but later made illegal. In a few states marijuana is now legal for medicinal use.

If drugs cannot be classified as good or bad by their molecular structure, then perhaps society classifies them by their effects. It might be reasonable to assume that addictive drugs are illegal, but that's not the case. Nicotine is highly addictive and is a legal drug, as are many prescription medicines. Drugs taken for the purpose of pleasure are not necessarily illegal (think of alcohol and Viagra), nor are drugs that alter consciousness or change personality (such as Prozac).

How a drug is defined as legal or illegal apparently is determined by example. The nationwide effort to stop Americans from drinking alcohol during the first decades of the twentieth century led to the passage of the Eighteenth Amendment and the ban on sales of alcohol from 1920 to 1933, known as Prohibition. Those who argued for Prohibition used examples of drunkenness, especially among the poor, to show how alcohol broke up families and left mothers and children penniless in the street. Those who opposed Prohibition initially pointed to the consumption of beer and wine in many cultural traditions. Later they raised examples of the bad effects of Prohibition—the rise of organized crime, the increase in alcohol abuse, and the general disregard for laws.

When you make a definition argument, it's important to think about what kind of definition you will use. Descriptions of three types follow.

Formal definitions

Formal definitions typically categorize an item into the next-higher classification and provide criteria that distinguish the item from other items within that classification. Most dictionary definitions are formal definitions. For example, fish are cold-blooded aquatic vertebrates that have jaws, fins, and scales and are distinguished from other cold-blooded aquatic vertebrates (such as sea snakes) by the presence of gills. If you can construct a formal definition with a specific classification and differentiating criteria that your audience will accept, then likely you will have a strong argument. The key is to get your audience to agree to your classification and criteria. Often your argument will amount to revising your audience's view of the classification or criteria (or both). For instance, imagine that you want to change your audience's view of contemporary universities. You might construct a thesis statement something like this: "While most people still think of universities as institutions [classification] of higher learning that prepare people for citizenship and the workplace [differentiating criteria], they are actually nothing more than big businesses" [revised classification].

Operational definitions

Many concepts cannot be easily defined by formal definitions. Researchers in the natural and social sciences must construct **operational definitions** that they use for their research. For example, researchers who study binge drinking among college students define a binge as five or more drinks in one sitting for a man, and four or more drinks for a woman. Some people think this standard is too low and should be raised to six to eight drinks to distinguish true problem drinkers from the general college population. No matter what the number, researchers must argue that the particular definition is one that suits the concept.

Definitions from example

Many human qualities such as honesty, courage, creativity, deceit, and love must be defined by examples that the audience accepts as representative of the concept. Few would not call the firefighters who entered the World Trade Center on September 11, 2001, courageous. Most people would describe someone with a diagnosis of terminal cancer who refuses to feel self-pity as courageous. But what about a student who declines to go to a concert with her friends so she can study for an exam? Her behavior might be admirable, but most people would hesitate to call it courageous. The key to arguing a **definition from example** is that the examples must strike the audience as typical of the concept, even if the situation is unusual.

Build a Definition Argument

Because definition arguments are so powerful, they are found at the center of some of the most important debates in American history. Definition arguments were at the heart of the abolition of slavery, for example, and many of the major arguments of the civil rights movement were based on definitions. Martin Luther King, Jr.'s, "Letter from Birmingham Jail" is one eloquent example.

King was jailed in April 1963 for leading a series of peaceful protests in Birmingham, Alabama. While he was being held in solitary confinement, Rev. King wrote a letter to eight white Birmingham clergymen. These religious leaders had issued a statement urging an end to the protests in their city. King argued that it was necessary to act now rather than wait for change. His purpose in writing the argument was to win acceptance for the protests and protestors and to make his audience see that the anti-segregationists were not agitators and rabble-rousers,

U.S. National Guard troops block off Beale Street in Memphis, Tennessee, as striking sanitation workers wearing placards reading, "I *AM* A MAN" pass by on March 29, 1968. Rev. Martin Luther King, Jr., returned to Memphis to lead the march and was assassinated a week later on April 4.

but citizens acting responsibly to correct a grave injustice. A critical part of King's argument is his definition of "just" and "unjust" laws.

Supporters of segregation in Birmingham had obtained a court order forbidding further protests, and the eight white clergymen urged King and his supporters to obey the courts. Our society generally assumes that laws, and the courts that enforce them, should be obeyed. King, however, argues that there are two categories of laws, and that citizens must treat one category differently from the other. Morally just laws, King argues, should be obeyed, but unjust ones should not. By distinguishing two different kinds of laws, King creates a rationale for obeying some laws and disobeying others. He then completes his definitional argument by showing how segregation laws fit the definition of "unjust." Once his audience accepts his placement of segregation laws in the "unjust" category, they must also accept that King and his fellow protestors were right to break those laws.

King maintains in his letter that people have a moral responsibility to obey just laws, and, by the same logic, "a moral responsibility to disobey unjust laws." His argument rests on the clear moral and legal criteria he uses to define just and unjust laws. Without these criteria, people could simply disobey any law they chose, which is what King's detractors accused him of advocating. King had to show that he was in fact acting on principle, and that he and his supporters wanted to establish justice, not cause chaos.

Here's how King makes the distinction between just and unjust laws:

> A just law is a man-made code that squares with the moral law of God. An unjust law is a code that is out of harmony with the moral law. . . . Any law that uplifts human personality is just. Any law that degrades human personality is unjust. All segregation statutes are unjust because segregation distorts the soul and damages the personality. It gives the segregator a false sense of superiority and the segregated a false sense of inferiority.

According to King, a just law meets the criteria of being consistent with moral law and uplifting human personality. An unjust law does not meet these criteria. Instead, it is out of harmony with moral law and damages human personality. King's claim that

> "All segregation laws are unjust because segregation distorts the soul and damages the personality"

uses the structure described at the beginning of this chapter:

Something is (or is not) a ___ because it has (does not have) features A, B, and C.

Building an extended definition argument like King's is a two-step process. First, you have to establish the criteria for the categories you wish to define. In King's letter, consistency with moral law and uplifting of the human spirit are set forth as criteria for a just law. King provides arguments from St. Thomas Aquinas, a religious authority likely to carry significant weight with Birmingham clergymen and others who will read the letter.

Second, you must convince your audience that the particular case in question meets or doesn't meet the criteria. King cannot simply state that segregation laws are unjust; he must provide evidence showing how they fail to meet the criteria for a just law. Specifically, he notes the segregation "gives the segregator a false sense of superiority and the segregated a false sense of inferiority." These false senses of self are a distortion or degradation of the human personality.

Sometimes definition arguments have to argue for the relevance of the criteria. King, in fact, spent a great deal of his letter laying out and defending his criteria for just and unjust laws. While he addressed his letter to clergymen, he knew that it would find a wider audience. Therefore, he did not rely solely on criteria linked to moral law, or the "law of God." People who were not especially religious might not be convinced by those parts of his argument. King presents two additional criteria for just laws that he knows will appeal to those who value the democratic process. He argues that "an unjust law is a code that a numerical or power majority group compels a minority group to obey but does not make binding on itself." In other words, a just law is the law for everyone. It is fairly easy to show how segregation laws fail to meet this criterion. These laws commonly prevented African Americans from using certain facilities reserved for whites, for example, but did not compel whites to stay out of African American seating areas on buses.

King also argues that a just law is a law created by representatives of the people the law will affect. He shows how segregation laws fail to match this criterion by pointing out that many African Americans had been denied the right to vote in Alabama. Consequently, the legislature that passed the segregation laws was not democratically elected.

When you build a definition argument, often you must put much effort into identifying and explaining your criteria. You must convince your readers that your criteria are the best ones for what you are defining and that they apply to the case you are arguing.

King's Extended Definition Argument

After establishing criteria for two kinds of laws, *just* and *unjust*, King argues that citizens must respond differently to laws that are unjust, by disobeying them. He then shows how the special case of *segregation laws* meets the criteria for unjust laws. If readers accept his argument, they will agree that segregation laws belong in the category of unjust laws, and therefore must be disobeyed.

Criteria for Just Laws	Criteria for Unjust Laws	Segregation Laws
Consistent with moral law	Not consistent with moral law	✓
Uplift human personality	Damage human personality	✓
Must be obeyed by all people	Must be obeyed by some people, but not others	✓
Made by democratically elected Representatives	Not made by democratically elected representatives	✓
Appropriate Response to Just Laws: All citizens should obey them.	Appropriate Response to Unjust Laws: All citizens should disobey them.	

Finding Good Reasons

What is Parody?

YouTube parody of an Apple iPad commercial as a "Big Ol' iPod Touch"

Downfall, a German film released in 2004 about Hitler's last days, has been used for hundreds of popular YouTube parodies. Most parodies use the same scene of a defeated Hitler, played by Bruno Ganz, unleashing a furious speech to his staff in German with YouTubers adding English subtitles on topics as varied as the plot of *Avatar*, the upgrade to Windows 7, Apple's iPad, academic grant reviews, and the failure of various sports teams to win big games.

The owner of the rights to the film, Constantin Films, demanded that YouTube take down the parodies in April 2010, and YouTube complied. Critics of the move complained that Constantin Films used YouTube's Content ID filter to determine what is acceptable rather than the fair use provisions of copyright law. They argue that fair-use law allows a film clip, a paragraph from an article, or a short piece of music to be adapted if the purpose is to create commentary or satire.

Write about it

1. Which of the following criteria do you think must be present for a work to be considered a parody? Are there any criteria you might change or add?
   - the work criticizes a previous work
   - the work copies the same structure, details, or style of the previous work
   - the connections to the previous work are clear to the audience
   - the work is humorous
   - the title is a play on the previous work
   - the work is presented in either a print, visual, or musical medium

2. Do the various uses of the *Downfall* clip meet the criteria above? Would you define them as parodies? Why or why not?

Steps to Writing a Definition Argument

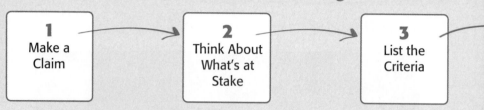

1 Make a Claim

2 Think About What's at Stake

3 List the Criteria

Step 1 Make a Claim

Make a definitional claim on a controversial issue that focuses on a key term.

Template

> _____ is (or is not) a _____ because it has (or does not have) features A, B, and C (or more).

Examples

- Hate speech (or pornography, literature, films, and so on) is (or is not) free speech protected by the First Amendment because it has (or does not have) these features.

- Hunting (or using animals for cosmetics testing, keeping animals in zoos, wearing furs, and so on) is (or is not) cruelty to animals because it has (or does not have) these features.

Step 2 Think About What's at Stake

- Does nearly everyone agree with you? If so, then your claim probably isn't interesting or important. If you can think of people who disagree, then something is at stake.
- Who argues the opposite of your claim?
- Why or how do they benefit from a different definition?

Step 3 List the Criteria

- Which criteria are necessary for _____ to be a _____?
- Which are the most important?
- Does your case in point meet all the criteria?

Step 4 Analyze Your Potential Readers

- Who are your readers?
- How does the definitional claim you are making affect them?
- How familiar are they with the issue, concept, or controversy that you're writing about?
- Which criteria are they most likely to accept with little explanation, and which will they disagree with?

Step 5 Write a Draft

Introduction
- Set out the issue, concept, or controversy.
- Give the background that your intended readers need.

Body
- Set out your criteria and argue for the appropriateness of the criteria.
- Anticipate where readers might question either your criteria or how they apply to your subject.
- Address opposing viewpoints by acknowledging how their definitions differ and by showing why your definition is better.

Conclusion
- Do more than simply summarize. You can, for example, go into more detail about what is at stake or the implications of your definition.

Step 6 Revise, Edit, Proofread

- For detailed instructions, see Chapter 4.
- For a checklist to use to evaluate your draft, see pages 48–49.

Michael Pollan

Eat Food: Food Defined

Michael Pollan is a journalism professor at the University of California, Berkeley, and the author of *In Defense of Food: An Eater's Manifesto* (2008), from which this excerpt is taken. *In Defense of Food* received many prizes and was named one of the ten best books of the year by the *New York Times* and the *Washington Post*. Pollan is also the author of *Second Nature* (1991), *A Place of My Own* (1997), *The Botany of Desire: A Plant's Eye View of the World* (2001), *The Omnivore's Dilemma: A Natural History of Four Meals* (2006), and *Food Rules* (2010). He is also a contributing writer for the *New York Times Magazine*.

Pollan asks why Americans worry so much about nutrition and yet seem so unhealthy. The title, *In Defense of Food*, is one of the many paradoxes that Pollan examines in the book. After all, why should food need defending if it is plentiful and we eat so much of it? Pollan argues that the answer lies in how we define food.

Pollan begins by asking why does food need to be defined?

The first time I heard the advice to "just eat food" it was in a speech by Joan Gussow, and it completely baffled me. Of course you should eat food—what else is there to eat? But Gussow, who grows much of her own food on a flood-prone finger of land jutting into the Hudson River, refuses to dignify most of the products for sale in the supermarket with that title. "In the thirty-four years I've been in the field of nutrition," she said in the same speech, "I have watched real food disappear from large areas of the supermarket and from much of the rest of the eating world." Taking food's place on the shelves has been an unending stream of foodlike substitutes, some seventeen thousand new ones every year—"products constructed largely around commerce and hope, supported by frighteningly little actual knowledge." Ordinary food is still out there, however, still being grown and even occasionally sold in the supermarket, and this ordinary food is what we should eat.

Pollan claims that everything that pretends to be food really isn't food, thus establishing the need for a definition.

2   But given our current state of confusion and given the thousands of products calling themselves food, this is more easily said than done. So consider these related rules of thumb. Each proposes a different sort of map to the contemporary food landscape, but all should take you to more or less the same place.

Don't eat anything your great grandmother wouldn't recognize as food.

3   Why your great grandmother? Because at this point your mother and possibly even your grandmother is as confused as the rest of us; to be safe we need to go back at least a couple generations, to a time before the advent of most modern foods. So depending on your age (and your grandmother), you may need to

go back to your great- or even great-great grandmother. Some nutritionists recommend going back even further. John Yudkin, a British nutritionist whose early alarms about the dangers of refined carbohydrates were overlooked in the 1960s and 1970s, once advised, "Just don't eat anything your Neolithic ancestors wouldn't have recognized and you'll be OK."

Pollan's first criterion of what is food offers a simple concept.

4   What would shopping this way mean in the supermarket? Well, imagine your great grandmother at your side as you roll down the aisles. You're standing together in front of the dairy case. She picks up a package of Go-Gurt Portable Yogurt tubes—and has no idea what this could possibly be. Is it a food or a toothpaste? And how, exactly, do you introduce it into your body? You could tell her it's just yogurt in a squirtable form, yet if she read the ingredients label she would have every reason to doubt that that was in fact the case. Sure, there's some yogurt in there, but there are also a dozen other things that aren't remotely yogurt like, ingredients she would probably fail to recognize as foods of any kind, including high-fructose corn syrup, modified corn starch, kosher gelatin, carrageenan, tri-calcium phosphate, natural and artificial flavors, vitamins, and so forth. (And there's a whole other list of ingredients for the "berry bubblegum bash" flavoring, containing everything but berries or bubblegum.) How did yogurt, which in your great grandmother's day consisted simply of milk inoculated with a bacterial culture, ever get to be so complicated? Is a product like Go-Gurt Portable Yogurt still a whole food? A food of any kind? Or is it just a food product?

Another way of defining food is to define what isn't food, but what Pollan calls "food products."

5   There are in fact hundreds of foodish products in the supermarket that your ancestors simply wouldn't recognize as food: breakfast cereal bars transected by bright white veins representing, but in reality having nothing to do with, milk; "protein waters" and "nondairy creamer"; cheeselike food-stuffs equally innocent of any bovine contribution; cakelike cylinders (with creamlike fillings) called Twinkies that never grow stale. Don't eat anything incapable of rotting is another personal policy you might consider adopting.

6   There are many reasons to avoid eating such complicated food products beyond the various chemical additives and corn and soy derivatives they contain. One of the problems with the products of food science is that, as Joan Gussow has pointed out, they lie to your body; their artificial colors and flavors and synthetic sweeteners and novel fats confound the senses we rely on to assess new foods and prepare our bodies to deal with them. Foods that lie leave us with little choice but to eat by the numbers, consulting labels rather than our senses.

7   It's true that foods have long been processed in order to preserve them, as when we pickle or ferment or smoke, but industrial processing aims to do much more than extend shelf life. Today foods are processed in ways specifically designed to sell us more food by pushing our evolutionary buttons—our inborn preferences

for sweetness and fat and salt. These qualities are difficult to find in nature but cheap and easy for the food scientist to deploy, with the result that processing induces us to consume much more of these ecological rarities than is good for us. "Tastes great, less filling!" could be the motto for most processed foods, which are far more energy dense than most whole foods: They contain much less water, fiber, and micronutrients, and generally much more sugar and fat, making them at the same time, to coin a marketing slogan, "More fattening, less nutritious!"

8   The great grandma rule will help keep many of these products out of your cart. But not all of them. Because thanks to the FDA's willingness, post–1973, to let food makers freely alter the identity of "traditional foods that everyone knows" without having to call them imitations, your great grandmother could easily be fooled into thinking that that loaf of bread or wedge of cheese is in fact a loaf of bread or a wedge of cheese. This is why we need a slightly more detailed personal policy to capture these imitation foods; to wit:

What food is can also be defined by what it isn't, hence a list of criteria for what isn't food.

Avoid food products containing ingredients that are a) unfamiliar set, b) unpronounceable, c) more than five in number, or that include d) high-fructose corn syrup.

9   None of these characteristics, not even the last one, is necessarily harmful in and of itself, but all of them are reliable markers for foods that have been highly processed to the point where they may no longer be what they purport to be. They have crossed over from foods to food products.

10   Consider a loaf of bread, one of the "traditional foods that everyone knows" specifically singled out for protection in the 1938 imitation rule. As your grandmother could tell you, bread is traditionally made using a remarkably small number of familiar ingredients: flour, yeast, water, and a pinch of salt will do it. But industrial bread— even industrial whole-grain bread—has become a far more complicated product of modern food science (not to mention commerce and hope). Here's the complete ingredients list for Sara Lee's Soft & Smooth Whole Grain White Bread. (Wait a minute—isn't "Whole Grain White Bread" a contradiction in terms? Evidently not any more.)

Pollan points out that the language used for food products is as convoluted as the ingredients.

> Enriched bleached flour [wheat flour, malted barley flour, niacin, iron, thiamin mononitrate (vitamin B), riboflavin (vitamin B_2), folic acid], water, whole grains [whole wheat flour, brown rice flour (rice flour, rice bran)], high fructose corn syrup [hello!], whey, wheat gluten, yeast, cellulose. Contains 2% or less of each of the following: honey, calcium sulfate, vegetable oil (soybean and/or cottonseed oils), salt, butter (cream, salt), dough conditioners (may contain one or more of the following: mono- and diglycerides, ethoxylated mono- and diglycerides, ascorbic acid, enzymes, azodicarbonamide),

guar gum, calcium propionate (preservative), distilled vinegar, yeast nutrients (monocalcium phosphate, calcium sulfate, ammonium sulfate), corn starch, natural flavor, beta-carotene (color), vitamin D_3, soy lecithin, soy flour.

11   There are many things you could say about this intricate loaf of "bread," but note first that even if it managed to slip by your great grandmother (because it is a loaf of bread, or at least is called one and strongly resembles one), the product fails every test proposed under rule number two: It's got unfamiliar ingredients (monoglycerides I've heard of before, but ethoxylated monoglycerides?); unpronounceable ingredients (try "azodicarbonamide"); it exceeds the maximum of five ingredients (by roughly thirty-six); and it contains high-fructose corn syrup. Sorry, Sara Lee, but your Soft & Smooth Whole Grain White Bread is not food and if not for the indulgence of the FDA could not even be labeled "bread."

12   Sara Lee's Soft & Smooth Whole Grain White Bread could serve as a monument to the age of nutritionism. It embodies the latest nutritional wisdom from science and government (which in its most recent food pyramid recommends that at least half our consumption of grain come from whole grains) but leavens that wisdom with the commercial recognition that American eaters (and American children in particular) have come to prefer their wheat highly refined—which is to say, cottony soft, snowy white, and exceptionally sweet on the tongue. In its marketing materials, Sara Lee treats this clash of interests as some sort of Gordian knot—it speaks in terms of an ambitious quest to build a "no compromise" loaf— which only the most sophisticated food science could possibly cut.

13   And so it has, with the invention of whole-grain white bread. Because the small percentage of whole grains in the bread would render it that much less sweet than, say, all-white Wonder Bread—which scarcely waits to be chewed before transforming itself into glucose—the food scientists have added high-fructose corn syrup and honey to to make up the difference; to overcome the problematic heft and toothsomeness of a real whole grain bread, they've deployed "dough conditioners," including guar gum and the aforementioned azodicarbonamide, to simulate the texture of supermarket white bread. By incorporating certain varieties of albino wheat, they've managed to maintain that deathly but apparently appealing Wonder Bread pallor.

14   Who would have thought Wonder Bread would ever become an ideal of aesthetic and gustatory perfection to which bakers would actually aspire—Sara Lee's Mona Lisa?

15   Very often food science's efforts to make traditional foods more nutritious make them much more complicated, but not necessarily any better for you. To make dairy products low fat, it's not enough to remove the fat. You then have to go to great lengths to

preserve the body or creamy texture by working in all kinds of food additives. In the case of low-fat or skim milk that usually means adding powdered milk. But powdered milk contains oxidized cholesterol, which scientists believe is much worse for your arteries than ordinary cholesterol, so food makers sometimes compensate by adding antioxidants, further complicating what had been a simple one-ingredient whole food. Also, removing the fat makes it that much harder for your body to absorb the fat-soluble vitamins that are one of the reasons to drink milk in the first place.

16   All this heroic and occasionally counterproductive food science has been undertaken in the name of our health—so that Sara Lee can add to its plastic wrapper the magic words "good source of whole grain" or a food company can ballyhoo the even more magic words "low fat." Which brings us to a related food policy that may at first sound counterintuitive to a health-conscious eater:

Avoid Food Products That Make Health Claims.

17   For a food product to make health claims on its package it must first have a package, so right off the bat it's more likely to be a processed than a whole food. Generally speaking, it is only the big food companies that have the wherewithal to secure FDA-approved health claims for their products and there trumpet them to the world. Recently, however, some of the tonier fruits and nuts have begun boasting about their health-enhancing properties, and there will surely be more as each crop council scrounges together the money to commission its own scientific study. Because all plants contain antioxidants, all these studies are guaranteed to find something on which to base a health oriented marketing campaign.

18   But for the most part it is the products of food science that make the boldest health claims, and these are often founded on incomplete and often erroneous science—the dubious fruits of nutritionism. Don't forget that trans-fat-rich margarine, one of the first industrial foods to claim it was healthier than the traditional food it replaced, turned out to give people heart attacks. Since that debacle, the FDA, under tremendous pressure from industry, has made it only easier for food companies to make increasingly doubtful health claims, such as the one Frito-Lay now puts on some of its chips—that eating them is somehow good for your heart. If you bother to read the health claims closely (as food marketers make sure consumers seldom do), you will find that there is often considerably less to them than meets the eye.

19   Consider a recent "qualified" health claim approved by the FDA for (don't laugh) corn oil. ("Qualified" is a whole new category of health claim, introduced in 2002 at the behest of industry.) Corn oil, you may recall, is particularly high in the omega-6 fatty acids we're already consuming far too many of.

> Very limited and preliminary scientific evidence suggests that eating about one tablespoon (16 grams) of corn oil daily may reduce the risk of heart disease due to the unsaturated fat content in corn oil.

20   The tablespoon is a particularly rich touch, conjuring images of moms administering medicine, or perhaps cod-liver oil, to their children. But what the FDA gives with one hand, it takes away with the other. Here's the small-print "qualification" of this already notably diffident health claim:

> [The] FDA concludes that there is little scientific evidence supporting this claim.

Close reading of labels undercuts health claims of food products.

> To achieve this possible benefit, corn oil is to replace a similar amount of saturated fat and not increase the total number of calories you eat in a day.

21   This little masterpiece of pseudoscientific bureaucratese was extracted from the FDA by the manufacturer of Mazola corn oil. It would appear that "qualified" is an official FDA euphemism for "all but meaningless." Though someone might have let the consumer in on this game: The FDA's own research indicates that consumers have no idea what to make of qualified health claims (how would they?), and its rules allow companies to promote the claims pretty much any way they want—they can use really big type for the claim, for example, and then print the disclaimers in teeny-tiny type. No doubt we can look forward to a qualified health claim for high-fructose corn syrup, a tablespoon of which probably does contribute to your health—as long as it replaces a comparable amount of, say, poison in your diet and doesn't increase the total number of calories you eat in a day.

22   When corn oil and chips and sugary breakfast cereals can all boast being good for your heart, health claims have become hopelessly corrupt. The American Heart Association currently bestows (for a fee) its heart-healthy seal of approval on Lucky Charms, Cocoa Puffs, and Trix cereals, Yoo-hoo lite chocolate drink, and Healthy Choice's Premium Caramel Swirl Ice Cream Sandwich—this at a time when scientists are coming to recognize that dietary sugar probably plays a more important role in heart disease than dietary fat. Meanwhile, the genuinely heart-healthy whole foods in the produce section, lacking the financial and political clout of the packaged goods a few aisles over, are mute. But don't take the silence of the yams as a sign that they have nothing valuable to say about health.

Pollan adds a playful touch by echoing the title of a popular movie to make a point.

Sample Student Definition Argument

Conley 1

Patrice Conley
Professor Douglas
English 101
15 Nov. 2010

Flagrant Foul: The NCAA's Definition of Student Athletes as Amateurs

Every year, thousands of student athletes across America sign the National Collegiate Athletic Association's Form 08-3a, the "Student-Athlete" form, waiving their right to receive payment for the use of their name and image (McCann). The form defines student athletes as amateurs, who cannot receive payment for playing their sports. While their schools and coaches may make millions of dollars in salaries and endorsement deals and are the highest-paid public employees in many states, student athletes can never earn a single penny from their college athletic careers.

Make no mistake: college athletics are big business. The most visible college sports—big-time men's football and basketball—generate staggering sums of money. For example, the twelve universities in the Southeastern Conference receive $205 million each year from CBS and ESPN for the right to broadcast its football games (Smith and Ourand). Even more money comes in from video games, clothing, and similar licenses. In 2010, the *New York Times* reported, "the NCAA's licensing deals are estimated at more than $4 billion" per year (Thamel). While the staggering executive pay at big corporations has brought public outrage, coaches' salaries are even more outlandish. Kentucky basketball coach, John Calipari, is paid over $4 million a year for a basketball program that makes about $35-40 million a year, more than 10% of the entire revenue. Tom Van Riper observes that no corporate CEO commands this large a share of the profits. He notes that if Steve Ballmer, the CEO at Microsoft, had Calipari's deal, Ballmer would make over $6 billion a year.

How can colleges allow advertisers, arena operators, concession owners, athletic gear manufacturers, retailers, game companies, and media moguls, along with coaches and university officials, to make millions and pay the stars of the show nothing? The answer is that colleges define

Patrice Conley sets out the definition she is attempting to rectify: amateurs are athletes who aren't paid.

Conley identifies what's at stake.

Conley disputes the definition that college sports are amateur sports.

The huge salaries paid to college coaches are comparable to those in professional sports.

Conley 2

Conley argues that colleges use the definition of athletes as amateurs to refuse to pay them.

athletes as amateurs. Not only are student athletes not paid for playing their sport, they cannot receive gifts and are not allowed to endorse products, which may be a violation of their right to free speech. The NCAA, an organization of colleges and schools, forces student athletes to sign away their rights because, it says, it is protecting the students. If student athletes could accept money from anyone, the NCAA argues, they might be exploited, cheated, or even bribed. Taking money out of the equation is supposed to let students focus on academics and preserve the amateur status of college sports.

The definition of amateur arose in the nineteenth century in Britain, when team sports became popular. Middle-class and upper-class students in college had ample time to play their sports while working-class athletes had only a half-day off (no sports were played on Sundays in that era). Teams began to pay top working-class sportsmen for the time they had to take off from work. Middle-class and upper-class sportsmen didn't want to play against the working-class teams, so they made the distinction between amateurs and professionals. The definition of amateur crossed the Atlantic to the United States, where college sports became popular in the 1880s. But it was not long until the hypocrisy of amateurism undermined the ideal. Top football programs like Yale had

Conley shows in this paragraph how the definition of college athletes as unpaid amateurs is based on outdated notions.

slush funds to pay athletes, and others used ringers—players who weren't students—and even players from other schools (Zimbalist 7). The Olympic Games maintained the amateur-professional distinction until 1988, but it was long evident that Communist bloc nations were paying athletes to train full-time and Western nations were paying athletes through endorsement contracts. The only Olympic sport that now requires amateur status is boxing. The college sports empire in the United States run by

Conley argues that everyone else has discarded that old idea of "amateurism as unpaid," so why won't the NCAA discard it?

the NCAA is the last bastion of amateurism for sports that draw audiences large enough to be televised.

Colleges might be able to defend the policy of amateurism if they extended this definition to all students. A fair policy is one that treats all students the same. A fair policy doesn't result in some students getting paid for professional work, while other students do not. Consider the

Conley 3

students in the Butler School of Music at the University of Texas at Austin, for example. Many student musicians perform at the professional level. Does the school prevent them from earning money for their musical performances? No. In fact, the school runs a referral service that connects its students with people and businesses who want to hire professional musicians. The university even advises its students on how to negotiate a contract and get paid for their performance ("Welcome").

Comparisons show that colleges do not apply the definition of amateur consistently.

Likewise, why are student actors and actresses allowed to earn money from their work and images, while student athletes are not? Think about actress Emma Watson, who enrolled at Brown University in Rhode Island. Can you imagine the university officials at Brown telling Watson that she would have to make the next two *Harry Potter* films for free, instead of for the $5 million she has been offered? Can you imagine Brown University telling Watson that all the revenue from Harry Potter merchandise bearing her likeness would have to be paid directly to the university for the rest of her life? They would if Watson were an athlete instead of an actress.

Do you think this analogy is effective?

In fact, compared to musicians and actors, student athletes have an even greater need to earn money while they are still in college. Athletes' professional careers are likely to be much shorter than musicians' or actors'. College may be the only time some athletes have the opportunity to capitalize on their success. (Indeed, rather than focusing student athletes on their academic careers, the NCAA policy sometimes forces students to leave college early, so they can earn a living before their peak playing years are over.) Student athletes often leave school with permanent injuries and no medical insurance or job prospects, whereas student musicians and actors rarely suffer career-ending injuries on the job.

Student athletes are prevented from profiting from their name and image. The NCAA says this rule preserves their standing as amateurs and protects them from the celebrity and media frenzy surrounding professional sports stars. Search for a "Tim Tebow Jersey" online, and you can buy officially branded Florida Gators shirts, ranging in price from $34.99 to $349.99 (autographed by Tebow). The NCAA, the University of Florida, Nike, and the other parties involved in the production and sale of these products get around the problem of using an amateur's name by

Conley 4

using his team number instead. Tebow's name doesn't appear anywhere on the jerseys—just his number, 15. Yet all these jerseys are identified as "Official Tim Tebow Gators merchandise," and they are certainly bought by fans of Tebow rather than by people who just happen to like the number fifteen. Nobody is saying how much money these jerseys have made for Nike, or for the NCAA. What we do know for sure is the amount Tim Tebow has made off the jerseys: nothing.

The example of Tim Tebow illustrates how the definition of amateur works against college athletes.

Defenders of the current system argue that student athletes on scholarships are paid with free tuition, free room and board, free books, and tutoring help. The total package can be the equivalent of $120,000 over four years. For those student athletes who are motivated to take advantage of the opportunity, the lifetime benefits can be enormous. Unfortunately, too few student athletes do take advantage of the opportunity. Seldom does a major college football and men's basketball program have graduation rates at or close to overall student body. A study by the University of North Carolina's College Sports Research Institute released in 2010 accuses the NCAA of playing fast and loose with graduation rates by counting part-time students in statistics for the general student body, making graduation rates for athletes look better in a comparison. Student athletes must be full-time students, thus they should be compared to other full-time students. The North Carolina Institute reports that 54.8% of major college (Football Bowl Subdivision) football players at 117 schools graduated within six years, compared to 73.7% of other full-time students. The gap between basketball players was even greater, with 44.6% of athletes graduating compared to 75.7% of the general student body (Zaiger). For the handful of talented

Conley gives evidence that undercuts the argument that college athletes are compensated with a college degree.

athletes who can play in the National Football League or the National Basketball Association, college sports provide training for their future lucrative, although short-lived, profession. But as the NCAA itself points out in its ads, the great majority of student athletes "go pro in something other than sports." For the 55% of college basketball players who fail to graduate, the supposed $120,000 package is an air ball.

The clever use of "air ball" reinforces Conley's argument that the NCAA's definition of amateur is outdated and unfair.

The NCAA would be wise to return to the older definition of *amateur*, which comes from Latin through old French, meaning "lover of." It doesn't

Conley 5

necessarily have to have anything to do with money. Whether it's a jazz performer or a dancer or an athlete, an amateur ought to be considered someone in love with an activity—someone who cares deeply about the activity, studies the activity in depth, and practices in order to be highly proficient. NBA players, Olympians, college athletes, high school players, and even bird watchers, star gazers, and open-source programmers: they're all amateurs. If they are lucky enough to be paid, so be it.

Conley concludes with her main claim. She proposes a new definition of amateur, one that would permit salaries and royalties to go to the college athlete.

Conley 6

Works Cited

McCann, Michael. "NCAA Faces Unspecified Damages, Changes in Latest Anti-Trust Case." *SI.com*. Time, Inc., 21 July 2009. Web. 3 Nov. 2010.

National Collegiate Athletic Association. Advertisement. *NCAA.org*. NCAA, 13 Mar. 2007. Web. 3 Nov. 2010.

Smith, Michael, and John Ourand. "ESPN Pays $2.25B for SEC Rights." *SportsBusiness Journal*. Smith and Street, 25 Aug. 2008. Web. 1 Nov. 2010.

Thamel, Pete. "N.C.A.A. Fails to Stop Licensing Lawsuit." *New York Times*. New York Times, 8 Feb. 2010. Web. 1 Nov. 2010.

Van Riper, Thomas. "The Highest-Paid College Basketball Coaches." *Forbes.com*. Forbes, 8 Mar. 2010. Web. 3 Nov. 2010.

"Welcome to the Music Referral Service." *Butler School of Music*. Univ. of Texas at Austin, n.d. Web. 5 Nov. 2010.

Zaiger, Alan Scher. "Study: NCAA Graduation Rate Comparisons Flawed." *ABC News*. ABC News, 20 Apr. 2010. Web. 1 Nov. 2010.

Zimbalist, Andrew. *Unpaid Professionals: Commercialism and Conflict in Big-Time College Sports*. Princeton UP, 2001. Print.

PEARSON
mycomplab

For support in learning this chapter's content, follow this path in MyCompLab:
> Resources > Writing > Writing Purposes > Writing to Argue or Persuade.
Review the Instruction and Multimedia resources, then complete the Exercises and click on Gradebook to measure your progress.

9 | Causal Arguments

In this chapter, you will learn that

1. Causal arguments take three basic forms (see page 114)
2. Causes can be identified using four methods (see page 115)
3. Effective causal arguments go beyond the obvious causes to explore complex relationships (see page 117)

Each year, we hear that American students are falling behind their international peers. Different groups argue that the solution lies in investing more in funding for additional teacher training, or smaller classrooms, or more technology in the classroom. Yet America invests billions more in education than some nations whose students surpass American students in achievement rankings. Still others have suggested that America's problem lies in a wide-scale cultural shift that has created an American student who is less motivated than those of the past. How can America's schools become world leaders again?

Understand How Causal Arguments Work

Causal claims can take three basic forms:

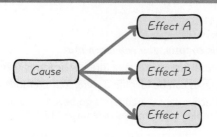

1. One cause leads to one or more effects.

The invention of the telegraph led to the commodities market, the establishment of standard time zones, and news reporting as we know it today.

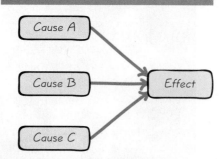

2. One effect has several causes.

Hurricanes are becoming more financially destructive to the United States because of the greater intensity of recent storms, an increase in the commercial and residential development of coastal areas, and a reluctance to enforce certain construction standards in coastal residential areas.

3. A series of events form a chain, where one event causes another, which then causes a third, and so on.

Making the HPV vaccination mandatory for adolescent girls will make unprotected sex seem safer, leading to greater promiscuity, ultimately resulting in more teenage pregnancies.

Find Causes

The causal claim is at the center of the causal argument. Writing a clear claim about cause and effect can be difficult because if a cause is worth writing about, it is likely to be complex. Obvious cases of cause and effect (staying out in the sun too long without skin protection causes sunburn) usually do not require written arguments because everyone is convinced that the causal relationship exists. Many of the causal claims that most people now accept without question—smoking causes cancer, shifting plates on the Earth's crust cause earthquakes, DDT causes eggshell thinning in bald eagles—were "settled" only after long and complex arguments.

The philosopher John Stuart Mill devised four ways for an investigator to go about finding causes.

- **The Common Factor Method.** Sometimes causes can be identified because two or more similar events share a common factor. The common factor may be the cause. For example, if two people in two different states both develop a rare disease, and both of them recently traveled to Madagascar, they were probably exposed to the illness while there.

- **The Single Difference Method.** Causes can often be identified when two situations or events have different outcomes. If there is a single difference in the two scenarios, that difference may be the cause. At the 1998 Winter Olympics in Nagano, Japan, the speed skating team from the Netherlands introduced a technological innovation to the sport—clap skates, which improve skaters' performance by keeping the skate blade in contact with the ice longer. Racing against the best skaters in the world, the Dutch on their clap skates won eleven of thirty medals, five of which were gold. By the 2002 Winter Olympics, all speed skaters had switched over to the new skates, and the medal count was much more evenly distributed. That year the United States, Netherlands, and Germany each won three gold medals, and a total of eight medals apiece. Clap skates were the most likely cause of the Netherlands' dominance four years earlier.

- **Concomitant Variation.** Some causes are discovered by observing a shared pattern of variation in a possible cause and possible effect. For example, scientists noticed that peaks in the 11-year sunspot cycle match disruptions in high-frequency radio transmission on earth, leading them to conclude that the solar activity somehow causes the disruptions.

- **Process of Elimination.** Another way to establish causation is to identify all the possible causes of something, and then test them one by one to eliminate those that can't be the cause. When an electrical appliance stops working, electricians often trace the problem this way, by checking switches one at a time to see if current can flow across them. The switch that doesn't show a continuous flow of current is the one that needs replacing.

A frequent error of people looking for cause and effect is to mistake correlation for causation. Just because one event happens after or at the same time as another one, you cannot assume that the first one caused the second. Sometimes it's just a coincidence. For example, you may observe that every time the mail carrier comes to your door, your dog barks at him, and then the mail carrier leaves. You might assume that your dog's barking causes the mail carrier to leave (your dog is probably convinced of this). However, the more likely cause is that the carrier has finished delivering your mail, so he goes on to the next house. Using Mills's methods will help you avoid mistaking correlation for causation in your own causal arguments.

To understand how you might use Mills's methods of identifying causes, suppose you want to research the cause of the increase in legalized lotteries in the United States. You research the history of lotteries in order to look for possible causes. You would discover that lotteries go back to colonial times, but were controversial because they were run by private companies that sometimes failed to pay the winners. Laws against lotteries were passed in 1840, but after the Civil War, the defeated states of the Confederacy needed money to rebuild bridges, buildings, and schools. Southerners ran lotteries and sold tickets throughout the nation. But once again, these lotteries were run by private companies, and some of them simply took people's money without paying out winnings. Eventually, lotteries were banned again.

In 1964, New Hampshire became the first state to authorize a lottery to fund the state's educational system. Soon other states, realizing that their citizens were spending their money on lottery tickets from New Hampshire, established lotteries of their own. During the 1980s, states began approving other forms of state-run gambling such as keno and video poker. By 1993 only Hawaii and Utah had no legalized gambling of any kind.

Knowing this background, you can begin using Mills's methods to look for the causes of lotteries' recent popularity. Using the common factor method, you consider what current lotteries have in common with earlier lotteries. That factor is easy to identify: It's economic. The early colonies and later the states have turned to lotteries again and again as a way of raising money without raising taxes. But, you wonder, why have lotteries spread so quickly since 1964, and raised so little concern? The single difference method shows you the likely reason: Lotteries in the past were run by private companies, and inevitably someone took off with the money instead of paying it out. Today's lotteries are operated by state agencies or contracted under state control. While they are not immune to scandal, they are much more closely monitored than lotteries in the past.

Mills's other methods might also lead you to potential causes. If you find, for example, that lotteries grow in popularity in the aftermath of wars, this concomitant variation might lead you to suspect that the economic damage of war can be one cause of lotteries' popularity. This in turn might suggest inflation caused by the Vietnam War as a possible contributing cause to the rise of state lotteries in the '60s and '70s. The process of elimination could also lead you to some probable causes for lotteries' popularity, though for such a complex topic, it would be time-consuming. You might begin by making a list of all the reasons you could think of: Perhaps people these days are more economically secure, and don't mind risking a few dollars on lottery tickets? Or maybe people are more desperate now, and lotteries represent one of the few ways they can accumulate wealth? Each of these possibilities would require research into history, economics, and psychology, but this might lead you to some interesting conclusions on the complex forces contributing to today's extensive lottery system.

Build a Causal Argument

Effective causal arguments move beyond the obvious to get at underlying causes. One great causal mystery today is global warming. Scientists generally agree that the average surface temperature on Earth has gone up by 1.3 degrees Fahrenheit or 0.7 degrees Celsius over the last hundred years, and that the amount of carbon dioxide in the atmosphere has increased by 25 percent since 1960. But the causes of those phenomena are disputed. Some people argue that the rise in temperature is caused by natural climate variations, and that the increase in carbon dioxide has little or nothing to do with it. Others argue that the rise in carbon dioxide traps heat in the atmosphere and has increased the earth's temperature. They argue further that the increased carbon dioxide is the result of human activity, especially the burning of fossil fuels and the destruction of tropical forests. The debate over global warming continues because the causation at work is not simple or easy to prove.

There are many events that may be caused by global warming, and they are more dramatically evident in arctic and subarctic regions. The decade from January 2000 to December 2009 is the warmest decade since modern temperature records began in the 1880s. Arctic sea ice shrank by 14 percent—an area the size of Texas—from 2004 to 2005, and Greenland's massive ice sheet has been thinning by more than 3 feet a year.

Many scientists consider these phenomena to be effects of global warming. They argue that a single cause—the rise in the Earth's temperature—has led to many dire effects, and will lead to more. If you wanted to make an argument along these lines, you would need to construct a causal chain:

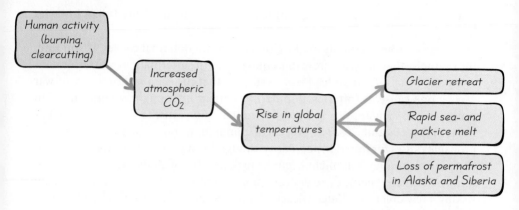

At each step, you would need to show the links between an event and its consequences, and you would need to convince readers that that link is real, not mere coincidence. You might find common factors, single differences, or concomitant variation that supports each causal link. You would also need to use a process of elimination to show that other possible causes are not in fact involved in your causal chain.

Some climate scientists have doubts about all these causal links. While the observable events—the loss of sea ice, glacier retreat, and so on—may be caused by human activity, they may be caused instead by naturally recurring cycles.

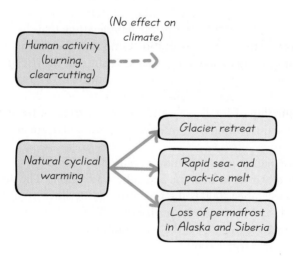

Or, the effects could be caused partly by natural cycles and partly by humans.

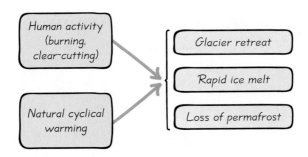

It is difficult to say for certain because much of the detailed data about the great melt in the north goes back only to the early 1990s—not long enough to rule out short-term climate cycles. However, computer models suggest a very low probability that such rapid change could occur naturally. So even if we are in a natural, short-term warming cycle, we still must ask if human activities are contributing to the documented warming, and making it even worse.

Identifying the causes of global warming is important because if we do not know the real causes, we cannot make the necessary changes to stop, reduce, or reverse it. If global warming continues unabated, the economic and human costs will be disastrous. But efforts to stop it are expensive and politically risky. Thus correctly establishing the causes of global warming is a crucial first step in solving the problem.

Glaciers in many parts of the world are melting at rates faster than scientists thought possible just a few years ago. Even major oil companies have acknowledged that global warming is real. Yet the American public has taken little notice of world climate change—perhaps because it's difficult to get excited about the mean temperature rising a few degrees and the sea level rising a few feet. What would get Americans thinking seriously about global warming?

Steps to Writing a Causal Argument

1
Make a Claim

2
What's at Stake in Your Claim?

3
Think of Possible Causes

Step 1 Make a Claim

Make a causal claim on a controversial trend, event, or phenomenon.

Template

> SOMETHING does (or does not) cause SOMETHING ELSE.

–or–

> SOMETHING causes SOMETHING ELSE, which, in turn, causes SOMETHING ELSE.

Examples

- One-parent families (or television violence, bad diet, and so on) are (or are not) the cause of emotional and behavioral problems in children.
- Firearms control laws (or right-to-carry-handgun laws) reduce (or increase) violent crimes.
- Putting grade school children into competitive sports teaches them how to succeed in later life (or puts undue emphasis on winning and teaches many who are slower to mature to have a negative self-image).

Step 2 What's at Stake in Your Claim?

- If the cause is obvious to everyone, then it probably isn't worth writing about.

Step 3 Think of Possible Causes

- Which are the immediate causes?
- Which are the background causes?
- Which are the hidden causes?
- Which are the causes that most people have not recognized?

Step 4 Analyze Your Potential Readers

- Who are your readers?
- How familiar will they be with the trend, event, or phenomenon that you're writing about?
- What are they likely to know and not know?
- How likely are they to accept your causal explanation?
- What alternative explanation might they argue for?

Step 5 Write a Draft

Introduction

- Describe the controversial trend, event, or phenomenon.
- Give the background that your intended readers will need.

Body

- Explain the cause or chain of causation of a trend, event, or phenomenon that is unfamiliar to your readers.
- Set out the causes that have been offered and reject them one by one. Then you can present the cause that you think is most important.
- Treat a series of causes one by one, analyzing the importance of each.

Conclusion

- Do more than simply summarize. Consider describing additional effects beyond those that have been noted previously.

Step 6 Revise, Edit, Proofread

- For detailed instructions, see Chapter 4.
- For a checklist to use to evaluate your draft, see pages 48–49.

Finding Good Reasons

Why Are Americans Gaining Weight?

Eric Schlosser, author of *Fast Food Nation* (2001), chows down on a grilled cheese sandwich, fries, and a soda. *Fast Food Nation* traces the rise of fast-food restaurants against the background of American culture based on the automobile. Schlosser claims that one of the effects of fast food is the increase in the number of overweight Americans.

There is no doubt that Americans have grown larger. A 2004 survey of Americans published in *JAMA: The Journal of the American Medical Association* found that nearly one-third (32.5 percent) of adults are obese and two-thirds (66.3 percent) are overweight. An especially disturbing aspect of this trend is that children are increasingly obese. The Center for Disease Control and Prevention reports that the percentage of obese children aged 6 to 11 almost quadrupled from 4 percent in 1974 to 15 percent in 2000, and the percentage of obese children aged 12 to 19 increased from 6 percent in 1974 to 15 percent in 2000.

Write about it

1. To what extent do you think fast food is the cause of the trend toward excess weight? To what extent do you think lifestyle changes and the content of food are causes? In addition to the amount of fast food Americans consume, consider the following:
   - more sedentary lifestyle with more driving and less walking
   - more time spent watching television, using computers, and playing video games
   - introduction of high-fructose corn syrup in many foods, from ketchup and peanut butter to chocolate milk and yogurt
   - inadequate physical education and reduced outdoor recess periods in schools
   - more food advertising directed at children

**Emily
Raine**

Why Should I Be Nice to You?
Coffee Shops and the Politics of
Good Service

Emily Raine recently received a master's degree in communication studies at McGill University in Montreal. She writes about graffiti and street art. This article appeared in the online journal *Bad Subjects* in 2005.

In this article, Raine explains why work in a coffee chain is worse than work in other kinds of service jobs. She also outlines the causes for what she sees as a destructive dynamic in the coffee chain culture and provides a possible alternative.

> "There is no more precious commodity than the relationship of trust and confidence a company has with its employees."
>
> —*Starbucks Coffee Company chairman Howard Schultz*

I actually like to serve. I'm not sure if this comes from some innate inclination to mother and fuss over strangers, or if it's because the movement and sociability of service work provides a much-needed antidote to the solitude of academic research, but I've always found something about service industry work satisfying. I've done the gamut of service jobs, from fine dining to cocktail waitressing to hip euro-bistro counter work, and the only job where I've ever felt truly whipped was working as a barista at one of the now-ubiquitous specialty coffee chains, those bastions of jazz and public solitude that have spread through urban landscapes over the last ten years or so. The pay was poor, the shifts long and oddly dispersed, the work boring and monotonous, the managers demanding, and the customers regularly displayed that unique spleen that emerges in even the most pleasant people before they've had the morning's first coffee. I often felt like an aproned Coke machine, such was the effect my sparkling personality had on the clientele. And yet, some combination of service professionalism, fear of termination and an imperative to be "nice" allowed me to suck it up, smile and continue to provide that intangible trait that the industry holds above all else, good service.

2   Good service in coffee shops doesn't amount to much. Unlike table service, where interaction with customers spans a minimum of half an hour, the average contact with a café customer lasts less than ten seconds. Consider how specialty cafés are laid

Raine establishes a credible, ethical stance in her introduction.

Even before identifying the effect that she intends to analyze, Raine identifies the cause—an efficient but impersonal assembly-line approach to service.

out: the customer service counter is arranged in a long line that clients move along to "use" the café. The linear coffee bar resembles an assembly line, and indeed, café labor is heavily grounded in the rationalism of Fordist manufacturing principles, which had already been tested for use in hospitality services by fast food chains. Each of the café workers is assigned a specific stage in the service process to perform exclusively, such as taking orders, using the cash registers, or handing clients cups of brewed coffee.

3   The specialization of tasks increases the speed of transactions and limits the duration of any one employee's interaction with the clientele. This means that in a given visit a customer might order from one worker, receive food from the next, then brewed coffee or tea from yet another, then pay a cashier before proceeding down the line of the counter, finishing the trip at the espresso machine which is always situated at its end. Ultimately, each of the café's products is processed and served by a different employee, who repeats the same preparation task for hours and attends to each customer only as they receive that one product.

Raine argues that the assembly-line service model precludes real interaction with customers.

4   Needless to say, the productive work in cafés is dreary and repetitive. Further, this style of service severely curtails interaction with the clientele, and the very brevity of each transaction precludes much chance for authentic friendliness or conversation—even asking about someone's day would slow the entire operation. The one aspect of service work that can be unpredictable—people—becomes redundant, and interaction with customers is reduced to a fatiguing eight-hour-long smile and the repetition of sentiments that allude to good service, such as injunctions to enjoy their purchases or to have a nice day. Rather than friendly exchanges with customers, barista workers' good service is reduced to a quick rictus in the customer's direction between a great deal of friendly interaction with the espresso machine.

Do you agree with this description of a typical coffee shop?

5   As the hospitality industry really took off in the sixties, good service became one of the trademarks of its advertising claims, a way for brands to distinguish themselves from the rest of the pack. One needn't think too hard to come up with a litany of service slogans that holler the good graces of their personnel—at Starbucks where the baristas make the magic, at Pacific Southwest Airlines where smiles aren't just painted on, or at McDonald's where smiles are free. Employee friendliness emerged as one of the chief distinguishing brand features of personal services, which means that the workers themselves become an aspect of the product for sale.

6   Our notions of good service revolve around a series of platitudes about professionalism—we're at your service, with a smile,

where the customer's always right—each bragging the centrality of the customer to everything "we" do. Such claims imply an easy and equal exchange between two parties: the "we" that gladly serves and the "you" that happily receives. There is, however, always a third party involved in the service exchange, and that's whoever has hired the server, the body that ultimately decides just what the dimensions of good service will be.

This "third party"—management, ownership—is the ultimate cause of the phenomenon under discussion.

7   Like most employees, a service worker sells labor to an employer at a set rate, often minimum wage, and the employer sells the product of that labor, the service itself, at market values. In many hospitality services, where gratuities make up the majority of employment revenue, the worker directly benefits from giving good service, which of course translates to good tips. But for the vast majority of service staff, and particularly those employed in venues yielding little or no gratuities—fast food outlets, café chains, cleaning and maintenance operations—this promises many workers little more than a unilateral imperative to be perpetually bright and amenable.

8   The vast majority of service personnel do not spontaneously produce an unaffected display of cheer and good will continuously for the duration of a shift. When a company markets its products on servers' friendliness, they must then monitor and control employees' friendliness, so good service is defined and enforced from above. Particularly in chains, which are premised upon their consistent reproduction of the same experience in numerous locations, organizations are obliged to impose systems to manage employees' interaction with their customers. In some chains, namely the fast food giants such as McDonald's and Burger King, employee banter is scripted into cash registers, so that as soon as a customer orders, workers are cued to offer, "would you like a dessert with that?" (an offer of dubious benefit to the customer) and to wish them a nice day. Ultimately, this has allowed corporations to be able to assimilate "good service"—or, friendly workers—into their overall brand image.

Does your experience as a customer (or worker) at fast food chains match this description?

9   While cafés genuflect toward the notion of good service, their layouts and management styles preclude much possibility of creating the warmth that this would entail. Good service is, of course, important, but not if it interferes with throughput. What's more, these cafés have been at the forefront of a new wave of organizations that not only market themselves on service quality but also describe employees' job satisfaction as the seed from which this flowers.

10   Perhaps the most glaring example of this is Starbucks, where cheerful young workers are displayed behind elevated

counters as they banter back and forth, calling out fancy Italian drink names and creating theatre out of their productive labor. Starbucks' corporate literature gushes not only about the good service its customers will receive, but about the great joy that its "partners" take in providing it, given the company's unique ability to "provide a great work environment and treat each other with respect and dignity," and where its partners are "emotionally and intellectually committed to Starbucks success." In the epigraph to this essay, Starbucks' chairman even describes the company's relationship with its workers as a commodity. Not only does Starbucks offer good service, but it attempts to guarantee something even better: good service provided by employees that are genuinely happy to give it.

The creation of 11 *this new kind of worker is in effect a public relations gimmick.*

Starbucks has branded a new kind of worker, the happy, wholesome, perfume-free barista. The company offers unusual benefits for service workers, including stock options, health insurance, dental plans and other perks such as product discounts and giveaways. Further, they do so very, very publicly, and the company's promotional materials are filled with moving accounts of workers who never dreamed that corporate America could care so much. With the other hand, though, the company has smashed unionization drives in New York, Vancouver and at its Seattle roaster; it schedules workers at oddly timed shifts that never quite add up to full-time hours; the company pays only nominally more than minimum wage, and their staffs are still unable to subsist schlepping lattes alone.

12   Starbucks is not alone in marketing itself as an enlightened employer. When General Motors introduced its Saturn line, the new brand was promoted almost entirely on the company's good relations with its staff. The company's advertising spots often featured pictures of and quotes from the union contract, describing their unique partnership between manufacturer, workers and union, which allowed blue-collar personnel to have a say in everything from automobile designs to what would be served for lunch. The company rightly guessed that this strategy would go over well with liberal consumers concerned about the ethics of their purchases. Better yet, Saturn could market its cars based on workers' happiness whether personnel were satisfied or not, because very few consumers would ever have the chance to interact with them.

13   At the specialty coffee chains, however, consumers *have* to talk to employees, yet nobody ever really asks. The café service counter runs like a smooth piece of machinery, and I found that most people preferred to pretend that they were interacting with an appliance. In such short transactions, it is exceedingly difficult

for customers to remember the humanity of each of the four to seven people they might interact with to get their coffees. Even fast food counters have one server who processes each customer's order, yet in cafés the workers just become another gadget in the well-oiled café machine. This is a definite downside for the employees—clients are much ruder to café staff than in any other sector of the industry I ever worked in. I found that people were more likely to be annoyed than touched by any reference to my having a personality, and it took no small amount of thought on my part to realize why.

14   Barista workers are hired to represent an abstract category of worker, not to act as individuals. Because of the service system marked by short customer interaction periods and a homogenous staff, the services rendered are linked in the consumer imagination to the company and not to any one individual worker. Workers' assimilation into the company image makes employees in chain service as branded as the products they serve. The chain gang, the workers who hold these eminently collegiate after-school jobs, are proscribed sales scripts and drilled on customer service scenarios to standardize interactions with customers. The company issues protocols for hair length, color and maintenance, visible piercings and tattoos as well as personal hygiene and acceptable odorific products. Workers are made more interchangeable by the use of uniforms, which, of course, serve to make the staff just that. The organization is a constant intermediary in every transaction, interjecting its presence in every detail of the service experience, and this standardization amounts to an absorption of individuals' personalities into the corporate image.

Raine spells out her thesis in this paragraph.

15   Many of the measures that chains take to secure the homogeneity of their employees do not strike us as particularly alarming, likely because similar restrictions have been in place for several hundred years. Good service today has inherited many of the trappings of the good servant of yore, including prohibitions against eating, drinking, sitting or relaxing in front the served, entering and exiting through back doors, and wearing uniforms to visually mark workers' status. These measures almost completely efface the social identities of staff during work hours, providing few clues to workers' status in their free time. Contact between service workers and their customers is thus limited to purely functional relations, so that the public only see them as workers, as makers of quality coffee, and never as possible peers.

16   Maintaining such divisions is integral to good service because this display of class distinctions ultimately underlies our

notions of service quality. Good service means not only serving well, but also allowing customers to feel justified in issuing orders, to feel okay about being served—which, in turn, requires demonstrations of class difference and the smiles that suggest servers' comfort with having a subordinate role in the service exchange.

17   Unlike the penguin-suited household servant staffs whose class status was clearly defined, service industry workers today often have much more in common from a class perspective with those that they serve. This not only creates an imperative for them to wear their class otherness on their sleeves, as it were, but also to accept their subordinate role to those they serve by being unshakably tractable and polite.

18   Faith Popcorn has rather famously referred to the four-dollar latte as a "small indulgence," noting that while this is a lot to pay for a glass of hot milk, it is quite inexpensive for the feeling of luxury that can accompany it. In this service climate, the class status of the server and the served—anyone who can justify spending this much on a coffee—is blurry, indeed. Coffee shops that market themselves on employee satisfaction assert the same happy servant that allows politically conscientious consumers, who are in many cases the workers' own age and class peers, to feel justified in receiving good service. Good service—as both an apparent affirmation of subordinate classes' desire to serve and as an enforced one-sided politeness—reproduces the class distinctions that have historically characterized servant-served relationships so that these are perpetuated within the contemporary service market.

Raine begins to shift attention to the customers' role in coffee shop culture.

19   The specialty coffee companies are large corporations, and for the twenty-somethings who stock their counters, barista work is too temporary to bother fighting the system. Mostly, people simply quit. Dissatisfied workers are stuck with engaging in tactics that will change nothing but allow them to make the best of their lot. These include minor infractions such as taking liberties with the uniforms or grabbing little bits of company time for their own pleasure, what Michel de Certeau calls *la perruque* and the companies themselves call "time theft." As my time in the chain gang wore on, I developed my own tactic, the only one I found that jostled the customers out of their complacency and allowed me to be a barista and a person.

20   There is no easy way to serve without being a servant, and I have always found that the best way to do so is to show my actual emotions rather than affecting a smooth display of interminable patience and good will. For café customers, bettering baristas' lots can be as simple as asking about their day,

addressing them by name—any little gesture to show that you noticed the person behind the service that they can provide. My tactic as a worker is equally simple, but it is simultaneously an assertion of individual identity at work, a refusal of the class distinctions that characterize the service environment and a rebuttal to the companies that would promote my satisfaction with their system: be rude. Not arbitrarily rude, of course—customers are people, too, and nobody gains anything by spreading bad will. But on those occasions when customer or management behavior warranted a zinging comeback, I would give it.

Were you expecting this "solution" to the situation Raine presents?

21   Rudeness, when it is demanded, undermines companies' claims on workers' personal warmth and allows them to retain their individuality by expressing genuine rather than affected feelings in at-work interpersonal exchanges. It is a refusal of the class distinctions that underlie consumers' unilateral prerogative of rudeness and servers' unilateral imperative to be nice. It runs contrary to everything that we have been taught, not only about service but about interrelating with others. But this seems to be the only method of asserting one's person-hood in the service environment, where workers' personalities are all too easily reduced to a space-time, conflated with the drinks they serve. Baristas of the world, if you want to avoid becoming a green-aproned coffee dispensary, you're just going to have to tell people off about it.

Raine reveals her specific audience, "baristias of the world," only at the end of her argument.

Sample Student Causal Argument

Armadi Tansal
Professor Stewart
English 115
29 October 2010

Modern Warfare: Video Games' Link to Real-World Violence

"John" is a nineteen-year-old college student who gets decent grades. He comes from a typical upper-middle-class family and plans to get his MBA after he graduates. John is also my friend, which is why I'm not using his real name.

John has been playing moderately violent video games since he was nine years old. I started playing video and console games around that age too, and I played a lot in junior high, but John plays more than anyone I know. John says that over the past year he has played video games at least four hours every day, and "sometimes all day and night on the weekends." I have personally witnessed John play *Call of Duty: Modern Warfare 2* for six hours straight, with breaks only to use the bathroom or eat something.

I've never seen John act violently, and he's never been in trouble with the law. But new research on violent video games suggests that John's gaming habit puts him at risk for violent or aggressive behavior. Dr. Craig Anderson, a psychologist at the University of Iowa, says "the active role required by video games . . . may make violent video games even more hazardous than violent television or cinema." When people like John play these games, they get used to being rewarded for violent behavior. For example, in the multiplayer version of *Modern Warfare 2*, if the player gets a five-kill streak, he can call in a Predator missile strike. If you kill 25 people in a row, you can call in a tactical nuclear strike. Missile strikes help you advance toward the mission goals more quickly, so the more people you kill, the faster you'll win.

Along with *Modern Warfare 2*, John plays games like *Left 4 Dead, Halo,* and *Grand Theft Auto*. All these games are rated M for Mature, which according to the Entertainment Software Rating Board means they "may contain intense violence, blood and gore, sexual content and/or strong

> Armadi Tansal establishes a personal relationship to his subject and audience.

Tansal 2

language." Some M-rated games, like *Grand Theft Auto,* feature random violence, where players can run amok in a city, beat up and kill people, and smash stuff for no reason. In others, like *Modern Warfare 2,* the violence takes place in the context of military action. To do well in all of these games, you have to commit acts of violence. But does acting violently in games make you more violent in real life?

Anderson says studies show that "violent video games are significantly associated with: increased aggressive behavior, thoughts, and affect [feelings]; increased physiological arousal; and decreased prosocial (helping) behavior." He also claims that "high levels of violent video game exposure have been linked to delinquency, fighting at school and during free play periods, and violent criminal behavior (e.g., self-reported assault, robbery)."

Being "associated with" and "linked to" violent behavior doesn't necessarily mean video games cause such behavior. Many people have argued that the links Anderson sees are coincidental, or that any effects video games might have on behavior are so slight that we shouldn't worry about them. Christopher Ferguson and John Kilburn, professors of Criminal Justice at Texas A&M International University, feel that the existing research does not support Anderson's claims. In a report published in the *Journal of Pediatrics,* they point out that in past studies, "the closer aggression measures got to actual violent behavior, the weaker the effects seen" (762).

From what I can tell, John doesn't have any more violent thoughts and feelings than most men his age. When I asked him if he thought the games had made him more violent or aggressive in real life, he said, "I'm actually less violent now. When we were kids we used to play 'war' with fake guns and sticks, chasing each other around the neighborhood and fighting commando-style. We didn't really fight but sometimes kids got banged up. No one ever gets hurt playing a video game."

Anderson admits that "a healthy, normal, nonviolent child or adolescent who has no other risk factors for high aggression or violence is not going to become a school shooter simply because they play five hours or 10 hours a week of these violent video games" (qtd. in St. George). But just because violent video games don't turn all players into

---

Tansal identifies the causal question at the heart of his argument.

Direct quotations from published sources build credibility.

Tansal is careful not to accept the easy answer that video games cause everyone to be more violent.

Tansal 3

mass murderers, that doesn't mean they have no effect on a player's behavior and personality. For example, my friend John doesn't get into fights or rob people, but he doesn't display a lot of prosocial "helping" behaviors either. He spends most of his free time gaming, so he doesn't get out of his apartment much. Also, the friends he does have mostly play video games with him.

Even though the games restrict his interactions with other humans and condition him to behave violently onscreen, John is probably not at high risk of becoming violent in real life. But according to researchers, this low risk of becoming violent is because none of the dozens of other risk factors associated with violent behavior are present in his life (Anderson et al. 160). If John was a high school dropout, came from a broken home, or abused alcohol and other drugs, his game playing might be more likely to contribute to violent behavior.

Anderson contends that violent video games are a "causal risk factor" for violence and aggression—not that they cause violent aggression. In other words, the games are a small piece of a much larger problem. People like my friend John are not likely to become violent because of the video games they play. But Anderson's research indicates that some people do. Although there is no simple way to tell who those people are, we should include video games as a possible risk factor when we think about who is likely to become violent.

Even if the risk contributed by violent video games is slight for each individual, the total impact of the games on violence in society could be huge. *Call of Duty: Modern Warfare 2* is the third-best-selling video game in the United States (Orry). Its creator, Activision Blizzard, had $1.3 billion dollars in sales in the just first three months of 2010 (Pham). Millions of people play this game, and games like it, and they aren't all as well-adjusted as John. If video games contribute to violent tendencies in only a small fraction of players, they could still have a terrible impact.

Tansal 4

Works Cited

Anderson, Craig. "Violent Video Games: Myths, Facts, and Unanswered Questions." *Psychological Science Agenda* 16.5 (2003): n. pag. Web. 6 Oct. 2010.

Anderson, Craig, et al. "Violent Video Game Effects on Aggression, Empathy, and Prosocial Behavior in Eastern and Western Countries." *Psychological Bulletin* 136 (2010): 151–73. Print.

Entertainment Software Rating Board. *Game Ratings and Descriptor Guide*. Entertainment Software Association, n. d. Web. 7 Oct. 2010.

Ferguson, Christopher J. and John Kilburn. "The Public Health Risks of Media Violence: A Meta-Analytic Review." *Journal of Pediatrics* 154.5 (2009): 759–63. Print.

John (pseudonym). Personal interview. 4 Oct. 2010.

Orry, James. "*Modern Warfare 2* the 3rd Best-Selling Game in the US." *Videogamer.com*. Pro-G Media Ltd., 12 Mar. 2010. Web. 6 Oct. 2010.

Pham, Alex. "Call of Duty: Modern Warfare 2 Propels Revenue, Profit for Activision Blizzard." *Los Angeles Times*. Los Angeles Times, 6 May 2010. Web. 7 Oct. 2010.

St. George, Donna. "Study Links Violent Video Games, Hostility." *Washington Post*. Washington Post, 3 Nov. 2008. Web. 5 Oct. 2010.

PEARSON
mycomplab

For support in learning this chapter's content, follow this path in MyCompLab:
> Resources > Writing > Writing Purposes > Writing to Analyze.
Review the Instruction and Multimedia resources, then complete the Exercises and click on Gradebook to measure your progress.

10 | Evaluation Arguments

QUICK TAKE

In this chapter, you will learn that

1. Evaluation arguments set out criteria and then judge something to be good or bad according to those criteria (see page 135)
2. Evaluation arguments are based on practical, aesthetic, and ethical criteria (see page 137)
3. Evaluation arguments often use comparisons (see page 138)

By some estimates, as many as five million animals are killed in shelters each year. Are "no-kill" shelters a good idea? Advocates of no-kill shelters argue that alternatives to euthanizing animals can be created by working to increase adoption demand for shelter animals. No-kill shelters also work to promote spaying and neutering to decrease the number of animals sent to shelters in the first place. Others argue that the term "no-kill" is divisive because it implies that some shelters are "kill" shelters and suggests that many shelter workers are cruel or uncaring. Are no-kill shelters an effective solution? What kind of evaluations would support or oppose the concept of the "no-kill" shelter? How can evaluation arguments be used to support more humane treatment of shelter animals?

Ｐeople make evaluations all the time. Newspapers, magazines, and television have picked up on this love of evaluation by running "best of" polls. They ask their readers to vote on the best Chinese restaurant, the best pizza, the best local band, the best coffeehouse, the best dance club, the best neighborhood park, the best swimming hole, the best bike ride (scenic or challenging), the best volleyball court, the best place to get married, and so on. If you ask one of your friends who voted in a "best" poll why she picked a particular restaurant as the best of its kind, she might respond by saying simply, "I like it." But if you ask her why she likes it, she might start offering good reasons such as these: the food is good, the service prompt, the prices fair, and the atmosphere comfortable. It's really not a mystery why these polls are often quite predictable or why the same restaurants tend to win year after year. Many people think that evaluations are matters of personal taste, but when we begin probing the reasons, we often discover that different people use similar criteria to make evaluations.

The key to convincing other people that your judgment is sound is establishing the criteria you will use to make your evaluation. Sometimes it will be necessary to argue for the validity of the criteria that you think your readers should consider. If your readers accept your criteria, it's likely they will agree with your conclusions.

Understand How Evaluation Arguments Work

Evaluation arguments set out criteria and then judge something to be good or bad (or better, or best) according to those criteria.

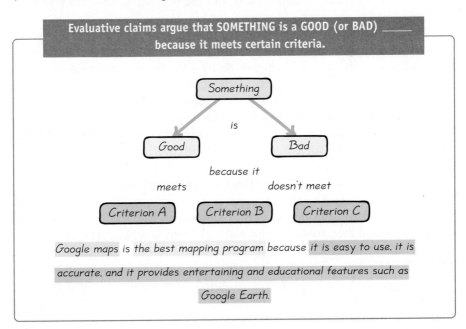

Evaluative claims argue that SOMETHING is a GOOD (or BAD) _____ because it meets certain criteria.

Something

is

Good   Bad

because it

meets   doesn't meet

Criterion A   Criterion B   Criterion C

Google maps is the best mapping program because it is easy to use, it is accurate, and it provides entertaining and educational features such as Google Earth.

Recognize Kinds of Evaluations

Arguments of evaluation are structured much like arguments of definition. Recall that the criteria in arguments of definition are set out in because clauses:

People often disagree about the relevance and appropriateness of criteria in an evaluation. Take as an example the question of which colleges are good schools. Until twenty years ago, most of the information that people used to evaluate a college came from the college itself. You could find out the price of tuition and what courses were offered, but other information was difficult to find, and it was hard to compare one college with another.

In 1983 the magazine *U.S. News & World Report* began ranking U.S. colleges and universities from a consumer's perspective. These rankings have remained controversial ever since. *U.S. News* evaluates schools using a complex set of criteria. Twenty-five percent of a school's ranking is based on a survey of reputation in which officials at each college rate the quality of schools in the same category as their own school. The remaining 75 percent is based on six kinds of statistical data. These measure retention of students, faculty resources, student selectivity, financial resources, alumni giving, and, for some schools, graduation rates (the difference between the number of students expected to graduate and the number who actually do).

U.S. News chooses specific types of information to look at in each category. For example, "faculty resources" are measured by the size of classes, average faculty pay, the percentage of professors with the highest degree in their field, the overall student-faculty ratio, and the percentage of faculty who are full-time.

Many college officials have criticized the criteria *U.S. News* uses to evaluate colleges. In an August 1998 *U.S. News* article, Gerhard Casper, the president of Stanford University (which is consistently near the top of the rankings), writes, "Much about these rankings—particularly their specious formulas and spurious precision—is utterly misleading." Casper argues that using graduation rates as a criterion rewards schools that pass low-achieving students. Other college presidents have argued that the magazine should use different criteria or weight the criteria differently, and some have called (without much success) for a boycott of the *U.S. News* rankings.

U.S. News replies in its defense that colleges and universities themselves do a lot of ranking, using data and methods that can be questioned. Schools rank students for admission, using SAT or ACT scores, high school GPA, class rank, and other factors, and then grade students and rank them against each other once they are enrolled in college. Schools also evaluate their faculty and take great interest in the national ranking of their departments. They care very much about how they stand in relation to one another. Why, then, *U.S. News* argues, shouldn't people be able to evaluate colleges and universities, since colleges and universities are in the business of evaluating people?

The magazine and the colleges have very different ideas about what constitute fair and relevant criteria for evaluating a college. But the *U.S. News* college rankings generate a tremendous amount of income for the magazine, suggesting that students and their parents agree with the criteria, and use them to help make their own decisions about college.

Some evaluation arguments rely more heavily on certain types of criteria than others. For example, a movie review (_____ is a good movie) is likely to focus most closely on aesthetic considerations: Engaging characters, an exciting story, beautiful cinematography. Ethical considerations may be relevant—say, if the film is exceptionally violent, or celebrates antisocial behavior—but usually don't predominate in a movie review. Practical considerations will probably be least important, since anyone reading a movie review is presumably willing to spend the price of admission to see a film.

Build an Evaluation Argument

Although evaluation arguments seem very similar to definition arguments, there is a key difference. Definition arguments seek to place something in the correct category by observing its qualities. They hinge on our judgments about similarity and difference. Evaluation arguments focus instead on what we value. Because of this, the criteria you choose when making an evaluation argument are very important. If your criteria do not appeal to the values of your audience, your readers will not feel that your evaluation is accurate.

Suppose that a city task force on downtown revitalization has a plan to demolish the oldest commercial building in your city. Your neighborhood association wants to preserve the building, perhaps by turning it into a museum. To persuade officials to do this, you must show that your plan for preservation is a good one, while the taskforce's plan for demolition is a bad one. You might argue that a museum would attract visitors to the downtown area, bringing in revenue. You might argue that the elaborately carved stone facade of the building is a rare example of a disappearing craft. Or you might argue that it is only fair to preserve the oldest commercial building in town, since the city's oldest house and other historic buildings have been saved.

Each of these arguments uses different criteria. The argument that a museum will bring in money is based on practical considerations. The argument about the rare and beautiful stonework on the building is based on aesthetic (artistic) considerations. The argument that an old commercial building deserves the same treatment as other old buildings is based on fairness, or ethical concerns. Depending on your audience, you might use all three kinds of criteria, or you might focus more on one or two kinds. If your city is in the middle of a budget crisis, it might be wise to stress the practical, economic benefits of a museum. If several City Council members are architects or amateur historians, your argument

Windmills produce energy without pollution and reduce dependence on foreign oil. Do you agree or disagree with people who do not want windmills built near them because they find them ugly?

might focus on the aesthetic criteria. You have to make assumptions about what your audience will value most as they consider your evaluation.

Evaluative arguments can look at just one case in isolation, but often they make comparisons. You could construct an argument about the fate of the old building that only describes your plan and its benefits. Or, you might also directly address the demolition proposal, showing how it lacks those benefits. Then your argument might be structured like this:

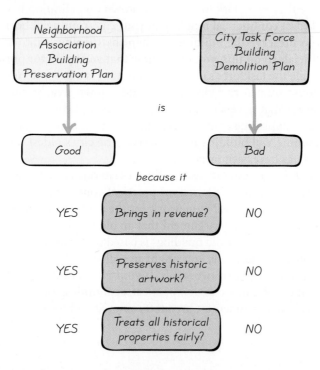

Finding Good Reasons

What's the best alternative fuel?

Biodiesel is an alternative fuel source that is made from vegetable oil (or animal fats) and alcohol. While biodiesel can be used alone, it is often mixed with petroleum diesel. Blends of up to 20 percent biodiesel can be used in a standard diesel engine without modifications—meaning that many cars on the road today would be capable of using biodiesel if it were to become widely available.

But is biodiesel a realistic solution to the world's dependence on fossil fuels? Many think yes. Proponents point to the reduction in greenhouse gas emissions and the lower dependence on foreign oil that would accompany wide-scale biodiesel adoption. Detractors point to millions of acres of land, which would typically be used for food production, that would be converted to fuel production, inevitably causing shortages and an overall rise in food prices.

Write about it

1. One way to assess a complicated issue like alternative fuel technologies is to evaluate each technology against a set of common criteria. Which of the following criteria are useful for evaluating fuel-efficient cars? Why are they useful?
   - cost of development and production
   - sticker price of cars using the technology
   - how long it takes for cars to reach the market
   - efficiency and reliability of cars using the technology
   - environmental impact
   - convenience of refueling and maintenance
   - driver's aesthetic experience

2. Are any of the above criteria more important than the others? If so, how would you rank them? Why? Are there any criteria you would add?

Steps to Writing an Evaluation Argument

Step 1 Make a Claim

Make an evaluative claim based on criteria.

Template

> SOMETHING is good (bad, the best, the worst) if measured by certain criteria (practicality, aesthetics, ethics).

Examples

- A book or movie review.
- An evaluation of a controversial aspect of sports (e.g., the current system of determining who is champion in Division I college football by a system of bowls and polls) or a sports event (e.g., this year's WNBA playoffs) or a team.
- An evaluation of the effectiveness of a social policy or law such as legislating 21 as the legal drinking age, current gun control laws, or environmental regulation.

Step 2 Think About What's at Stake

- Does nearly everyone agree with you? Then your claim probably isn't interesting or important. If you can think of people who disagree, then something is at stake.
- Who argues the opposite of your claim?
- Why do they make a different evaluation?

Step 3 List the Criteria

- Which criteria make something either good or bad?
- Which criteria are the most important?
- Which criteria are fairly obvious, and which will you have to argue for?

Step 4 Analyze Your Potential Readers

- Who are your readers?
- How familiar will they be with what you are evaluating?
- Which criteria are they most likely to accept with little explanation, and which will they disagree with?

Step 5 Write a Draft

Introduction

- Introduce the person, group, institution, event, or object that you are going to evaluate. You might want to announce your stance at this point or wait until the concluding section.
- Give the background that your intended readers will need.

Body

- Describe each criterion and then analyze how well what you are evaluating meets that criterion.
- If you are making an evaluation according to the effects someone or something produces, describe each effect in detail.
- Anticipate where readers might question either your criteria or how they apply to your subject.
- Address opposing viewpoints by acknowledging how their evaluations might differ and by showing why your evaluation is better.

Conclusion

- If you have not yet announced your stance, conclude that, on the basis of the criteria you set out or the effects you have analyzed, something is good (bad, the best, the worst).
- If you have made your stance clear from the beginning, end with a compelling example or analogy.

Step 6 Revise, Edit, Proofread

- For detailed instructions, see Chapter 4.
- For a checklist to use to evaluate your draft, see pages 48–49.

P. J. O'Rourke

The End of the Affair

P. J. O'Rourke is a humorist and satirist who follows in the tradition of the New Journalism where there is no pretense of objectivity and the biases of the writer are in the foreground. Even those who don't agree with his libertarian conservative political views still find him funny, like Bill Maher, who invites O'Rourke on his HBO show. O'Rourke was editor-in-chief of the satirical *National Lampoon* magazine and worked at *Rolling Stone* from 1986 to 2001. The titles of his book suggest his sense of humor: *Modern Manners: An Etiquette Book for Rude People* (1983), *The Bachelor's Home Companion: A Practical Guide to Keeping House like a Pig* (1987), *Holidays in Hell* (1988), *Parliament of Whores: A Lone Humorist Attempts to Explain the Entire U.S. Government* (1991), *Give War a Chance: Eyewitness Accounts of Mankind's Struggle against Tyranny, Injustice, and Alcohol-free Beer* (1992), and *Peace Kills: America's Fun New Imperialism* (2004). O'Rourke's humor is infused with outrage over the influence of government in ordinary life, which you will find in this evaluation argument.

O'Rourke begins by announcing that he is from an older generation. What does he gain and lose from this strategy?

2   The phrase "bankrupt General Motors," which we expect to hear uttered on Monday, leaves Americans my age in economic shock. The words are as melodramatic as "Mom's nude photos." And, indeed, if we want to understand what doomed the American automobile, we should give up on economics and turn to melodrama.

Politicians, journalists, financial analysts and other purveyors of banality have been looking at cars as if a convertible were a business. Fire the MBAs and hire a poet. The fate of Detroit isn't a matter of financial crisis, foreign competition, corporate greed, union intransigence, energy costs or measuring the shoe size of the footprints in the carbon. It's a tragic romance—unleashed passions, titanic clashes, lost love and wild horses. Foremost are the horses. Cars can't be comprehended without them. A hundred and some years ago Rudyard Kipling wrote "The Ballad of the King's Jest," in which an Afghan tribesman avers: Four things greater than all things are—Women and Horses and Power and War.

Note how his favored criteria—romance, passion, horses—have to do with aesthetics, not practical issues like safety or environmental impact.

3   Insert another "power" after the horse and the verse was as true in the suburbs of my 1950s boyhood as it was in the Khyber Pass.

4   Horsepower is not a quaint leftover of linguistics or a vague metaphoric anachronism. James Watt, father of the steam engine

and progenitor of the industrial revolution, lacked a measurement for the movement of weight over distance in time—what we call energy. (What we call energy wasn't even an intellectual concept in the late 18th century—in case you think the recent collapse of global capitalism was history's most transformative moment.) Mr. Watt did research using draft animals and found that, under optimal conditions, a dray horse could lift 33,000 pounds one foot off the ground in one minute. Mr. Watt—the eponymous watt not yet existing—called this unit of energy "1 horse-power."

Note how this paragraph establishes O'Rourke's expertise, his credibility.

O'Rourke's favored criteria—status and being cool—have nothing to do with practicality and everything to do with aesthetics.

5   In 1970 a Pontiac GTO (may the brand name rest in peace) had horsepower to the number of 370. In the time of one minute, for the space of one foot, it could move 12,210,000 pounds. And it could move those pounds down every foot of every mile of all the roads to the ends of the earth for every minute of every hour until the driver nodded off at the wheel. Forty years ago the pimply kid down the block, using $3,500 in saved-up soda-jerking money, procured might and main beyond the wildest dreams of Genghis Khan, whose hordes went forth to pillage mounted upon less oomph than is in a modern leaf blower.

6   Horses and horsepower alike are about status and being cool. A knight in ancient Rome was bluntly called "guy on

horseback," Equesitis. Chevalier means the same, as does Cavalier. Lose the capitalization and the dictionary says, "insouciant and debonair; marked by a lofty disregard of others' interests, rights, or feelings; high-handed and arrogant and supercilious." How cool is that? Then there are cowboys—always cool—and the U.S. cavalry that coolly comes to their rescue plus the proverbially cool-handed "Man on Horseback" to whom we turn in troubled times.

O'Rourke uses predominantly male references. Do you think he was writing only for men?

7   Early witnesses to the automobile urged motorists to get a horse. But that, in effect, was what the automobile would do—get a horse for everybody. Once the Model T was introduced in 1908 we all became Sir Lancelot, gained a seat at the Round Table and were privileged to joust for the favors of fair maidens (at drive-in movies). The pride and prestige of a noble mount was vouchsafed to the common man. And woman, too. No one ever tried to persuade ladies to drive sidesaddle with both legs hanging out the car door.

More "status" and "being cool."

"Schlub" is Yiddish slang for an unattractive person. Why does O'Rourke use this term?

8   For the purpose of ennobling us schlubs, the car is better than the horse in every way. Even more advantageous than cost, convenience and not getting kicked and smelly is how much easier it is to drive than to ride. I speak with feeling on this subject, having taken up riding when I was nearly 60 and having begun to drive when I was so small that my cousin Tommy had to lie on the transmission hump and operate the accelerator and the brake with his hands.

9   After the grown-ups had gone to bed, Tommy and I shifted the Buick into neutral, pushed it down the driveway and out of earshot, started the engine and toured the neighborhood. The sheer difficulty of horsemanship can be illustrated by what happened to Tommy and me next. Nothing. We maneuvered the car home, turned it off and rolled it back up the driveway. (We were raised in the blessedly flat Midwest.) During our foray the Buick's speedometer reached 30. But 30 miles per hour is a full gallop on a horse. Delete what you've seen of horse riding in movies. Possibly a kid who'd never been on a horse could ride at a gallop without killing himself. Possibly one of the Jonas Brothers could land an F-14 on a carrier deck.

Cars in the 1950s and 1960s represented the triumph of aesthetics over practical issues like gas mileage and safety.

10   Thus cars usurped the place of horses in our hearts. Once we'd caught a glimpse of a well-turned Goodyear, checked out the curves of the bodywork and gaped at that swell pair of headlights, well, the old gray mare was not what she used to be. We embarked upon life in the fast lane with our new paramour. It was a great love story of man and machine. The road to the future was paved with bliss.

11   Then we got married and moved to the suburbs. Being away from central cities meant Americans had to spend more of their

time driving. Over the years away got farther away. Eventually this meant that Americans had to spend all of their time driving. The play date was 40 miles from the Chuck E. Cheese. The swim meet was 40 miles from the cello lesson. The Montessori was 40 miles from the math coach. Mom's job was 40 miles from Dad's job and the three-car garage was 40 miles from both.

O'Rourke describes how practicality gained the upper hand over aesthetics.

12   The car ceased to be object of desire and equipment for adventure and turned into office, rec room, communications hub, breakfast nook and recycling bin—a motorized cup holder. Americans, the richest people on Earth, were stuck in the confines of their crossover SUVs, squeezed into less space than tech-support call-center employees in a Mumbai cubicle farm. Never mind the six-bedroom, eight-bath, pseudo-Tudor with cathedral-ceilinged great room and 1,000-bottle controlled-climate wine cellar. That was a day's walk away.

O'Rourke mocks how practicality rules—that the romance of cars is reduced to cup holders.

13   We became sick and tired of our cars and even angry at them. Pointy-headed busybodies of the environmentalist, new urbanist, utopian communitarian ilk blamed the victim. They claimed the car had forced us to live in widely scattered settlements in the great wasteland of big-box stores and the Olive Garden. If we would all just get on our Schwinns or hop a trolley, they said, America could become an archipelago of cozy gulags on the Portland, Oregon, model with everyone nestled together in the most sustainably carbon-neutral, diverse and ecologically unimpactful way.

14   But cars didn't shape our existence; cars let us escape with our lives. We're way the heck out here in Valley Bottom Heights and Trout Antler Estates because we were at war with the cities. We fought rotten public schools, idiot municipal bureaucracies, corrupt political machines, rampant criminality and the pointy-headed busybodies. Cars gave us our dragoons and hussars, lent us speed and mobility, let us scout the terrain and probe the enemy's lines. And thanks to our cars, when we lost the cities we weren't forced to surrender, we were able to retreat.

Note how O'Rourke characterizes the unfortunate practicalities of modern life.

15   But our poor cars paid the price. They were flashing swords beaten into dull plowshares. Cars became appliances. Or worse. Nobody's ticked off at the dryer or the dishwasher, much less the fridge. We recognize these as labor-saving devices. The car, on the other hand, seems to create labor. We hold the car responsible for all the dreary errands to which it needs to be steered. Hell, a golf cart's more fun. You can ride around in a golf cart with a six-pack, safe from breathalyzers, chasing Canada geese on the fairways and taking swings at gophers with a mashie.

O'Rourke reverses the usual positive meaning of the metaphor of turning swords into plowshares.

Now the new cars are tied explicitly to "busybodies"—the practical-minded regulators that O'Rourke despises.

16   We've lost our love for cars and forgotten our debt to them and meanwhile the pointy-headed busybodies have been exacting their revenge. We escaped the poke of their noses once, when we lived downtown, but we won't be able to peel out so fast the next time. In the name of safety, emissions control and fuel economy, the simple mechanical elegance of the automobile has been rendered ponderous, cumbersome and incomprehensible. One might as well pry the back off an iPod as pop the hood on a contemporary motor vehicle. An aging shade-tree mechanic like myself stares aghast and sits back down in the shade. Or would if the car weren't squawking at me like a rehearsal for divorce. You left the key in. You left the door open. You left the lights on. You left your dirty socks in the middle of the bedroom floor.

17   I don't believe the pointy-heads give a damn about climate change or gas mileage, much less about whether I survive a head-on with one of their tax-sucking mass-transit projects. All they want to is to make me hate my car. How proud and handsome would Bucephalas look, or Traveler or Rachel Alexandra,

It's romantic aesthetics vs. ugly practicality.

with seat and shoulder belts, air bags, 5-mph bumpers and a maze of pollution-control equipment under the tail?

18   And there's the end of the American automobile industry. When it comes to dull, practical, ugly things that bore and annoy me, Japanese things cost less and the cup holders are more conveniently located.

19   The American automobile is—that is, was—never a product of Japanese-style industrialism. America's steel, coal, beer, beaver pelts and PCs may have come from our business plutocracy, but American cars have been manufactured mostly by romantic fools. David Buick, Ransom E. Olds, Louis Chevrolet, Robert and Louis Hupp of the Hupmobile, the Dodge brothers, the Studebaker brothers, the Packard brothers, the Duesenberg brothers, Charles W. Nash, E. L. Cord, John North Willys, Preston Tucker and William H. Murphy, whose Cadillac cars were designed by the young Henry Ford, all went broke making cars. The man who founded General Motors in 1908, William Crapo (really) Durant, went broke twice. Henry Ford, of course, did not go broke, nor was he a romantic, but judging by his opinions he certainly was a fool.

20   America's romantic foolishness with cars is finished,
however, or nearly so. In the far boondocks a few good old boys
haven't got the memo and still tear up the back roads. Doubtless
the Obama administration's Department of Transportation is even
now calculating a way to tap federal stimulus funds for mandatory
OnStar installations to locate and subdue these reprobates.

Is O'Rourke himself one of those good old boys?

21   Among certain youths—often first-generation Americans—
there remains a vestigial fondness for Chevelle low-riders or
Honda "tuners." The pointy-headed busybodies have yet to enfold
these youngsters in the iron-clad conformity of cultural diversity's
embrace. Soon the kids will be expressing their creative energy in
a more constructive way, planting bok choy in community gardens
and decorating homeless shelters with murals of Che.

22   I myself have something old-school under a tarp in the
basement garage. I bet when my will has been probated, some
child of mine will yank the dust cover and use the proceeds of the
eBay sale to buy a mountain bike. Four things greater than all
things are, and I'm pretty sure one of them isn't bicycles. There
are those of us who have had the good fortune to meet with
strength and beauty, with majestic force in which we were willing
to trust our lives. Then a day comes, that strength and beauty
fails, and a man does what a man has to do. I'm going downstairs
to put a bullet in a V-8.

Sample Student Evaluation Argument

Rashaun Giddens

Professor Chen

English 1302

21 April 2009

Stop Loss or "Loss of Trust"

Looking back on my high school career, my social and extracurricular lives were filled with countless highs: hanging out with my friends, prom, and varsity track to name a few. My academic career, however, was a bit shakier. So busy with what I saw then as the important things in life, I often procrastinated or altogether avoided my schoolwork. My senior year, the recruiter from the U.S. Army Reserves spoke at a school assembly. He asked that we as seniors consider the prospect of becoming "weekend warriors." In the wake of September 11, we could help protect our country and simultaneously work toward paying for a college education, which seemed like a great idea to many students. For those who could not otherwise afford college, the prospect of receiving a higher education in return for patriotism and some good hard work sounded fair enough. My life, however, took a different turn. When I received my track scholarship, I decided to head off to college right away. Many of my friends, however, heeded the call to service. So far, their realities have been far from the lives that were pitched to them; rather, this was the beginning of a path to broken dreams and broken promises.

My cousin, moved to action by a charismatic recruiter, an Army announcement of fifteen-month active tours, and the prospect of a paid college education, chose to join the United States Army Reserves. The Army, suffering from a recruitment shortfall, had recently announced a policy that would allow recruits to serve in active duty for a mere fifteen months. For serving for just over a year, my cousin could do his national duty and put himself on a path to self-improvement. The recruiter did not, however, highlight the fine print to this new program. No one told my cousin that he could be called back to active duty for up to eight years under the government's "stop loss" policy. Further, no one told him that just one day after the Army announced the incentive program, an

[Margin note:] Note how the introduction creates a connection with the audience; while anyone can be persuaded by this essay, Giddens is especially addressing people around his own age.

[Margin note:] Here the Giddens names the specific issue, "stop loss," and indicates some of what is at stake.

Giddens 2

appeals court ruled that the Army could, under stop loss, compel soldiers to remain beyond the initial eight-year obligation (Wickham).

The stop loss policy forces thousands of soldiers to serve beyond their volunteer enlistment contracts. The all-volunteer Army—on which the government prides itself—is slowly developing into a disgruntled mass of men and women being held against their will. These men and women wanted to serve their countries and their families, and they signed what they believed were binding agreements with a trustworthy employer—the United States government—only to find that their government didn't bargain in good faith.

> "Against their will" raises an ethical issue.

> Giddens announces the point he will defend and that his argument will be based in part on ethical considerations.

As far back as the Civil War, the government needed incentives to retain its troops. (Although we all want freedom, few actually want to put our own lives on the line in the pursuit of that goal.) Both the Union and the Confederacy needed to make tough decisions to maintain strong armed forces when soldiers' contracts were expiring. The Union chose to offer financial incentives to keep its young men in uniform, while the Confederacy instituted a series of (not so) "voluntary" reenlistment policies (Robertson). During World War II all soldiers were forced to remain active until they reached a designated number of points. Vietnam saw the last stage of a mandatory draft, with soldiers serving one-year tours (Hockstader). Today's military relies on stop loss, making soldiers stay in the military after their commitment ends. Congress first gave the military the authority to retain soldiers after the Vietnam War when new volunteers were too few to replace departing soldiers. In November 2002, the Pentagon gave stop loss orders for Reserve and National Guard units activated to fight terrorism (Robertson).

> The research in this paragraph builds Giddens's credibility. He has done his homework.

> The definition of "stop loss" is embedded in the larger argument.

This policy is neither forthcoming, safe, nor compassionate toward those most directly impacted—the soldiers and their families. As the United States became more and more entrenched in the conflicts in Iraq and later in Afghanistan, the military was stretched thinner and thinner. By 2004, approximately 40% of those serving in Iraq and Afghanistan came from the ranks of the part-time soldiers: the Reserves and the National Guard (Gerard). While these individuals did know that their countries could call if they enlisted, they continue to bear an inordinate burden of actual combat time, and this new policy continues

> This specific thesis defines the three criteria that the essay will discuss, in order.

Giddens presents his first criterion in this paragraph: the "stop loss" policy is not forthcoming.

to create situations further removed from the job for which they enlisted. Recruiters often pitch the military—including the Reserves and the Guard—to young, impressionable, and often underprivileged kids. I have experienced this pitch firsthand and have seen the eyes of my classmates as the recruiter promised them a better and richer tomorrow. Seeing a golden opportunity for self-respect and achievement, young men and women sign on the dotted line. Today, other young men and women are buying a bill of goods. These recruits—and those who came before them—deserve to have an honest relationship with the government they protect. As policymakers tout the all-volunteer Army, those who serve find their rights threatened. The military claims to teach soldiers respect and honor. Is misleading your employees honest?

Giddens argues that if the policy is not forthcoming, it isn't fair.

Giddens introduces his second criterion—the "stop loss" policy isn't safe.

Aside from being less than forthright, stop loss may be putting our soldiers in harm's way. The policy forces these soldiers to suffer the strain of combat for extended periods of time. Because of the way the policy works, troops may learn of tour extensions mere hours before they had planned to return stateside to lower-stress positions and their loved ones. These troops need to be ready, alert, and equipped with a morale which allows them to fight effectively. Stop loss instead forces these soldiers—often those trained for short stints—to work beyond their experience and training. This policy may prove to overextend, both emotionally and physically, our fighting men and women. As they repeatedly suffer disappointment because of changes in their orders and delays of departure, morale is likely to drop. Based on reports from families, this practice has been devastating to their soldiers. Nancy Durst, wife of United States Reservist Staff Sergeant Scott Durst, told *Talk of the Nation*'s Neal Conan that the military detained her husband's unit just thirty minutes before it was to board the bus scheduled to deliver it to a stateside flight. The unit was later informed that tours had been extended for another four months (Durst). War breeds stress, but how can soldiers be expected to function at an optimal level when forced to suffer disappointments at the hands of their own government?

This second criterion, safety, is based on practicality— on the policy's negative consequences.

Finally, this policy simply runs contrary to the current administration's stated interest in the preservation of family and the bolstering of small

Giddens 4

businesses. First (and most obviously), this less-than-forthright policy keeps families separated. Husbands, wives, and children find themselves separated for longer periods of time, left with uncertainty and ambiguity for comfort. How does this aid in preserving the family? Second, when the government deploys reservists, soldiers often take a severe pay cut. Forced to leave their regular jobs, soldiers—and their families—must survive on an often much smaller government wage. Stop loss extends tours of duty and consequently the economic struggles of the families in question. Third, the policy has proven detrimental to the small-business owner. Men and women have used their military experience, discipline, and training to further themselves economically. The United States prides itself on the power of the small businessman; however, individuals such as Chief Warrant Officer Ronald Eagle have been hurt by this policy. After twenty years of service, Eagle was set to retire from the Army and focus on his aircraft-maintenance business. Instead, the Army has indefinitely moved his retirement date. As a consequence, Eagle has taken a $45,000 pay cut and wonders whether his business will survive his hiatus (Hockstader). Is this the way the government and military fight to preserve the family—emotionally and economically?

Because American men and women risk their lives in the name of bettering those of Iraqis and Afghans, the military should think about how their policy affects the lives of their soldiers and those back home. While the stop loss policy does allow the armed forces to build a larger active force without the public backlash (and political suicide) of instituting the draft, this policy comes at a cost. Those who have chosen to serve their country—whether for the training, educational possibilities, economic support, or expression of patriotism—are being bamboozled.

Watch the television commercials that, even now, tout training and part-time service. Read the stories of those serving and the families left behind. The sales pitch and the real picture do not match. The United States is undeniably one of the strongest nations in the world and a bastion of freedom. For these very reasons, the armed forces and the United States government, which represents all citizens, must find a way to lead this war (or conflict or crusade) honestly. If we have to pay soldiers double what they currently make in order to get them to reenlist, we should

> Giddens's third criterion maintains that the policy hurts families and small businesses.

> Giddens raises the practical consequences on individual soldiers.

> This third criterion is not just a matter of impracticality; it's also a matter of fairness.

> Giddens sums up what is at stake.

Giddens 5

Giddens ends by emphasizing the ethical issue because ethical consideration typically are the strongest ones to include in an evaluation argument.

do so. Even a draft would at least be aboveboard and honest. But we cannot continue to trick people into risking their lives for our national security. Our country must show the honor and respect deserved by those who fight, and stop loss undeniably dishonors and shows disrespect to our soldiers. The military must take a cue from its own advertising and "be all they can be." Be honest.

Giddens 6

Works Cited

Durst, Nancy. Interview with Neal Conan. *Talk of the Nation*. Natl. Public Radio. WNYC, New York. 19 Apr. 2004. Radio.

Gerard, Philip. "When the Cry Was 'Over the Hill in October.'" *Charleston Gazette* 16 May 2004: 1E. *LexisNexis Academic*. Web. 6 Apr. 2009.

Hockstader, Lee. "Army Stops Many Soldiers from Quitting; Orders Extend Enlistments to Curtail Troop Shortages." *WashingtonPost* 29 Dec. 2003: A01. *LexisNexis Academic*. Web. 8 Apr. 2009.

Robertson, John. "The Folly of Stop Loss." *Pittsburgh Post-Gazette* 19 Dec. 2004: J1. *LexisNexis Academic*. Web. 7 Apr. 2009.

Wickham, DeWayne. "A 15-Month Enlistment? Check Army's Fine Print." *USA Today* 17 May 2005: 13A. *LexisNexis Academic*. Web. 6 Apr. 2009.

PEARSON
mycomplab

For support in learning this chapter's content, follow this path in MyCompLab:
> Resources > Writing > Writing Purposes > Writing to Evaluate.
Review the Instruction and Multimedia resources, then complete the Exercises and click on Gradebook to measure your progress.

11 | Narrative Arguments

QUICK TAKE

In this chapter, you will learn that

1. Narrative arguments rely on concrete individual stories rather than large-scale statistics (see below)
2. Narrative arguments should allow readers to draw their own conclusions (see page 154)
3. Narrative arguments must strike readers as truthful and representative of larger issues (see page 156)

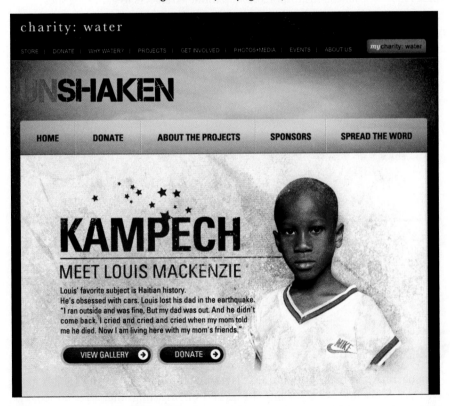

charity: water

STORE | DONATE | WHY WATER? | PROJECTS | GET INVOLVED | PHOTOS+MEDIA | EVENTS | ABOUT US   *my* charity: water

UNSHAKEN

HOME   DONATE   ABOUT THE PROJECTS   SPONSORS   SPREAD THE WORD

KAMPECH
MEET LOUIS MACKENZIE

Louis' favorite subject is Haitian history.
He's obsessed with cars. Louis lost his dad in the earthquake.
"I ran outside and was fine, But my dad was out. And he didn't come back. I cried and cried and cried when my mom told me he died. Now I am living here with my mom's friends."

VIEW GALLERY ●   DONATE ●

Charity: water understands the persuasive power of personal stories. Their online campaign features narratives like the story of Louis Mackenzie, a young boy who lost his father in the January 2010 earthquake in Haiti. "I cried and cried and cried when my mom told me he died," the text reads. As many organizations have learned, people often feel more compelled to donate money when they read personal stories like Louis's than when they are barraged with abstract numbers and statistics. Why are such stories effective as arguments? What makes some stories more compelling than others? © 2010 Charitywater.org. Used with permission.

Understand How Narrative Arguments Work

A single, detailed personal story sometimes makes a stronger case than large-scale statistical evidence. The Annenberg Public Policy Center reported that an estimated 1.6 million of 17 million U.S. college students gambled online in 2005, but it was the story of Greg Hogan that made the problem real for many Americans. Hogan, the son of a Baptist minister, was an extraordinarily talented musician, who played onstage twice at Carnegie Hall by age 13. He chose to attend Lehigh University in Pennsylvania, where he was a member of the orchestra and class president. At Lehigh he also acquired an addiction to online poker. He lost $7,500, much of which he borrowed from fraternity brothers. To pay them back, he robbed a bank, only to be arrested a few hours later. Eventually he received a long prison sentence. Hogan's story helped to influence Congress to pass the Unlawful Internet Gambling Enforcement Act, which requires financial institutions to stop money transfers to gambling sites.

Successful narrative arguments typically don't have a thesis statement but instead tell a compelling story. From the experience of one individual, readers infer a claim and the reasons that support the claim.

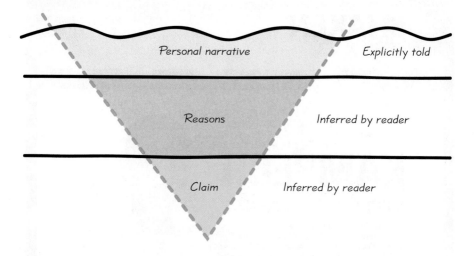

Recognize Kinds of Narrative Arguments

Using narrative to make an argument is part of human nature. As far back as we have records, we find people telling stories and singing songs that argue for change. During periods of history where explicit arguments are dangerous to make, stories allow people to safely criticize authority or imagine how life could be different. The history of folk music is a continuous recycling of old tunes, phrases, and narratives to engage new political situations. Anti-war ballads popular in Ireland in the 1840s were sung in the 1960s by Americans protesting their country's involvement in Vietnam. All the popular narrative genres—short stories, novels, movies, and theater—have been used as ways to make arguments for change.

Singer/songwriter Shawn Colvin is one of many contemporary folk, blues, rock, and rap artists who continue the tradition of making narrative arguments in their songs. Can you think of a song that makes a narrative argument?

Narrative arguments allow readers to fill in the good reasons, and come to their own conclusions. The personal connection readers can feel with the writer of a narrative argument makes this strategy a compelling means of persuasion. Moreover, because the writer usually refrains from making an outright claim, people reading narrative arguments are more likely to feel that they are "making up their own minds" rather than being reluctantly persuaded.

Narrative arguments can be representative anecdotes or they can be longer accounts of particular events that express larger ideas. One such story is George Orwell's account of a hanging in Burma (the country now known as Myanmar) while he was a British colonial administrator in the late 1920s. In "A Hanging," first published in 1931, Orwell narrates the story of an execution of a nameless prisoner who was convicted of a nameless crime. Everyone present quietly and dispassionately performs his job—the prison guards, the hangman, the superintendent, and even the prisoner, who offers no resistance when he is bound and led to the gallows. All is totally routine until a very small incident makes Orwell realize what is happening:

> It was about forty yards to the gallows. I watched the bare brown back of the
> prisoner marching in front of me. He walked clumsily with his bound arms,
> but quite steadily, with that bobbing gait of the Indian who never straightens
> his knees. At each step his muscles slid neatly into place, the lock of hair on

his scalp danced up and down, his feet printed themselves on the wet gravel. And once, in spite of the men who gripped him by each shoulder, he stepped slightly aside to avoid a puddle on the path.

It is curious, but till that moment I had never realized what it means to destroy a healthy, conscious man. When I saw the prisoner step aside to avoid the puddle, I saw the mystery, the unspeakable wrongness, of cutting a life short when it is in full tide. This man was not dying, he was alive just as we were alive. All the organs of his body were working—bowels digesting food, skin renewing itself, nails growing, tissues forming—all toiling away in solemn foolery. His nails would still be growing when he stood on the drop, when he was falling through the air with a tenth of a second to live. His eyes saw the yellow gravel and the grey walls, and his brain still remembered, foresaw, reasoned— reasoned even about puddles. He and we were a party of men walking together, seeing, hearing, feeling, understanding the same world; and in two minutes, with a sudden snap, one of us would be gone—one mind less, one world less.

Orwell's narrative leads to a dramatic moment of recognition, which gives this story its lasting power. His sudden realization of what execution means to both the prisoner and his executioners is a powerful argument to reconsider the morality of the death penalty.

Build a Narrative Argument

Because storytelling is such a familiar activity, it is easy for writers to get carried away with their narrative, and lose sight of the point they are trying to make. Readers find narrative compelling, but not if the narrative is long-winded, full of unnecessary detail, or has no obvious point. Furthermore, readers are quickly put off if they feel they are being given a lecture.

There are two keys to making effective narrative arguments: establishing that the narrative is truthful, and showing its relevance to a wider problem or question. Writing from personal experience can increase the impact of your argument, but that impact diminishes greatly if readers doubt you are telling the truth. And while the story you tell may be true, it is important that it also be representative— something that has happened to many other people, or something that could happen to your readers. Narrative arguments are useful for illustrating how people are affected by particular issues or events, but they are more effective if you have evidence that goes beyond a single incident.

One rule of thumb that you can keep in mind when building a narrative argument is to start out with as much detail and as many events as you can recall, then revise and edit heavily. It's hard to select the best details and events for your argument until you have written them all down, and often the process of writing and remembering will bring up new details that you had forgotten, or hadn't seen the relevance of before. Once you can see the big picture you have painted with your narrative, it is easier to see what your readers do not need, and remove it. This strategy brings your story, and your argument, into sharper focus.

Finding Good Reasons

Can a Story Make an Argument?

This photo shows two polar bears standing atop a small ice flow in the Arctic Ocean. The National Wildlife Foundation describes the plight of the polar bear, struggling to survive in the face of a changing climate.

As climate change melts sea ice, the U.S. Geological Survey projects that two-thirds of polar bears will disappear by 2050. This dramatic decline of polar bears is occurring in our lifetime, which is but a minuscule fraction of the time polar bears have roamed the vast Arctic seas. The retreat of ice has implications beyond the obvious habitat loss. The larger gap of open water between the ice and land also contributes to rougher wave conditions, making the bears' swim from shore to sea ice more hazardous. Exacerbating the problems of the loss of hunting areas, the shrinking polar ice cap will also cause a decline in polar bears' prey—seals. The polar bear is the proverbial "canary in the coal mine" of the serious threat global warming poses to wildlife species around the world, unless we take immediate and significant action to reduce global warming pollution.
The National Wildlife Foundation

Write about it

1. What argument might the National Wildlife Foundation be making about the state of climate change? What details reveal their argument?

2. Why might the National Wildlife Foundation have chosen the polar bear to personify the effects of climate change? What other types of animals would have made good choices? Poor choices?

3. How does the National Wildlife Foundation's account of climate change differ from other accounts that you have heard? What is the other side of this issue? Does this story change your thinking about climate change? Why or why not?

Steps to Writing a Narrative Argument

1
Identify an Experience That Makes an Implicit Argument

2
List All the Details You Can Remember

3
Examine the Significance of the Event

Step 1 Identify an Experience That Makes an Implicit Argument

Think about experiences that made you realize that something is wrong or that things need to be changed. The experience does not have to be one that leads to a moral lesson at the end, but it should be one that makes your readers think.

Examples

- Being accused of and perhaps even arrested and hauled to jail for something you didn't do or for standing up for something you believed in.
- Moving from a well-financed suburban school to a much poorer rural or urban school in the same state.
- Experiencing stereotyping or prejudice in any way—for the way you look, the way you act, your age, your gender, your race, or your sexual orientation.

Step 2 List All the Details You Can Remember

- When did it happen?
- How old were you?
- Why were you there?
- Who else was there?
- Where did it happen? If the place is important, describe what it looked like.

Step 3 Examine the Significance of the Event

- How did you feel about the experience when it happened?
- How did it affect you then?
- How do you feel about the experience now?
- What long-term effects has it had on your life?

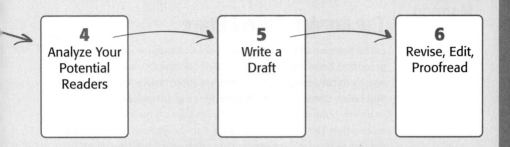

Step 4 Analyze Your Potential Readers

- Who are your readers?
- How much will your readers know about the background of the experience you are describing?
- Would anything similar ever likely have happened to them?
- How likely are they to agree with your feelings about the experience?

Step 5 Write a Draft

- You might need to give some background first, but if you have a compelling story, often it's best to launch right in.
- You might want to tell the story as it happened (chronological order), or you might want to begin with a striking incident and then go back to tell how it happened (flashback).
- You might want to reflect on your experience at the end, but you want your story to do most of the work. Avoid drawing a simple moral lesson. Your readers should share your feelings if you tell your story well.

Step 6 Revise, Edit, Proofread

- For detailed instructions, see Chapter 4.
- For a checklist to use to evaluate your draft, see pages 48–49.

Leslie
Marmon
Silko

The Border Patrol State

Leslie Marmon Silko (1948–) was born in Albuquerque and graduated from the University of New Mexico. She has received much critical acclaim for her writings about Native Americans. Her first novel, *Ceremony* (1977), describes the struggles of a veteran returning home after World War II to civilian life on a New Mexico reservation. Her incorporation of Indian storytelling techniques in *Ceremony* drew strong praise. One critic called her "the most accomplished Indian writer of her generation." She has since published two more novels, *Almanac of the Dead* (1991) and *Gardens in the Dunes* (1999); a collection of essays, *Yellow Woman* and a *Beauty of the Spirit: Essays on Native American Life Today* (1996); two volumes of poems and stories; and many shorter works. Silko's talents as a storyteller are evident in this essay, which first appeared in the magazine *The Nation* in 1994.

I used to travel the highways of New Mexico and Arizona with a wonderful sensation of absolute freedom as I cruised down the open road and across the vast desert plateaus. On the Laguna Pueblo reservation, where I was raised, the people were patriotic despite the way the U.S. government had treated Native Americans. As proud citizens, we grew up believing the freedom to travel was our inalienable right, a right that some Native Americans had been denied in the early twentieth century. Our cousin, old Bill Pratt, used to ride his horse 300 miles overland from Laguna, New Mexico, to Prescott, Arizona, every summer to work as a fire lookout.

Silko establishes freedom of travel 2 as a fundamental human, as well as American, right—an important assumption underlying her argument. 3

In school in the 1950s, we were taught that our right to travel from state to state without special papers or threat of detainment was a right that citizens under communist and totalitarian governments did not possess. That wide open highway told us we were U.S. citizens; we were free. . . .

Not so long ago, my companion Gus and I were driving south from Albuquerque, returning to Tucson after a book promotion for the paperback edition of my novel *Almanac of the Dead*. I had settled back and gone to sleep while Gus drove, but I was awakened when I felt the car slowing to a stop. It was nearly midnight on New Mexico State Road 26, a dark, lonely stretch of two-lane highway between Hatch and Deming. When I sat up, I saw the headlights and emergency flashers of six vehicles—Border Patrol cars and a van were blocking both lanes of the highway. Gus stopped the car and rolled down the window to ask what was wrong. But the closest Border Patrolman and his companion did not reply; instead, the first agent ordered us to "step out of the car." Gus asked why, but his question seemed to set them off. Two more Border Patrol agents immediately approached our car, and one of them snapped, "Are you looking for trouble?" as if he would relish it.

Specific details paint a vivid picture of the experience and establish credibility.

4   I will never forget that night beside the highway. There was an awful feeling of menace and violence straining to break loose. It was clear that the uniformed men would be only too happy to drag us out of the car if we did not speedily comply with their request (asking a question is tantamount to resistance, it seems). So we stepped out of the car and they motioned for us to stand on the shoulder of the road. The night was very dark, and no other traffic had come down the road since we had been stopped. All I could think about was a book I had read—*Nunca Mas*—the official report of a human rights commission that investigated and certified more than 12,000 "disappearances" during Argentina's "dirty war" in the late 1970s.

5   The weird anger of these Border Patrolmen made me think about descriptions in the report of Argentine police and military officers who became addicted to interrogation, torture and the murder that followed. When the military and police ran out of political suspects to torture and kill, they resorted to the random abduction of citizens off the streets. I thought how easy it would be for the Border Patrol to shoot us and leave our bodies and car beside the highway, like so many bodies found in these parts and ascribed to "drug runners."

Silko connects her experience with border patrol to more extreme incidents to establish the potential danger inherent in these searches.

6   Two other Border Patrolmen stood by the white van. The one who had asked if we were looking for trouble ordered his partner to "get the dog," and from the back of the van another patrolman brought a small female German shepherd on a leash. The dog apparently did not heel well enough to suit him, and the handler jerked the leash. They opened the doors of our car and pulled the dog's head into it, but I saw immediately from the expression in her eyes that the dog hated them, and that she would not serve them. When she showed no interest in the inside of the car, they brought her around back to the trunk, near where we were standing. They half-dragged her up into the trunk, but still she did not indicate any stowed-away human beings or illegal drugs.

7   The mood got uglier; the officers seemed outraged that the dog could not find any contraband, and they dragged her over to us and commanded her to sniff our legs and feet. To my relief, the

strange violence the Border Patrol agents had focused on us now seemed shifted to the dog. I no longer felt so strongly that we would be murdered. We exchanged looks—the dog and I. She was afraid of what they might do, just as I was. The dog's handler jerked the leash sharply as she sniffed us, as if to make her perform better, but the dog refused to accuse us: She had an innate dignity that did not permit her to serve the murderous impulses of those men. I can't forget the expression in the dog's eyes; it was as if she were embarrassed to be associated with them. I had a small amount of medicinal marijuana in my purse that night, but she refused to expose me. I am not partial to dogs, but I will always remember the small German shepherd that night.

8   Unfortunately, what happened to me is an everyday occurrence here now. Since the 1980s, on top of greatly expanding border checkpoints, the Immigration and Naturalization Service and the Border Patrol have implemented policies that interfere with the rights of U.S. citizens to travel freely within our borders. I.N.S. agents now patrol all interstate highways and roads that lead to or from the U.S.–Mexico border in Texas, New Mexico, Arizona and California. Now, when you drive east from Tucson on Interstate 10 toward El Paso, you encounter an I.N.S. check station outside Las Cruces, New Mexico. When you drive north from Las Cruces up Interstate 25, two miles north of the town of Truth or Consequences, the highway is blocked with orange emergency barriers, and all traffic is diverted into a two-lane Border Patrol checkpoint—ninety-five miles north of the U.S.–Mexico border.

9   I was detained once at Truth or Consequences, despite my and my companion's Arizona driver's licenses. Two men, both Chicanos, were detained at the same time, despite the fact that they too presented ID and spoke English without the thick Texas accents of the Border Patrol agents. While we were stopped, we watched as other vehicles—whose occupants were white—were waved through the checkpoint. White people traveling with brown people, however, can expect to be stopped on suspicion they work with the sanctuary movement, which shelters refugees. White people who appear to be clergy, those who wear ethnic clothing or jewelry and women with very long hair or very short hair (they could be nuns) are also frequently detained; white men with beards or men with long hair are likely to be detained, too, because Border Patrol agents have "profiles" of "those sorts" of white people who may help political refugees. (Most of the political refugees from Guatemala and El Salvador are Native American or mestizo because the indigenous people of the Americas have continued to resist efforts by invaders to displace them from their

---

Silko implicitly asks, if even the dog recognizes the border patrol's barbarity, how can any reasonable person defend their actions?

ancestral lands.) Alleged increases in illegal immigration by people of Asian ancestry mean that the Border Patrol now routinely detains anyone who appears to be Asian or part Asian, as well.

10   Once your car is diverted from the Interstate Highway into the checkpoint area, you are under the control of the Border Patrol, which in practical terms exercises a power that no highway patrol or city patrolman possesses: They are willing to detain anyone, for no apparent reason. Other law-enforcement officers need a shred of probable cause in order to detain someone. On the books, so does the Border Patrol; but on the road, it's another matter. They'll order you to stop your car and step out; then they'll ask you to open the trunk. If you ask why or request a search warrant, you'll be told that they'll have to have a dog sniff the car before they can request a search warrant, and the dog might not get there for two or three hours. The search warrant might require an hour or two past that. They make it clear that if you force them to obtain a search warrant for the car, they will make you submit to a strip search as well.

11   Traveling in the open, though, the sense of violation can be even worse. Never mind high-profile cases like that of former Border Patrol agent Michael Elmer, acquitted of murder by claiming self-defense, despite admitting that as an officer he shot an "illegal" immigrant in the back and then hid the body, which remained undiscovered until another Border Patrolman reported the event. (Last month, Elmer was convicted of reckless endangerment in a separate incident, for shooting at least ten rounds from his M-16 too close to a group of immigrants as they were crossing illegally into Nogales in March 1992.) Or that in El Paso a high school football coach driving a vanload of players in full uniform was pulled over on the freeway and a Border Patrol agent put a cocked revolver to his head. (The football coach was Mexican-American, as were most of the players in his van; the incident eventually caused a federal judge to issue a restraining order against the Border Patrol.) We've a mountain of personal experiences like that which never make the newspapers. A history professor at U.C.L.A. told me she had been traveling by train from Los Angeles to Albuquerque twice a month doing research. On each of her trips, she had noticed that the Border Patrol agents were at the station in Albuquerque scrutinizing the passengers. Since she is six feet tall and of Irish and German ancestry, she was not particularly concerned. Then one day when she stepped off the train in Albuquerque, two Border Patrolmen accosted her, wanting to know what she was doing, and why she was traveling between Los Angeles and Albuquerque twice a month. She

Have you ever crossed an international border? What experiences have you had?

In paragraphs 11 and 12, Silko offers additional stories to exemplify the unnerving nature of these searches.

presented identification and an explanation deemed "suitable" by the agents, and was allowed to go about her business.

12   Just the other day, I mentioned to a friend that I was writing this article and he told me about his 73-year-old father, who is half Chinese and who had set out alone by car from Tucson to Albuquerque the week before. His father had become confused by road construction and missed a turnoff from Interstate 10 to Interstate 25; when he turned around and circled back, he missed the turnoff a second time. But when he looped back for yet another try, Border Patrol agents stopped him and forced him to open his trunk. After they satisfied themselves that he was not smuggling Chinese immigrants, they sent him on his way. He was so rattled by the event that he had to be driven home by his daughter.

13   This is the police state that has developed in the southwestern United States since the 1980s. No person, no citizen, is free to travel without the scrutiny of the Border Patrol. In the city of South Tucson, where 80 percent of the respondents were Chicano or Mexicano, a joint research project by the University of Wisconsin and the University of Arizona recently concluded that one out of every five people there had been detained, mistreated verbally or nonverbally, or questioned by I.N.S. agents in the past two years.

Silko uses statistics from a research study conducted by respected universities as evidence for her claim.

14   Manifest Destiny may lack its old grandeur of theft and blood—"lock the door" is what it means now, with racism a trump card to be played again and again, shamelessly, by both major political parties. "Immigration," like "street crime" and "welfare fraud," is a political euphemism that refers to people of color. Politicians and media people talk about "illegal aliens" to dehumanize and demonize undocumented immigrants, who are for the most part people of color. Even in the days of Spanish and Mexican rule, no attempts were made to interfere with the flow of people and goods from south to north and north to south. It is the U.S. government that has continually attempted to sever contact between the tribal people north of the border and those to the south.

Having established the injustice of U.S. methods for defending its borders, Silko changes her focus to question the idea of borders themselves.

15   Now that the "Iron Curtain" is gone, it is ironic that the U.S. government and its Border Patrol are constructing a steel wall ten feet high to span sections of the border with Mexico. While politicians and multinational corporations extol the virtues of NAFTA and "free trade" (in goods, not flesh), the ominous curtain is already up in a six-mile section at the border crossing at Mexicali; two miles are being erected but are not yet finished at Naco; and at Nogales, sixty miles south of Tucson, the steel wall has been

all rubber-stamped and awaits construction likely to begin in March. Like the pathetic multimillion-dollar "antidrug" border surveillance balloons that were continually deflated by high winds and made only a couple of meager interceptions before they blew away, the fence along the border is a theatrical prop, a bit of pork for contractors. Border entrepreneurs have already used blowtorches to cut passageways through the fence to collect "tolls," and are doing a brisk business. Back in Washington, the I.N.S. announces a $300 million computer contract to modernize its record-keeping and Congress passes a crime bill that shunts $255 million to the I.N.S. for 1995, $181 million earmarked for border control, which is to include 700 new partners for the men who stopped Gus and me in our travels, and the history professor, and my friend's father, and as many as they could from South Tucson.

Silko extends her thesis further.

16   It is no use; borders haven't worked, and they won't work, not now, as the indigenous people of the Americas reassert their kinship and solidarity with one another. A mass migration is already under way; its roots are not simply economic. The Uto–Aztecan languages are spoken as far north as Taos Pueblo near the Colorado border, all the way south to Mexico City. Before the arrival of the Europeans, the indigenous communities throughout this region not only conducted commerce, the people shared cosmologies, and oral narratives about the Maize Mothers, the Twin Brothers and their Grandmother, Spider Woman, as well as Quetzalcoatl the benevolent snake. The great human migration within the Americas cannot be stopped; human beings are natural forces of the Earth, just as rivers and winds are natural forces.

17   Deep down the issue is simple: The so-called "Indian Wars" from the days of Sitting Bull and Red Cloud have never really ended in the Americas. The Indian people of southern Mexico, of Guatemala and those left in El Salvador, too, are still fighting for their lives and for their land against the "cavalry" patrols sent out by the governments of those lands. The Americas are Indian country, and the "Indian problem" is not about to go away.

18   One evening at sundown, we were stopped in traffic at a railroad crossing in downtown Tucson while a freight train passed us, slowly gaining speed as it headed north to Phoenix. In the twilight I saw the most amazing sight: Dozens of human beings, mostly young men, were riding the train; everywhere, on flat cars, inside open boxcars, perched on top of boxcars, hanging off ladders on tank cars and between boxcars. I couldn't count fast

Silko concludes with another story as evidence for her thesis that people cannot be bound by artificial borders.

enough, but I saw fifty or sixty people headed north. They were dark young men, Indian and mestizo; they were smiling and a few of them waved at us in our cars. I was reminded of the ancient story of Aztlán, told by the Aztecs but known in other Uto–Aztecan communities as well. Aztlán is the beautiful land to the north, the origin place of the Aztec people. I don't remember how or why the people left Aztlán to journey farther south, but the old story says that one day, they will return.

For support in learning this chapter's content, follow this path in MyCompLab:
> Resources > Writing > Writing Purposes > Writing to Describe.

Review the Instruction and Multimedia resources, then complete the Exercises and click on Gradebook to measure your progress.

12 | Rebuttal Arguments

QUICK TAKE

In this chapter, you will learn that

1. Rebuttal arguments use two basic strategies: refutation and counter-argument (see page 168)
2. Refutation arguments focus on the shortcomings of the opposing argument (see page 169)
3. Counterarguments acknowledge opposing positions but go on to maintain that the writer has the better argument (see page 170)

Whaling is an ancient form of hunting that greatly expanded in the nineteenth century due to a worldwide demand for whale oil. By 1986 the worldwide whale populations were so seriously depleted that the International Whaling Committee banned commercial whaling to allow whale populations to replenish. Limited whaling continues for scientific research, but environmental organizations such as Greenpeace insist that "science" is a guise for the continuation of commercial whaling. Greenpeace protests all whaling vigorously—both by peaceful means and by open ocean confrontations with whaling vessels. Could their protests at sea be considered a rebuttal argument?

Understand How Rebuttal Arguments Work

There are two basic approaches to rebutting an argument: you can refute the argument, or you can counterargue. In the first case, **refutation**, you demonstrate the shortcomings of the argument you wish to discredit, and you may or may not offer a positive claim of your own. In the second case, **counterargument**, you focus on the strengths of the position you support, and spend little time on the specifics of the argument you are countering. There can be substantial overlap between these two tactics, and good rebuttal arguments often employ both refutation and counterargument.

Because they focus on the shortcomings in the opposition's argument, a refutation argument often takes much of its structure from the argument being refuted.

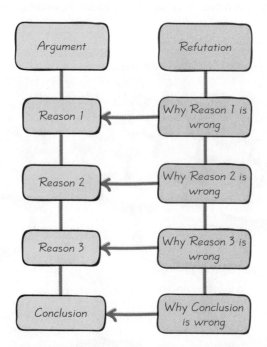

Many college students believe that using technology to "multitask" makes them more productive, believing that studying, texting a friend, and listening to music all at once is an efficient use of their time. But research shows that engaging in multiple tasks is distracting, interferes with memory, and makes it difficult to switch from one task to another, making multitaskers less productive than people focusing on one task at a time.

Counterarguments more often take up ideas the opposing claims has not addressed at all, or they take a very different approach to the problem. By largely ignoring the specifics of the argument being countered, they make the implicit claim that the counterargument is superior.

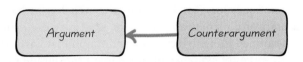

Those who argue for tariffs on goods from China claim that tariffs will protect American manufacturing jobs, but tariffs are a bad idea because they would increase prices on clothing, furniture, toys, and other consumer goods for everyone, and would cause the loss of retailing jobs as well.

Recognize Kinds of Rebuttal Arguments

Refutation

A refutation can either challenge the assumptions underlying a claim, or it can question the evidence supporting a claim. Until about five hundred years ago, people believed that the sky, and everything in it, moved, while the Earth remained still. They observed the stars moving from west to east in a regular, circular motion, and concluded that all the heavenly bodies orbited around an axis between Earth and Polaris, the northern star. This theory, however, did not explain the movement of the planets. If you watch the path of Mars over several nights, for example, you will notice that it moves, like the stars, from east to west. But occasionally, it will appear to move backward, from west to east, before reversing itself and resuming an east-to-west course. This phenomenon is called retrograde motion, and it is exhibited by all the planets in our solar system. In fact, our word *planet* derives from the Greek term *planetes*, meaning "wanderer." The ancient Greeks assumed that the planets and stars orbited the Earth, but that the planets sometimes wandered from their paths.

In the second century CE, the Greek astronomer Ptolemy made precise and detailed observations of the planets and created a model to predict their retrograde motion. In his treatise, the *Almagest,* he theorized that Mars and the other "wanderers" periodically deviated from their path around the Earth, making small circles, or epicycles, before moving on again. It was a complicated system, but it predicted the movements of the planets very accurately, and so it went unchallenged for over a thousand years.

In the early sixteenth century, the Polish astronomer Nicolaus Copernicus recognized that Ptolemy's observations could be explained more simply if the Earth and other planets circled the Sun. Copernicus's theory, later confirmed by the German astronomer Johannes Kepler, eventually replaced the Ptolemaic model of the solar system as the accepted explanation for observed planetary motion.

Copernicus did not question Ptolemy's evidence—the data he had collected showing where the stars and planets appear in the sky to an Earth-bound observer. Instead, he questioned Ptolemy's central assumption that Earth is the center of the solar system. Because evidence of the planet's retrograde motion had been observed by people over such a long period of time, it was unlikely to be wrong. Instead, it was the theory Ptolemy constructed to explain his data that was incorrect.

But sometimes evidence is wrong. Sometimes, too, evidence is incomplete or not representative, and sometimes counterevidence can be found. People who are bent on persuading others may leave out information that weakens their case, or employ evidence in questionable ways to try to bolster their claims. Dermatologists argue that indoor tanning is harmful to people's health because it exposes them to ultraviolet radiation, a known cause of cancer. The tanning industry, not surprisingly, disagrees, arguing that indoor tanning is safer than outdoor tanning because it assures safe levels of UV radiation exposure. While sunbathers often get sunburned, indoor tanners only get safe levels of radiation. This is an intriguing claim, but the AMA has discovered that in fact people who use tanning beds *do* get burned—as many of 50 percent of them. The tanning industry also claims indoor tanning provides people with a "protective" tan that reduces the amount of harmful UV radiation they absorb when they do go out in the sun. Doctors counter this claim by pointing out that a "base tan" provides only as much protection as a sunblock with a Sun Protection Factor, or SPF, of 3, and that the minimum recommended SPF for sunscreen is 15. The protection offered by an indoor tan is minimal at best. Both sides continue to argue over what evidence is valid, and accurate, when assessing the safety of indoor tanning.

Counterargument

Another way to rebut is to counterargue. In a counterargument, you might acknowledge an opposing point of view, but you might not consider it in detail. Rather, you put the main effort into your own argument. A counterarguer, in effect, says, "I hear your argument. But there is more to it than that. Now listen while I explain why another position is stronger." Counterargument is an effective way of persuading audiences, but sometimes it is used as a way to avoid addressing opposing views honestly. People's tendency to be persuaded by counterargument also makes them susceptible to red herrings, when an irrelevant but dramatic detail is put forward as if it were important, or *ad hominem* attacks, where someone makes spurious accusations about an opponent instead of engaging in real debate.

The counterarguer depends on the wisdom of his or her audience members to hear all sides of an issue and make up their own minds about the merits of the case. In the following short poem, Wilfred Owen, a veteran of the horrors of World War I trench warfare, offers a counterargument to those who argue that war is noble, to those who believe along with the poet Horace that "dulce et decorum est pro patria mori"—that it is sweet and fitting to die for one's country. This poem gains in popularity whenever there is an unpopular war for it rebuts the belief that it is noble to die for one's country in modern warfare.

Dulce Et Decorum Est

Bent double, like old beggars under sacks,
Knock-kneed, coughing like hags, we cursed through sludge,
Till on the haunting flares we turned our backs
And towards our distant rest began to trudge.
Men marched asleep. Many had lost their boots
But limped on, blood-shod. All went lame; all blind;
Drunk with fatigue; deaf even to the hoots
Of tired, outstripped Five-Nines that dropped behind.

Gas! Gas! Quick, boys! — An ecstasy of fumbling,
Fitting the clumsy helmets just in time;
But someone still was yelling out and stumbling,
And flound'ring like a man in fire or lime . . .
Dim, through the misty panes and thick green light,
As under a green sea, I saw him drowning.
In all my dreams, before my helpless sight,
He plunges at me, guttering, choking, drowning.

If in some smothering dreams you too could pace
Behind the wagon that we flung him in,
And watch the white eyes writhing in his face,
His hanging face, like a devil's sick of sin;
If you could hear, at every jolt, the blood
Come gargling from the froth-corrupted lungs,
Obscene as cancer, bitter as the cud
Of vile, incurable sores on innocent tongues,
My friend, you would not tell with such high zest
To children ardent for some desperate glory,
The old Lie; Dulce et Decorum est
Pro patria mori.

Owen does not summarize the argument in favor of being willing to die for one's country and then refute that argument point by point. Rather, his poem presents an opposing argument, supported by a narrative of the speaker's experience in a poison-gas attack, that he hopes will more than counterbalance what he calls "the old Lie." Owen simply ignores the reasons people give for being willing to die for one's country and argues instead that there are good reasons not to do so. And he hopes that the evidence he summons for his position will outweigh for his audience (addressed as "My friend,") the evidence in support of the other side.

Rebuttal arguments frequently offer both refutation and counterargument. Like attorneys engaged in a trial, people writing rebuttals must make their own cases based on good reasons and hard evidence, but they also do what they can to undermine their opponent's case. In the end the jury—the audience—decides.

Build a Rebuttal Argument

As you prepare to rebut an argument, look closely at what your opponent says. What exactly are the claims? What is the evidence? What are the assumptions? What do you disagree with? Are there parts you agree with? Are there assumptions you share? Do you agree that the evidence is accurate?

Knowing where you agree with someone helps you focus your rebuttal on differences. Having points of agreement can also help you build credibility with your audience, if you acknowledge that your opponent makes some logical points, or makes reasonable assumptions.

Consider using counterargument if you generally agree with a claim but do not think it goes far enough, if you feel an argument proposes the wrong solution to a problem, or if you think that, while accurate, it misses the "big picture." Counterargument lets you frame your own, stronger take on the question at hand without spending a lot of time trying to find flaws in the opposing position when there may not be many there.

If you do have serious objections to an argument, plan to refute it, and start by looking for the most important differences in your respective positions. What are the biggest "red flags" in the argument you disagree with? What are the weakest points of your opponent's argument? What are the strongest points of your own? You will probably want to highlight these differences in your rebuttal. You may find many problems with evidence and logic, in which case you will probably want to prioritize them. You do not necessarily need to point out the flaws in every single element of an argument. Direct your audience to the ones that matter the most.

You can also use counterargument in combination with refutation, first showing why an existing argument is wrong, and then offering an alternative. This is one of the more common forms of rebuttal. As you examine your opponent's claims and evidence, look closely for fallacies and faulty logic (see pages 17–19). How do these distort the problem or lead the audience to mistaken conclusions? Pointing them out to your readers will strengthen your position.

Look too at sources. Check your opponent's facts. Scrutinize the experts he or she relies on. And consider the purpose and motivation behind arguments you rebut. Groups funded by major industries, political parties, and special interest groups may have hidden or not-so-hidden agendas driving the arguments they make. Pointing these out to your readers can strengthen your own position.

Finding Good Reasons

Can the Web be trusted for research?

Most Web users are familiar with the huge and immensely popular Wikipedia, the online encyclopedia. What makes Wikipedia so different from traditional, print encyclopedias is that entries can be contributed or edited by anyone.

In 2007, Jimmy Wales, president of Wikimedia and one of its founders, debated the legitimacy of Wikipedia with Dale Hoiberg, editor-in-chief of *Encyclopedia Britannica.* Hoiberg's main criticism of Wikipedia is that its structure—an open-source wiki without the formal editorial control that shapes traditional, print encyclopedias— allows for inaccurate entries.

In response, Wales argues that *Britannica* and newspapers also contain errors, but Wikipedia has the advantage that they are easily corrected. Furthermore, he asserts that Wikipedia's policy of using volunteer administrators to delete irrelevant entries and requiring authors of entries to cite reliable, published sources ensures quality. Nonetheless, some universities including UCLA and the University of Pennsylvania along with many instructors strongly discourage and even ban students from citing Wikipedia in their work. (Wikipedia also cautions against using its entries as a primary source for serious research.)

Write about it

1. If your college decided to ban the use of Wikipedia as a reference because it lacked the authority of a traditional encyclopedia, would you want to challenge it? Why or why not?

2. If you chose to challenge the college's policy, how would you do so? Would it be effective to refute the college's claims point by point, noting fallacies in logic and reasoning? Would it be effective to build a counterargument in which you examine the assumptions on which the college's claims are based? Which strategy would you choose, and why?

Steps to Writing a Rebuttal Argument

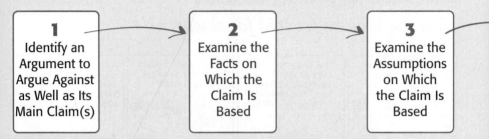

1 Identify an Argument to Argue Against as Well as Its Main Claim(s)

2 Examine the Facts on Which the Claim Is Based

3 Examine the Assumptions on Which the Claim Is Based

Step 1 Identify an Argument to Argue Against as Well as Its Main Claim(s)

- What exactly are you arguing against?
- Are there secondary claims attached to the main claim?
- Include a fair summary of your opponent's position in your finished rebuttal.

Examples

- Arguing against raising taxes for the purpose of building a new sports stadium (examine how proponents claim that a new sports facility will benefit the local economy).
- Arguing for raising the minimum wage (examine how opponents claim that a higher minimum wage isn't necessary and negatively affects small-business owners).

Step 2 Examine the Facts on Which the Claim Is Based

- Are the facts accurate, current, and representative?
- Is there another body of facts that you can present as counterevidence?
- If the author uses statistics, can the statistics be interpreted differently?
- If the author quotes from sources, how reliable are those sources?
- Are the sources treated fairly, or are quotations taken out of context?

Step 3 Examine the Assumptions on Which the Claim Is Based

- What are the primary and secondary assumptions of the claim you are rejecting?
- How are those assumptions flawed?
- Does the author resort to name calling, use faulty reasoning, or ignore key facts (see pages 17–19)?

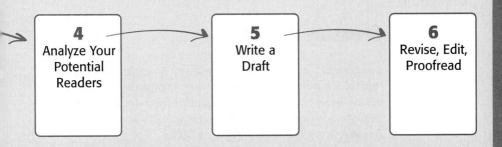

Step 4 Analyze Your Potential Readers

- To what extent do your potential readers support the claim that you are rejecting?
- If they strongly support that claim, how might you appeal to them to change their minds?
- What common assumptions and beliefs do you share with them?

Step 5 Write a Draft

Introduction

Identify the issue and the argument you are rejecting.

- Provide background if the issue is unfamiliar to most of your readers.
- Give a quick summary of the competing positions even if the issue is familiar to your readers.
- Make your aim clear in your thesis statement.

Body

Take on the argument that you are rejecting. Consider questioning the evidence that is used to support the argument by doing one or more of the following.

- Challenge the facts and the currency and relevance of examples.
- Present counterevidence and countertestimony.
- Challenge the credibility of sources cited.
- Question the way in which statistical evidence is presented and interpreted.
- Argue that quotations are taken out of context.

Conclusion

- Conclude on a firm note by underscoring your objections.
- Consider closing with a counterargument or counterproposal.

Step 6 Revise, Edit, Proofread

- For detailed instructions, see Chapter 4.
- For a checklist to use to evaluate your draft, see pages 48–49.

Dan Stein

Crossing the Line

Dan Stein is president of the Federation for American Immigration Reform, a Washington D.C.–based nonprofit organization that seeks to stop illegal immigration. He frequently speaks and writes about immigration issues. "Crossing the Line" was published in the *Los Angeles Business Journal* in February 2007.

Stein uses a fact from a respected polling agency to bolster his assumption that the majority of Americans strongly oppose illegal immigration.

The timing could not have been worse for Bank of America to announce that it would begin issuing credit cards to illegal aliens in Los Angeles. News of Bank of America's decision was published in the *Wall Street Journal* on February 13, the same day that a new Harris Poll revealed that Americans perceive the two greatest threats to their security to be illegal immigration and the outsourcing of American jobs.

2   Even more than the prospect of the Iranians or the North Koreans with nukes, Americans believe that their security is threatened by millions of people pouring across our borders and by corporations that appear willing to sell out the interests of American workers. In one decision, Bank of America managed to pluck two raw nerves by appearing to encourage illegal immigration, while sending the message that it would not let any national interest stand in the way of it making a buck.

3   The Bank of America decision and the overwhelming negative public reaction to it illustrates the growing disconnect between the elite and everyone else in this country. To the elite—including the current occupant of the White House—the traditional idea of the nation has become a bothersome anachronism. To the extent that the entity known as the United States has any relevance at all to them, it is to secure their ability to conduct business and maximize their corporate bottom lines. Concepts of patriotism and loyalty are marketing tools and nothing more.

Stein connects his argument to other issues his audience is likely to relate to.

4   To Bank of America and other large corporations, illegal immigrants are a source of low wage labor and an untapped customer market. It matters not that illegal immigrants are breaking the laws of the United States, taking jobs from and driving down wages for middle class workers, burdening schools (not the ones the children of Bank of America executives attend, of course) and other vital public services. What matters to the banking industry is that the estimated 12 to 15 million illegal aliens living in the United States have purchasing power and that there is money to be made off of serving them.

5   It is true that Bank of America did not create the illegal immigration crisis in the United States, although banking industry decisions to allow illegal aliens to open bank accounts, take out home mortgages and now obtain credit cards has certainly added to the problem. But the fact that the federal government has done little to resolve the problem of illegal immigration does not mean that banks and other business interests have an unfettered right to profit from illegal immigration. Bank of America did not create the illegal drug problem in the United States, but that does not entitle it to market services to the drug cartels, even though it would be enormously profitable to do so.

Stein alludes to the drug industry to assert that corporations' obligation to respect the laws of the country trump their obligation to make a profit.

OVERTLY DISCRIMINATORY

6   The plan to issue credit cards to illegal aliens is also overtly discriminatory, giving a new meaning to their corporate slogan: "Bank of America, Higher Standards" (for some). While American citizens and legal U.S. residents are held to one standard in order to obtain credit, illegal aliens will be held to a lower standard. The plastic that any of us tote around in our wallets required us to open our entire lives to our creditors and to provide verification of our identities and credit-worthiness. In their hunger to make money off of illegal aliens Bank of America is prepared to accept easily counterfeited Mexican matricula cards as proof of identity, and maintaining a checking account for three months as a credit history.

7   Bank of America has obviously felt the sting of a public backlash, as evidenced by their sudden reluctance to discuss it in the media. Some people have gone so far as to pull their accounts out of Bank of America. But given the consolidation of the banking industry generally, and the fact that a handful of banks have a corner on the credit card market, it will require government action to stop financial institutions from pursuing profits in blatant disregard of the law and the public interest.

Stein uses refutation heavily in his rebuttal, never straying too far from the issue: the legality and morality of Bank of America's new policy.

8   Existing federal law clearly prohibits "encouraging or inducing unauthorized aliens to enter the United States, and engaging in a conspiracy or aiding and abetting" people who violate U.S. immigration laws. Products and services specifically marketed to illegal aliens, intended to make it easier to live and work in the U.S. illegally, violate the spirit if not the letter of the law.

9   To Bank of America, illegal aliens are just customers and the United States nothing more than a market. To the American people, illegal immigration and corporate greed are seen as serious threats to their security. Bank of America has provided the proof that both are inexorably intertwined.

Stein summarizes his thesis in the conclusion.

Gregory Rodriguez

Illegal Immigrants—They're Money

Gregory Rodriguez is a Los Angeles–based Irvine Senior Fellow at the New America Foundation, a nonpartisan think tank in Washington, D.C. He has written widely about issues of national identity, social cohesion, assimilation, race relations, religion, immigration, demographics, and social and political trends. He published "Illegal Immigrants—They're Money," a rebuttal to Dan Stein's article about the Bank of America, as a column in the *Los Angeles Times* on March 4, 2007.

Dan Stein, the premier American nativist and president of the Federation for American Immigration Reform, is shocked, shocked. He's mad at Bank of America for issuing credit cards to illegal immigrants. He says that to Bank of America "and other large corporations, illegal immigrants are a source of low-wage labor and an untapped customer market." You bet they are, and that's the American way.

In paragraphs 2 and 3, Rodriguez defines his vision of the realities of the American dream.

2   Sure, I'm proud to be a citizen of a nation that portrays itself as a refuge for the "tired," "the poor" and the "huddled masses yearning to breathe free." But let's face it, Emma Lazarus, the poet who wrote those words, may have laid it on a bit thick. The truth, no less beautiful in its way, is a little more crass and self-serving. But it wouldn't have sounded nearly as poetic to say, "bring us your able-bodied, poor, hardworking masses yearning for a chance to climb out of poverty, establish a credit history and. . . ." We all love to rhapsodize about immigrants' embrace of the American dream, but it's more like a hard-nosed American deal—you come here, you work your tail off under grueling conditions, and you can try your damnedest to better your lot over time.

3   In their generational struggle for acceptance and security, from outsider to insider and, dare I say, from exploited to exploiter, immigrants could avail themselves of those inalienable rights that stand at the core of our national political philosophy—life, liberty and the pursuit of happiness.

Rodriguez makes a transition to his thesis by pointing out that illegal immigration is a recent construct.

4   But that, of course, was before the invention of illegal immigration.

5   Until the early 1900s, pretty much anybody who wasn't diseased, a criminal, a prostitute, a pauper, an anarchist or a Chinese laborer could gain entrance to the U.S. Between 1880 and 1914, only 1% of a total of 25 million European immigrants were excluded from this country. But after transatlantic crossings had already been halted by World War I, Congress buckled to anti-foreign sentiment and closed the proverbial Golden Door by passing a series of restrictionist laws in 1917, 1921 and 1924.

6   Yet even as the historical front door of the nation was being closed, business interests were busy prying open a new side-door. Only three months after the passage of the Immigration Act of 1917, which required all newcomers to pass a literacy test and pay a head tax, the U.S. Secretary of Commerce waived the regulations for Mexican workers. Thus began America's dishonorable relationship with Mexican immigrant labor.

7   For the next several decades, Mexican workers were brought in when the economy expanded and kicked out when times got bad. They were recruited in the 1920s, only to be deported in the 1930s. They were brought in again during the labor shortage in the 1940s. By the 1950s, one branch of the government recruited Mexican workers, under the illusion that they were "temporary," while another sought to keep them out.

Rodriquez establishes a longstanding tradition of fairweather treatment of Mexican immigrants by U.S. policy.

8   The *piece de resistance* in the creation of the illegal immigrant is the Immigration Act of 1965. Although touted as a great piece of liberal legislation that ended discriminatory immigration barriers, it imposed an annual cap on migrants from the Western Hemisphere that was 40% less than the number that had been arriving yearly before 1965. A decade later, Congress placed a 20,000 limit per country in this hemisphere.

9   In other words, after importing millions of Mexicans over the decades, particularly during the bracero guest-worker program from 1942 to 1963, and establishing well-trod routes to employment north of the border, the U.S. drastically reduced the number of visas available to Mexicans. This reduction, of course, coincided with a rapid rise in Mexico's population. And guess what? When jobs were available on this side of the border, Mexicans just kept coming, whether they had papers or not.

10   Clearly, today as ever, mass migration to the U.S. is being driven by economic need—the immigrants' and our economy's. But the hard-nosed American deal has become unfair because, on top of the handicaps we have always imposed on new arrivals, we've added a rather brutal one—criminal status. Good luck with that pursuit of happiness as you engage in backbreaking labor when your place in society is summed up with that one cutting word, "illegal."

Rodriguez asserts his thesis in this paragraph.

11   No, I'm not advocating open borders. Nor do I believe that immigrants should be guaranteed anything but a chance to achieve their end of the nation's cruel bargain. For hardworking illegal immigrants who've established roots here, we should uphold our end of the bargain and give them a chance to achieve their piece of the American dream. Bank of America is not wrong to give illegal immigrants the tools with which to compete legitimately in the marketplace. We as a nation are wrong for treating all these people as illegitimate.

Rodriquez addresses Stein only briefly in the introduction and here in the conclusion. Why?

Sample Student Rebuttal Argument

Ramos 1

Marta Ramos
Professor Jacobs
English 1010
30 April 2010

Oversimplifying the Locavore Ethic

James McWilliams's argument in his essay "On Locavorism" is based on an overly simplistic understanding of the locavore ethic. His claim, that eating locally is an unrealistic goal, fails to take into account the flexibility of locavorism, the ways consumer food preferences drive the free market system, and the realities of food processing infrastructure.

> Ramos identifies the source that she will refute and the source's claim in the first paragraph.

McWilliams's criticism of locavorism would make sense if, as he implies, locavores were a single-minded group of people demanding the complete conversion of the agricultural systems to uniform, regimented local production and consumption. In fact, there is no reason that locavorism has to completely replace the existing agricultural system, and hardly any locavores advocate this. Locavorism, the practice of eating food that is grown locally and in season, is not an all-or-nothing policy. It is a direction in which individuals and communities can move. Locavores.com, a Web site run by the chef Jessica Prentice, who coined the term "locavore," spells out local-eating strategies:

> Ramos defines the term "locavore" and asserts that McWilliams misunderstands the movement.

> If not LOCALLY PRODUCED, then ORGANIC.
> If not ORGANIC, then FAMILY FARM.
> If not FAMILY FARM, then LOCAL BUSINESS.
> If not LOCAL BUSINESS, then TERROIR—foods famous for the region they are grown in. ("Guidelines")

This hierarchy of food sources prefers local sources over distant ones, and prioritizes local farms and businesses to receive local food dollars. Eating locally, according to Locavores, represents "A step toward regional food self reliance" ("Top"). Given the political instability of many areas of the world that grow our food and the way energy costs can drastically affect food prices, it makes sense to reduce our dependence on distant food sources. As Jennifer Maiser, one of the founders of the locavore movement, puts it,

> Ramos uses a direct quotation from a respected voice in the locavore community to build credibility.

Ramos 2

Locavores are people who pay attention to where their food
comes from and commit to eating local food as much as
possible. The great thing about eating local is that it's not
an all-or-nothing venture. Any small step you take helps the
environment, protects your family's health and supports
small farmers in your area.

The goal is not to end completely our importation of food.

McWilliams cites Phoenix as an example of why locavorism won't work.
Certainly cities like Phoenix, which lacks the water to grow much food,
will always rely on external supply chains to feed their populations. But
the obstacles to local eating in Phoenix should not prevent residents of
San Francisco, Sarasota, or Charleston from eating locally grown foods.
Locavorism doesn't have to work everywhere to be beneficial.

In addition to misrepresenting locavorism's goals, McWilliams
illogically claims that it cannot meet people's food needs. "At current
levels of fruit production," he warns, "apples are the only crop that could
currently feed New Yorkers at a level that meets the U.S. Recommended
Dietary Allowances." McWilliams is wrong when he claims that if New
Yorkers ate locally grown fruits, they could "rarely indulge in a pear,
peach, or basket of strawberries." That might be the case if New York
farmers continued to grow nothing but apples and grapes. But if some of
those crops were replaced with other fruits, New York could have a very
diverse supply of produce that would come reasonably close to meeting
the nutritional needs of its citizens. In fact, if committed locavores seek
out locally grown strawberries, peaches, and pears, and are willing to pay
more money for them than they do for apples, local farmers will have
sound economic reasons for replacing some of their aging apple trees
with peach and pear trees instead. McWilliams makes locavorism sound
impractical because he tries to imagine it working within current agricultural realities. In fact, locavores seek to change the way food is produced
and consumed. Moreover, locavorism works toward this change not, as
McWilliams suggests, by advocating laws that restrict food producers but
by encouraging consumers to vote with their wallets.

McWilliams's argument about New York also rests on the peculiar
assumption that every person in the state has to eat the same fruits in

In her refuta-
tion Ramos ad-
dresses
McWilliams's
argument point
by point.

Ramos quotes
McWilliams
and then dis-
proves the
quoted claim.

Ramos 3

the same amounts in order for locavorism to work. He points out that except for apples and grapes, "every other fruit the state produces is not being harvested at a level to provide all New Yorkers with an adequate supply." McWilliams implies that if you can't grow enough of a crop to supply every single person in the state, there is no point in growing it; however, the goal of locavorism is choice, not total local supply of all food, a fact McWilliams seems to willfully ignore.

Ramos questions McWilliams's assumptions and finds them lacking.

Finally, McWilliams claims that the cost and inconvenience of processing food locally will prevent communities from moving toward local eating. He notes that "whereas the conventional system of production and distribution has in place a series of large-scale processing centers capable of handling these tasks in a handful of isolated locations," smaller communities do not. There are two problems with this argument. First, many of the "processing centers" McWilliams is thinking of *aren't* capable of handling the task of food production. The National Resources Defense Council reports that "from 1995 to 1998, 1,000 spills or pollution incidents occurred at livestock feed-lots in 10 states and 200 manure-related fish kills resulted in the death of 13 million fish" ("Facts"). In 2009, Fairbank Farms recalled over half a million pounds of ground beef after nineteen people were hospitalized and two died from E. coli bacteria in the meat (United States). Also in 2009, the King Nut Companies of Solon, Ohio, sickened over 400 people, including three who died, by producing and distributing peanut butter infected with salmonella ("Virginia"). Large-scale processing plants are not a solution to our food security needs. They are part of the problem.

Ramos addresses the claim that she takes greatest issue with last. She then gives it further emphasis by providing two distinct counterarguments.

Second, the cost of changing the country's food-processing system from large-scale to small-scale is not as prohibitive as McWilliams makes it sound. Factories age. Machines wear out and have to be replaced. Food production facilities are replaced all the time. Newer facilities could easily be built on a smaller, more regional scale. In fact, given the cost of recalls and lawsuits when tainted food is distributed over a large area, food producers have good reason to think about smaller, more localized production and distribution.

McWilliams either does not understand locavorism or understands it and prefers to misrepresent its goals and methods. His arguments in favor of our current food production system ignore both the very real benefits of local eating, and the considerable cost of the existing system.

Ramos closes with an appeal to the benefits of locavorism.

Ramos 4

Works Cited

"Facts about Pollution from Livestock Farms." *Natural Resources Defense Council*. Natural Resources Defense Council, 15 July 2005. Web. 7 Apr. 2010.

"Guidelines for Eating Well." *Locavores*. Locavores, 3 June 2009. Web. 9 Apr. 2010.

Maiser, Jennifer. "10 Steps to Becoming a Locavore." *PBS: NOW*. Jump Start Productions, 2 Nov. 2007. Web. 8 Apr. 2010.

McWilliams, James. "On Locavorism." *New York Times*. New York Times, 26 Aug. 2008. Web. 8 Apr. 2010.

"Top Twelve Reasons to Eat Locally." *Locavores*. Locavores, 3 June 2009. Web. 9 Apr. 2010.

United States. Dept. of Health and Human Services. "Multistate Outbreak of E. coli 0157:H7 Infections Associated with Beef from Fairbanks Farms." *Centers for Disease Control and Prevention*. Dept. of Health and Human Services, 24 Nov. 2009. Web. 8 Apr. 2010.

"Virginia, Minnesota Confirms Salmonella Deaths Related to Tainted Peanut Butter." *Fox News*. Fox News Network, 13 Jan. 2009. Web. 10 Apr. 2010.

PEARSON
mycomplab

For support in learning this chapter's content, follow this path in MyCompLab:
> Resources > Writing > Writing Purposes > Writing to Argue or Persuade.
Review the Instruction and Multimedia resources, then complete the Exercises and click on Gradebook to measure your progress.

13 | Proposal Arguments

QUICK TAKE

In this chapter, you will learn that

1. Proposal arguments identify a problem and offer a solution (see page 185)

2. Successful proposal arguments convince readers that the solution will work (see page 186)

3. Successful proposal arguments acknowledge other possible solutions and argue why the proposed solution is better (see page 186)

The San Francisco Bicycle Coalition, "dedicated to creating safer streets and more livable communities," is an organization whose primary goal is to build a citywide bike network in San Francisco. The success of the coalition's efforts to increase bicycle ridership for commuters created its own problem: Caltrain commuter trains ran out of room for bicycles, and riders were "bumped" because the trains' bike storage cars were filled to capacity. The coalition crafted a new proposal called Bikes On Board to persuade Caltrain to add more bike storage capacity on its trains. The coalition's proposal encourages riders to report "bumps" in order to document exactly how many times cyclists are denied rides on trains due to limited bike storage. This well-defined proposal forms part of a larger campaign and organizational mission encompassing environmental, economic, and personal fitness issues. What local issues inspire you to propose action? How would you go about crafting a proposal argument to promote interest in a cause or solution?

Understand How Proposal Arguments Work

Proposal arguments make the case that someone should do something: "The federal government should raise grazing fees on public lands." "The student union should renovate the old swimming pool in Butler Gymnasium." "All parents should secure their children in booster seats when driving, even for short distances." Proposals can also argue that something should *not* be done, or that people should stop doing something: "The plan to extend Highway 45 is a waste of tax dollars and citizens should not vote for it." "Don't drink and drive."

The challenge for writers of proposal arguments is to convince readers to take action. It's easy for readers to agree that something should be done, as long as they don't have to do it. It's much harder to get readers involved with the situation or convince them to spend their time or money trying to carry out the proposal. A successful proposal argument conveys a sense of urgency to motivate readers, and describes definite actions they should take.

The key to a successful proposal is using good reasons to convince readers that if they act, something positive will happen (or something negative will be avoided). If your readers believe that taking action will benefit them, they are more likely to help bring about what you propose.

Proposal arguments take the form shown here.

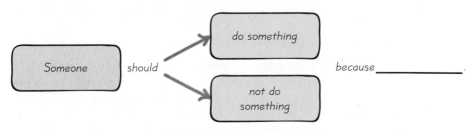

We should convert existing train tracks in the downtown areas to a light-rail system and build a new freight track around the city because we need to relieve traffic and parking congestion downtown.

Recognize Components of Proposal Arguments

Most successful proposals have four major components:

- **Identifying and defining the problem.** Sometimes, your audience is already fully aware of the problem you want to solve. If your city frequently tears up streets and then leaves them for months without fixing them, you shouldn't have much trouble convincing citizens that streets should be repaired more quickly. But if you raise a problem unfamiliar to your readers, first you will have to convince them that the problem is real. Citizens will not see the need to replace miles of plumbing lines running under the streets, for example, unless you convince them that the pipes are old and corroded and are a risk to everyone's safety. You will also need to define the scope of the problem—does every single pipe need replacing, or only those more than forty years old? Is this a job for the city, or do federal clean water regulations mean that other government officials must be involved? The clearer you are about what must be done, and by whom, the stronger your argument will be.

■ **Stating a proposed solution.** A strong proposal offers a clear, definite statement of exactly what you are proposing. Vague statements that "Something must be done!" may get readers stirred up about the issue, but are unlikely to lead to constructive action. A detailed proposal also adds credibility to your argument, showing that you are concerned enough to think through the nuts and bolts of the changes to be made. You can state your proposed solution near the beginning of your argument, or introduce it later—for example, after you have considered and rejected other possible solutions.

■ **Convincing readers that the proposed solution is fair and will work.** Once your readers agree that a problem exists and a solution should be found, you have to convince them that your solution is the best one. Perhaps you want your city to fire the planning committee members who are responsible for street repair. You will need to show that those officials are indeed responsible for the delays, and that, once they are fired, the city will be able to quickly hire new, more effective planners.

■ **Demonstrating that the solution is feasible.** Your solution not only has to work; it must be feasible, or practical, to implement. You might be able to raise money for street repairs by billing property owners for repairs to the streets in front of their houses, but opposition to such a proposal would be fierce. Most Americans will object to making individuals responsible for road repair costs when roads are used by all drivers.

You may also have to show how your proposal is better than other possible actions that could be taken. Perhaps others believe your city should hire private contractors to repair the streets more quickly, or reward work crews who finish quickly with extra pay or days off. If there are multiple proposed solutions, all perceived as equally good, then there is no clear course of action for your audience to work for. Very often, that means nothing will happen.

Build a Proposal Argument

At this moment, you might not think that you feel strongly enough about anything to write a proposal argument. But if you write a list of things that make you mad or at least a little annoyed, then you have a start toward writing a proposal argument. Some things on your list are not going to produce proposal arguments that many people would want to read. If your roommate is a slob, you might be able to write a proposal for that person to start cleaning up more, but who else would be interested? Similarly, it might be annoying to you that where you live is too far from the ocean, but it is hard to imagine making a serious proposal to move your city closer to the coast. Short of those extremes, however, are many things that might make you think, "Why hasn't someone done something about this?" If you believe that others have something to gain if a problem is solved, or at least that the situation can be made a little better, then you might be able to develop a good proposal argument.

For instance, suppose you are living off campus, and you buy a student parking sticker when you register for courses so that you can park in the student lot. However, you quickly find out that there are too many cars and trucks for the number of available spaces, and unless you get to campus by 8:00 A.M., you aren't going to find a place to park in your assigned lot. The situation makes you angry because you believe that if you pay for a sticker, you should have a reasonable chance of finding a place to park. You see that there are unfilled lots reserved for faculty and staff next to the student parking lot, and you wonder why more spaces aren't allotted to students. You decide to write to the president of your college. You want her to direct parking and traffic services to give more spaces to students or else to build a parking garage that will accommodate more vehicles.

When you start talking to other students on campus, however, you begin to realize that the problem may be more complex than your first view of it. Your college has taken the position that if fewer students drive to campus, there will be less traffic on and around your campus. The administration wants more students to ride shuttle buses, to form car pools, or to bicycle to campus instead of driving alone. You also find out that faculty and staff members pay ten times as much as students for their parking permits, so they pay a very high premium for a guaranteed space—much too high for most students. If the president of your college is your primary audience, you first have to argue that a problem really exists. You have to convince the president that many students have no choice but to drive if they are to attend classes. You, for example, are willing to ride the shuttle buses, but they don't run often enough for you to make your classes, get back to your car that you left at home, and then drive to your job.

Next, you have to argue that your solution will solve the problem. An eight-story parking garage might be adequate to park all the cars of students who want to drive, but parking garages are very expensive to build. Even if a parking garage is the best solution, the question remains: who is going to pay for it? Many problems in life could be solved if you had access to unlimited resources, but very few people—or organizations—have such resources at their command. It's not enough to propose a solution that can resolve the problem. You have to be able to argue for the feasibility of your solution. If you want to argue that a parking garage is the solution to the parking problem on your campus, then you must also propose how to finance the garage.

Steps to Writing a Proposal Argument

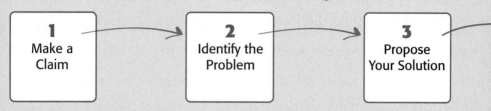

1 Make a Claim

2 Identify the Problem

3 Propose Your Solution

Step 1 Make a Claim

Make a proposal claim advocating a specific change or course of action.

Template

We should (or should not) do SOMETHING.

Examples

- Redesigning the process of registering for courses, getting e-mail, or making appointments to be more efficient.
- Creating bicycle lanes to make cycling safer and to reduce traffic.
- Streamlining the rules for recycling newspapers, bottles, and cans to encourage increased participation.

Step 2 Identify the Problem

- What exactly is the problem, what causes it, and who is most affected?
- Has anyone tried to do anything about it? If so, why haven't they succeeded?
- What is likely to happen in the future if the problem isn't solved?

Step 3 Propose Your Solution

State your solution as specifically as you can.

- What exactly do you want to achieve?
- How exactly will your solution work? Can it be accomplished quickly, or will it have to be phased in over a few years?
- Has anything like it been tried elsewhere? If so, what happened?
- If your solution costs money, how do you propose to pay for it?

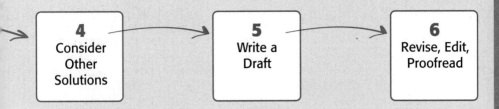

Step 4 Consider Other Solutions

- What other solutions have been or might be proposed for this problem, including doing nothing?
- Why is your solution better?

Step 5 Write a Draft

Introduction

- Set out the issue or problem, perhaps by telling about your experience or the experience of someone you know.
- Argue for the seriousness of the problem.
- Give some background about the problem if necessary.

Body

- Present your solution. Consider setting out your solution first, explaining how it will work, discussing other possible solutions, and arguing that yours is better. Or consider discussing other possible solutions first, arguing that they don't solve the problem or are not feasible, and then presenting your solution.
- Make clear the goals of your solution. Many solutions cannot solve problems completely.
- Describe in detail the steps in implementing your solution and how they will solve the problem you have identified.
- Explain the positive consequences that will follow from your proposal. What good things will happen, and what bad things will be avoided, if your advice is taken?

Conclusion

- Issue a call to action—if your readers agree with you, they will want to take action.
- Restate and emphasize exactly what readers need to do to solve the problem.

Step 6 Revise, Edit, Proofread

- For detailed instructions, see Chapter 4.
- For a checklist to use to evaluate your draft, see pages 48–49.

Finding Good Reasons

Who should make decisions about economic development?

Cape Cod, Massachusetts, is a peninsula that expands from the southern portion of Massachusetts into the Atlantic Ocean. Famous for its beautiful shoreline, Cape Cod is a popular destination for summer vacationers. The Cape Wind Project is a proposed 24-square-mile offshore wind farm that would be built beginning a little less than 5 miles off of the Cape's southern coast. Proponents of the plan cite the benefits of clean energy. Strong opposition, however, has been voiced by the Alliance to Protect Nantucket Sound, which claims that the proposed wind farm will not only destroy property values, but also irrevocably damage the Cape's priceless views, threaten the vital tourist industry, dislocate necessary shipping lanes, disrupt fish populations, and pose a hazard to birds. The Cape Wind Project has brought a prolonged battle in Massachusetts courts that no doubt will continue with a series of appeals.

Write about it

1. If you were the spokesperson for the Cape Wind Project, what reasons would you give to the Massachusetts State Courts to persuade them to begin construction of the wind farm?

2. If you were the spokesperson for the Alliance to Protect Nantucket Sound, what reasons would you give to the Massachusetts State Courts to persuade them to block the construction of the wind farm?

3. If you were a judge on the Massachusetts State Bench, what reasons might you expect to hear from these two groups? Draft a proposal that would win your vote.

Glenn Loury

A Nation of Jailers

Glenn Loury is Merton P. Stoltz Professor of the Social Sciences at Brown University and a guest on many television and radio news programs. He is the author of *One by One, From the Inside Out: Essays and Reviews on Race and Responsibility in America* (1995), *Anatomy of Racial Inequality* (2001), *Ethnicity, Social Mobility and Public Policy: Comparing the US and the UK* (2005), and over two hundred essays and reviews on racial inequality and social policy.

The most challenging problems of social policy in the modern world are never merely technical. In order properly to decide how we should govern ourselves, we must take up questions of social ethics and human values. What manner of people are we Americans? What vision would we affirm, and what example would we set, before the rest of the world? What kind of society would we bequeath to our children? How shall we live? Inevitably, queries such as these lurk just beneath the surface of the great policy debates of the day. So, those who would enter into public argument about what ails our common life need make no apology for speaking in such terms.

2   It is precisely in these terms that I wish to discuss a preeminent moral challenge for our time — that imprisonment on a massive scale has become one of the central aspects of our nation's social policy toward the poor, powerfully impairing the lives of some of the most marginal of our fellow citizens, especially the poorly educated black and Hispanic men who reside in large numbers in our great urban centers.

3   The bare facts of this matter — concerning both the scale of incarceration and its racial disparity — have been much remarked upon of late. Simply put, we have become a nation of jailers and, arguably, racist jailers at that. The past four decades have witnessed a truly historic expansion, and transformation, of penal institutions in the United States — at every level of government, and in all regions of the country. We have, by any measure, become a vastly more punitive society. Measured in constant dollars and taking account of all levels of government, spending on corrections and law enforcement in the United States has more than quadrupled over the last quarter century. As a result, the American prison system has grown into a leviathan unmatched in human history. This development should be deeply troubling to anyone who professes to love liberty.

4   Here, as in other areas of social policy, the United States is a stark international outlier, sitting at the most rightward end of

Instead of immediately announcing his thesis, Loury asks the big question: what is our ideal vision of society?

In paragraph 2, Loury narrows the focus to the massive-scale imprisonment of poor Americans.

the political spectrum: We imprison at a far higher rate than the other industrial democracies — higher, indeed, than either Russia or China, and vastly higher than any of the countries of Western Europe. According to the International Centre for Prison Studies in London, there were in 2005 some 9 million prisoners in the world; more than 2 million were being held in the United States. With approximately one twentieth of the world's population, America had nearly one fourth of the world's inmates. At more than 700 per 100,000 residents, the U.S. incarceration rate was far greater than our nearest competitors (the Bahamas, Belarus, and Russia, which each have a rate of about 500 per 100,000.) Other industrial societies, some of them with big crime problems of their own, were less punitive than we by an order of magnitude: the United States incarcerated at 6.2 times the rate of Canada, 7.8 times the rate of France, and 12.3 times the rate of Japan.

> Comparisons with other nations make a strong argument that the United States has an incarceration problem.

5   The demographic profile of the inmate population has also been much discussed. In this, too, the U.S. is an international outlier. African Americans and Hispanics, who taken together are about one fourth of the population, account for about two thirds of state prison inmates. Roughly one third of state prisoners were locked up for committing violent offenses, with the remainder being property and drug offenders. Nine in ten are male, and most are impoverished. Inmates in state institutions average fewer than eleven years of schooling.

6   The extent of racial disparity in imprisonment rates exceeds that to be found in any other arena of American social life: at eight to one, the black to white ratio of male incarceration rates dwarfs the two to one ratio of unemployment rates, the three to one nonmarital child bearing ratio, the two to one ratio of infant mortality rates and the one to five ratio of net worth. More black male high school dropouts are in prison than belong to unions or are enrolled in any state or federal social welfare programs. The brute fact of the matter is that the primary contact between black American young adult men and their government is via the police and the penal apparatus. Coercion is the most salient feature of their encounters with the state. According to estimates compiled by sociologist Bruce Western, nearly 60% of black male dropouts born between 1965 and 1969 had spent at least one year in prison before reaching the age of 35.

> Statistics show the degree to which the problem applies to black men.

7   For these men, and the families and communities with which they are associated, the adverse effects of incarceration will extend beyond their stays behind bars. My point is that this is not merely law enforcement policy. It is social policy writ large. And no other country in the world does it quite like we do.

8   This is far more than a technical issue — entailing more, that is, than the task of finding the most efficient crime control policies. Consider, for instance, that it is not possible to conduct a cost-benefit analysis of our nation's world-historic prison buildup over the past 35 years without implicitly specifying how the costs imposed on the persons imprisoned, and their families, are to be reckoned. Of course, this has not stopped analysts from pronouncing on the purported net benefits to "society" of greater incarceration without addressing that question! Still, how — or, indeed, whether — to weigh the costs born by law-breakers — that is, how (or whether) to acknowledge their humanity — remains a fundamental and difficult question of social ethics. Political discourses in the United States have given insufficient weight to the collateral damage imposed by punishment policies on the offenders themselves, and on those who are knitted together with offenders in networks of social and psychic affiliation.

Loury asserts that imprisonment policies cause far greater costs than simply keeping criminals in jail.

9   Whether or not one agrees, two things should be clear: social scientists can have no answers for the question of what weight to put on a "thug's," or his family's, well-being; and a morally defensible public policy to deal with criminal offenders cannot be promulgated without addressing that question. To know whether or not our criminal justice policies comport with our deepest values, we must ask how much additional cost borne by the offending class is justifiable per marginal unit of security, or of peace of mind, for the rest of us. This question is barely being asked, let alone answered, in the contemporary debate.

10   Nor is it merely the scope of the mass imprisonment state that has expanded so impressively in the United States. The ideas underlying the doing of criminal justice — the superstructure of justifications and rationalizations — have also undergone a sea change. Rehabilitation is a dead letter; retribution is the thing. The function of imprisonment is not to reform or redirect offenders. Rather, it is to keep *them* away from *us*. "The prison," writes sociologist David Garland, "is used today as a kind of reservation, a quarantine zone in which purportedly dangerous individuals are segregated in the name of public safety." We have elaborated what are, in effect, a "string of work camps and prisons strung across a vast country housing millions of people drawn mainly from classes and racial groups that are seen as politically and economically problematic." We have, in other words, marched quite a long way down the punitive road, in the name of securing public safety and meting out to criminals their just deserts.

11   And we should be ashamed of ourselves for having done so. Consider a striking feature of this policy development, one that is

crucial to this moral assessment: the ways in which we now deal with criminal offenders in the United States have evolved in recent decades in order to serve expressive and not only instrumental ends. We have wanted to "send a message," and have done so with a vengeance. Yet in the process we have also, in effect, provided an answer for the question: who is to blame for the maladies that beset our troubled civilization? That is, we have constructed a narrative, created scapegoats, assuaged our fears, and indulged our need to feel virtuous about ourselves. We have met the enemy and the enemy, in the now familiar caricature, is *them* — a bunch of anomic, menacing, morally deviant "thugs." In the midst of this dramaturgy — unavoidably so in America — lurks a potent racial subplot.

Loury introduces a personal narrative argument to give a concrete example to the statistics he has provided.

12   This issue is personal for me. As a black American male, a baby-boomer born and raised on Chicago's South Side, I can identify with the plight of the urban poor because I have lived among them. I am related to them by the bonds of social and psychic affiliation. As it happens, I have myself passed through the courtroom, and the jailhouse, on my way along life's journey. I have sat in the visitor's room at a state prison; I have known, personally and intimately, men and women who lived their entire lives with one foot to either side of the law. Whenever I step to a lectern to speak about the growth of imprisonment in our society, I envision voiceless and despairing people who would have me speak on their behalf. Of course, personal biography can carry no authority to compel agreement about public policy. Still, I prefer candor to the false pretense of clinical detachment and scientific objectivity. I am not running for high office; I need not pretend to a cool neutrality that I do not possess. While I recognize that these revelations will discredit me in some quarters, this is a fate I can live with.

13   So, my racial identity is not irrelevant to my discussion of the subject at hand. But, then, neither is it irrelevant that among the millions now in custody and under state supervision are to be found a vastly disproportionate number of the black and the brown. There is no need to justify injecting race into this discourse, for prisons are the most race-conscious public institutions that we have. No big city police officer is "colorblind" nor, arguably, can any afford to be. Crime and punishment in America have a color — just turn on a television, or open a magazine, or listen carefully to the rhetoric of a political campaign — and you will see what I mean. The fact is that, in this society as in any other, order is maintained by the threat and the use of force. We enjoy our good lives because we are shielded by the forces of law and order upon which we rely to keep the unruly at bay. Yet, in this society to an extent unlike virtually any other, those bearing the

heavy burden of order-enforcement belong, in numbers far exceeding their presence in the population at large, to racially defined and historically marginalized groups. Why should this be so? And how can those charged with the supervision of our penal apparatus sleep well at night knowing that it is so?

14   This punitive turn in the nation's social policy is intimately connected, I would maintain, with public rhetoric about responsibility, dependency, social hygiene, and the reclamation of public order. And such rhetoric, in turn, can be fully grasped only when viewed against the backdrop of America's often ugly and violent racial history: There is a reason why our inclination toward forgiveness and the extension of a second chance to those who have violated our behavioral strictures is so stunted, and why our mainstream political discourses are so bereft of self-examination and searching social criticism. An historical resonance between the stigma of race and the stigma of prison has served to keep alive in our public culture the subordinating social meanings that have always been associated with blackness. Many historians and political scientists — though, of course, not all — agree that the shifting character of race relations over the course of the nineteenth and twentieth centuries helps to explain why the United States is exceptional among democratic industrial societies in the severity of its punitive policy and the paucity of its social-welfare institutions. Put directly and without benefit of euphemism, the racially disparate incidence of punishment in the United States is a morally troubling residual effect of the nation's history of enslavement, disenfranchisement, segregation, and discrimination. It is not merely the accidental accretion of neutral state action, applied to a racially divergent social flux. It is an abhorrent expression of who we Americans are as a people, even now, at the dawn of the twenty-first century.

In this paragraph, Loury makes a causal argument: the present situation is the result of a history of racism in the United States.

15   My recitation of the brutal facts about punishment in today's America may sound to some like a primal scream at this monstrous social machine that is grinding poor black communities to dust. And I confess that these facts do at times leave me inclined to cry out in despair. But my argument is intended to be moral, not existential, and its principal thesis is this: we law-abiding, middle-class Americans have made collective decisions on social and incarceration policy questions, and we benefit from those decisions. That is, we benefit from a system of suffering, rooted in state violence, meted out at our behest. Put differently our society — the society we together have made — first tolerates crime-promoting conditions in our sprawling urban ghettos, and then goes on to act out rituals of punishment against them as some awful form of human sacrifice.

After expressing anger Loury returns to a reasoned argument about public policy.

16   It is a central reality of our time that a wide racial gap has opened up in cognitive skills, the extent of law-abidingness, stabil-

ity of family relations, and attachment to the work force. This is the basis, many would hold, for the racial gap in imprisonment. Yet I maintain that this gap in human development is, as a historical matter, rooted in political, economic, social, and cultural factors peculiar to this society and reflective of its unlovely racial history. That is to say, *it is a societal, not communal or personal, achievement.* At the level of the individual case we must, of course, act as if this were not so. There could be no law, and so no civilization, absent the imputation to persons of responsibility for their wrongful acts. But the sum of a million cases, each one rightly judged fairly on its individual merits, may nevertheless constitute a great historic wrong. This is, in my view, now the case in regards to the race and social class disparities that characterize the very punitive policy that we have directed at lawbreakers. And yet, the state does not only deal with individual cases. It also makes policies in the aggregate, and the consequences of these policies are more or less knowable. It is in the making of such aggregate policy judgments that questions of social responsibility arise.

17   This situation raises a moral problem that we cannot avoid. We cannot pretend that there are more important problems in our society, or that this circumstance is the necessary solution to other, more pressing problems — unless we are also prepared to say that we have turned our backs on the ideal of equality for all citizens and abandoned the principles of justice. We ought to be asking ourselves two questions: Just what manner of people are we Americans? And in light of this, what are our obligations to our fellow citizens — even those who break our laws?

18   Without trying to make a full-fledged philosophical argument here, I nevertheless wish to gesture — in the spirit of the philosopher John Rawls — toward some answers to these questions. I will not set forth a policy manifesto at this time. What I aim to do is suggest, in a general way, how we ought to be thinking differently about this problem. Specifically, given our nation's history and political culture, I think that there are severe limits to the applicability in this circumstance of a pure ethic of personal responsibility, as the basis for distributing the negative good of punishment in contemporary America. I urge that we shift the boundary toward greater acknowledgment of social responsibility in our punishment policy discourse — even for wrongful acts freely chosen by individual persons. In suggesting this, I am not so much making a "root causes" argument — he did the crime, but only because he had no choice — as I am arguing that the society at large is implicated in his choices because we have acquiesced in structural arrangements which work to our benefit and his detriment, and yet which shape his consciousness and sense of identity in such a way that

Loury returns to the question that he set out in the opening paragraph: what is our collective vision of the ideal society?

the choices he makes. We condemn those choices, but they are nevertheless compelling to him. I am interested in the moral implications of what the sociologist Loïc Wacquant has called the "double-sided production of urban marginality." I approach this problem of moral judgment by emphasizing that closed and bounded social structures — like racially homogeneous urban ghettos — create contexts where "pathological" and "dysfunctional" cultural forms emerge, but these forms are not intrinsic to the people caught in these structures. Neither are they independent of the behavior of the people who stand outside of them.

19   Several years ago, I took time to read some of the nonfiction writings of the great nineteenth-century Russian novelist Leo Tolstoy. Toward the end of his life he had become an eccentric pacifist and radical Christian social critic. I was stunned at the force of his arguments. What struck me most was Tolstoy's provocative claim that the core of Christianity lies in Jesus' Sermon on the Mount: You see that fellow over there committing some terrible sin? Well, if you have ever lusted, or allowed jealousy, or envy or hatred to enter your own heart, then you are to be equally condemned! This, Tolstoy claims, is the central teaching of the Christian faith: we're all in the same fix.

Loury makes a surprising move by appealing to the teachings of Jesus.

20   Now, without invoking any religious authority, I nevertheless want to suggest that there is a grain of truth in this religious sentiment that is relevant to the problem at hand: That is, while the behavioral pathologies and cultural threats that we see in society — the moral erosions "out there" — the crime, drug addiction, sexually transmitted disease, idleness, violence and all manner of deviance — while these are worrisome, nevertheless, our moral crusade against these evils can take on a pathological dimension of its own. We can become self-righteous, legalistic, ungenerous, stiff-necked, and hypocritical. We can fail to see the beam in our own eye. We can neglect to raise questions of social justice. We can blind ourselves to the close relationship that actually exists between, on the one hand, behavioral pathology in the so-called urban underclass of our country and, on the other hand, society-wide factors — like our greed-driven economy, our worship of the self, our endemic culture of materialism, our vacuous political discourses, our declining civic engagement, and our aversion to sacrificing private gain on behalf of much needed social investments. We can fail to see, in other words, that the problems of the so-called underclass — to which we have reacted with a massive, coercive mobilization — are but an expression, at the bottom of the social hierarchy, of a more profound and widespread moral deviance — one involving all of us.

21   Taking this position does not make me a moral relativist. I merely hold that, when thinking about the lives of the disadvantaged in our society, the fundamental premise that should guide us is that we are all in this together. *Those* people languishing in the corners of our society are *our* people — they are *us* – whatever may be their race, creed, or country of origin, whether they be the crack-addicted, the HIV-infected, the mentally ill homeless, the juvenile drug sellers, or worse. Whatever the malady, and whatever the offense, we're all in the same fix. We're all in this thing together.

22   Just look at what we have wrought. We Americans have established what, to many an outside observer, looks like a system of racial caste in the center of our great cities. I refer here to millions of stigmatized, feared, and invisible people. The extent of disparity in the opportunity to achieve their full human potential, as between the children of the middle class and the children of the disadvantaged — a disparity that one takes for granted in America — is virtually unrivaled elsewhere in the industrial, advanced, civilized, free world.

23   Yet too many Americans have concluded, in effect, that those languishing at the margins of our society are simply reaping what they have sown. Their suffering is seen as having nothing to do with us — as not being evidence of systemic failures that can be corrected through collective action. Thus, as I noted, we have given up on the ideal of rehabilitating criminals, and have settled for simply warehousing them. Thus we accept — despite much rhetoric to the contrary — that it is virtually impossible effectively to educate the children of the poor. Despite the best efforts of good people and progressive institutions — despite the encouraging signs of moral engagement with these issues that I have seen in my students over the years, and that give me hope — despite these things, it remains the case that, speaking of the country as a whole, there is no broadly based demand for reform, no sense of moral outrage, no anguished self-criticism, no public reflection in the face of this massive, collective failure.

The main work of the essay is getting readers to acknowledge the problem. If the problem is recognized, then various solutions will follow.

24   The core of the problem is that the socially marginal are not seen as belonging to the same general public body as the rest of us. It therefore becomes impossible to do just about anything with them. At least implicitly, our political community acts as though some are different from the rest and, because of their culture — because of their bad values, their self-destructive behavior, their malfeasance, their criminality, their lack of responsibility, their unwillingness to engage in hard work — they *deserve* their fate.

25   But this is quite wrongheaded. What we Americans fail to recognize — not merely as individuals, I stress, but as a political

community — is that these ghetto enclaves and marginal spaces of our cities, which are the source of most prison inmates, are products of our own making: Precisely because we do not want those people near us, we have structured the space in our urban environment so as to keep *them* away from *us*. Then, when they fester in their isolation and their marginality, we hypocritically point a finger, saying in effect: "Look at those people. They threaten to the civilized body. They must therefore be expelled, imprisoned, controlled." It is not *we* who must take social responsibility to reform our institutions but, rather, it is *they* who need to take personal responsibility for their wrongful acts. It is not we who must set our *collective* affairs aright, but they who must get their *individual* acts together. This posture, I suggest, is inconsistent with the attainment of a just distribution of benefits and burdens in society.

26   Civic inclusion has been the historical imperative in Western political life for 150 years. And yet — despite our self-declared status as a light unto the nations, as a beacon of hope to freedom-loving peoples everywhere — despite these lofty proclamations, which were belied by images from the rooftops in flooded New Orleans in September 2005, and are contradicted by our overcrowded prisons — the fact is that this historical project of civic inclusion is woefully incomplete in these United States.

27   At every step of the way, reactionary political forces have declared the futility of pursuing civic inclusion. Yet, in every instance, these forces have been proven wrong. At one time or another, they have derided the inclusion of women, landless peasants, former serfs and slaves, or immigrants more fully in the civic body. Extending to them the franchise, educating their children, providing health and social welfare to them has always been controversial. But this has been the direction in which the self-declared "civilized" and wealthy nations have been steadily moving since Bismarck, since the revolutions of 1848 and 1870, since the American Civil War with its Reconstruction Amendments, since the Progressive Era and through the New Deal on to the Great Society. This is why we have a progressive federal income tax and an estate tax in this country, why we feed, clothe and house the needy, why we (used to) worry about investing in our cities' infrastructure, and in the human capital of our people. What the brutal facts about punishment in today's America show is that *this American project of civic inclusion remains incomplete*. Nowhere is that incompleteness more evident than in the prisons and jails of America. And this as yet unfulfilled promise of American democracy reveals a yawning chasm between an ugly and uniquely American reality, and our nation's exalted image of herself.

Loury proposes that if Americans would embrace the ideals of the United States, the conditions that lead to massive-scale imprisonment would change.

Sample Student Proposal Argument

Lee 1

Kim Lee

Professor Patel

RHE 306

31 March 2009

Let's Make It a Real Melting Pot with Presidential Hopes for All

The image the United States likes to advertise is a country that embraces diversity and creates a land of equal opportunity for all. As the Statue of Liberty cries out, "give me your tired, your poor, your huddled masses yearning to breathe free," American politicians gleefully evoke such images to frame the United States as a bastion for all things good, fair, and equal. As a proud American, however, I must nonetheless highlight one of the cracks in this façade of equality. Imagine that an infertile couple decides to adopt an orphaned child from China. They follow all of the legal processes deemed necessary by both countries. They fly abroad and bring home their (once parentless) six-month-old baby boy. They raise and nurture him, and while teaching him to embrace his ethnicity, they also teach him to love Captain Crunch, baseball, and *The Three Stooges*. He grows and eventually attends an ethnically diverse American public school. One day his fifth-grade teacher tells the class that anyone can grow up to be president. To clarify her point, she turns to the boy, knowing his background, and states, "No, you could not be president, Stu, but you could still be a senator. That's something to aspire to!" How do Stu's parents explain this rule to this American-raised child? This scenario will become increasingly common, yet as the Constitution currently reads, only "natural-born" citizens may run for the offices of president and vice president. Neither these children nor the thousands of hardworking Americans who chose to make America their official homeland may aspire to the highest political position in the land. While the huddled masses may enter, it appears they must retain a second-class citizen ranking.

The "natural-born" stipulation regarding the presidency stems from the self-same meeting of minds that brought the American people the Electoral College. During the Constitutional Convention of 1787, the

> Lee sets out the problem with a concrete scenario.

Lee 2

Congress formulated the regulatory measures associated with the office of the president. A letter sent from John Jay to George Washington during this period reads as follows:

> "Permit me to hint," Jay wrote, "whether it would not be wise and seasonable to provide a strong check to the admission of foreigners into the administration of our national government; and to declare expressly that the Commander in Chief of the American army shall not be given to, nor devolve on, any but a natural-born citizen." (Mathews A1)

Shortly thereafter, Article II, Section I, Clause V, of the Constitution declared that "No Person except a natural born Citizen, or a Citizen of the United States at the time of the Adoption of this Constitution, shall be eligible to the Office of President." Jill A. Pryor states in the *Yale Law Journal* that "some writers have suggested that Jay was responding to rumors that foreign princes might be asked to assume the presidency" (881). Many cite disastrous examples of foreign rule in the eighteenth century as the impetus for the "natural-born" clause. For example, in 1772—only fifteen years prior to the adoption of the statute—Poland had been divided up by Prussia, Russia, and Austria (Kasindorf). Perhaps an element of self-preservation and not ethnocentrism led to the questionable stipulation. Nonetheless, in the twenty-first century this clause reeks of xenophobia.

> Lee gives the historical background of the "natural-born" restriction.

The Fourteenth Amendment clarified the difference between "natural-born" and "native-born" citizens by spelling out the citizenship status of children born to American parents outside of the United States (Ginsberg 929). This clause qualifies individuals such as Senator John McCain—born in Panama—for presidency. This change, however, is not adequate. I propose that the United States abolish the natural-born clause and replace it with a stipulation that allows naturalized citizens to run for president. This amendment would state that a candidate must have been naturalized and must have lived in residence in the United States for a period of at least twenty-five years. The present time is ideal for this change. This amendment could simultaneously honor the spirit of the Constitution, protect and ensure the interests of the United States, promote an international image of

> Lee states her proposal in this paragraph.

Lee 3

inclusiveness, and grant heretofore-withheld rights to thousands of legal and loyal United States citizens.

In our push for change, we must make clear the importance of this amendment. It would not provide special rights for would-be terrorists. To the contrary, it would fulfill the longtime promises of the nation. The United States claims to allow all people to blend into the great stew of citizenship. It has already suffered embarrassment and international cries of ethnic bias as a result of political moves such as Japanese American internment and the Guantanamo Bay detention center. This amendment can help mend the national image as every American takes one more step toward equality. Naturalized citizens have been contributing to the United States for centuries. Many nameless Mexican, Irish, and Asian Americans sweated and toiled to build the American railroads. The public has welcomed naturalized Americans such as Bob Hope, Albert Pujols, and Peter Jennings into their hearts and living rooms. Individuals such as German-born Henry Kissinger and Czechoslovakian-born Madeleine Albright have held high posts in the American government and have served as respected aides to its presidents. The amendment must make clear that it is not about one man's celebrity. Approximately seven hundred foreign-born Americans have won the Medal of Honor and over sixty thousand proudly serve in the United States military today (Siskind 5). The "natural-born" clause must be removed to provide each of these people—over half a million naturalized in 2003 alone—with equal footing to those who were born into citizenship rather than working for it (United States).

Since the passing of the Bill of Rights, only seventeen amendments have been ratified. This process takes time and overwhelming congressional and statewide support. To alter the Constitution, a proposed amendment must pass with a two-thirds "super-majority" in both the House of Representatives and the Senate. In addition, the proposal must find favor in two-thirds (38) of state legislatures. In short, this task will not be easy. In order for this change to occur, a grassroots campaign must work to dispel misinformation regarding naturalized citizens and to force the hands of senators and representatives wishing to retain their congressional seats. We must take this proposal to ethnicity-specific political

> Lee gives examples of people who are qualified to become president yet are ineligible.

> Lee explains the process of amending the Constitution and ends with a call for action.

Lee 4

groups from both sides of the aisle, business organizations, and community activist groups. We must convince representatives that this issue matters. Only through raising voices and casting votes can the people enact change. Only then can every American child see the possibility for limitless achievement and equality. Only then can everyone find the same sense of pride in the possibility for true American diversity in the highest office in the land.

Lee 5

Works Cited

Ginsberg, Gordon. "Citizenship: Expatriation: Distinction between Naturalized and Natural Born Citizens." *Michigan Law Review* 50 (1952): 926–29. *JSTOR*. Web. 6 Mar. 2009.

Kasindorf, Martin. "Should the Constitution Be Amended for Arnold?" *USA Today* 2 Dec. 2004. *LexisNexis Academic*. Web. 8 Mar. 2009.

Mathews, Joe. "Maybe Anyone Can Be President." *Los Angeles Times* 2 Feb. 2005: A1. *LexisNexis Academic*. Web. 6 Mar. 2009.

Pryor, Jill A. "The Natural Born Citizen Clause and Presidential Eligibility: An Approach for Resolving Two Hundred Years of Uncertainty." *Yale Law Journal* 97.5 (1988): 881–99. Print.

Siskind, Lawrence J. "Why Shouldn't Arnold Run?" *Recorder* 10 Dec. 2004: 5. *LexisNexis Academic*. Web. 10 Mar. 2009.

United States. Dept. of Commerce. Census Bureau. "The Fourth of July 2005." *Facts for Features*. US Dept. of Commerce, 27 June 2005. Web. 17 Mar. 2009.

PEARSON
mycomplab

Designing and Presenting Arguments

PART

4

14 | Designing Multimedia Arguments

QUICK TAKE

In this chapter, you will learn that

1. The choice of media is critical for persuading particular audiences (see below)
2. Images and graphics, when used purposefully, can be used as evidence to support your argument (see page 208)
3. Printed documents need to be carefully designed to engage and persuade your audience (see page 209)
4. Multimedia arguments can be designed and delivered to meet the needs of college audiences (see page 210)

Arguments do not communicate with words alone. Even written arguments that do not contain graphics or images have a look and feel that also communicate meaning. Many arguments depend on presenting information visually, in multimedia, or in images, in addition to using written language. Using effective design strategies will make your arguments more engaging and compelling.

Think About Which Media Will Reach Your Audience

Before you graduate from college, likely you will find occasions when you want to persuade an audience beyond your teacher, classmates, and friends—possibly for your work, possibly for an organization you belong to, or possibly because an issue concerns you. You may have a clear sense of your message and the good reasons to support that message. But no matter how good your argument, nothing will happen unless you can command the scarcest commodity in our multitasking world—the attention of your audience.

Most college assignments specify the medium, which is typically a printed paper that you submit to the instructor. In the workplace and in life outside college, the choice of medium often isn't immediately evident. For example, if you want to address a neighborhood issue, would a brochure or a Web site be more effective?

Think about your options.

PRINTED TEXT

- Advantages: Low technological requirements to produce; complex, in-depth arguments are possible.
- Disadvantages: Unless published in an established forum like a newspaper, it can be difficult to get people to read the argument.

WEB SITE

- Advantages: Inexpensive to create and allows images, video, audio, and animations to be embedded.
- Disadvantages: How do people find your Web site among the millions of other sites?

BLOG

- Advantages: Inexpensive to create and many sites host blogs.
- Disadvantages: Requires frequent, interesting content to keep readers coming back.

AUDIO PODCAST

- Advantages: Inexpensive to create and can be downloaded from a Web site.
- Disadvantages: Requires some audio editing skills. Like other Web-based media, you have to have a strategy for getting people to listen.

VIDEO

- Advantages: Can be uploaded to sites like YouTube and Vimeo.
- Disadvantages: Producing quality original video takes time, equipment, and editing skills.

Know When to Use Visual Evidence

Personal computers, digital cameras, scanners, printers, and the Web have made it easy to include images and graphics in writing and link to audio and video. But these technologies don't tell you if, when, or how images and graphics should be used.

Think about what an image or graphic communicates

- **What are your readers' expectations for the medium you are using?** Most essays don't include images; most Web sites and brochures do.

- **What is the purpose for an image or graphic?** Does it illustrate a concept? Does it highlight an important point? Does it show something that is hard to explain with words alone? If you don't know the purpose, you may not need the image.

- **Where should an image or graphic be placed in your text?** Images should be as close as possible to the relevant point in your text.

- **What will readers focus on when they see the image?** Will they focus on the part that matters? If not, you may need to crop the image.

- **What explanation do readers need in order to understand the image?** Provide informative captions for the images and graphics you use, and refer to them in your text.

Think About the Argument an Image Makes

Images don't speak for themselves, but if they are referenced in your text and captioned, they can make supporting arguments. Think strategically when you include arguments.

Say, for example, you are making a proposal argument for more students to become more involved in feeding homeless people in your city. Students are aware that there are homeless people, but many students are not aware of organizations that deliver food to hungry people. You might want to photograph the volunteers instead of homeless people.

Volunteers work to make sandwiches that will be distributed by a food truck to homeless people.

Think about the argument a chart or graph makes

Charts and graphs are useful for visually representing statistical trends and for making comparisons. For example, the rising national debt became a hotly debated issue during the administrations of George H. W. Bush and Barack Obama. Many graphs were used in the debate to show the dramatic rise of federal debt. But if you want to make a causal argument that lowering the income tax rate for the rich contributed to the rise in the debt, you might use a line graph.

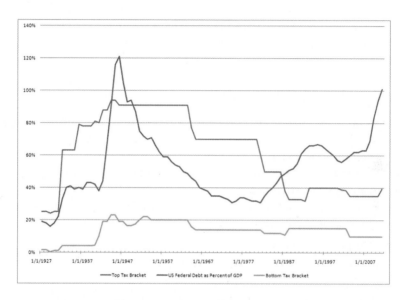

Line graph comparing the national debt with the highest and lowest income tax rates.

Design Arguments for Print

Writing on a computer gives you a range of options for designing a page that is appropriate to your assignment. Thinking about design will lead to a more effective presentation of your argument.

- **Choose the orientation, size of your page, and number of columns.** You can usually use the defaults on your computer for academic essays (remember to select double-spacing for line spacing if the default is single-spaced). For other kinds of texts you may want a horizontal rather than a vertical orientation, a size other than a standard sheet of paper, and two or more columns rather than one.

- **Divide your text into units.** The paragraph is the basic unit of extended writing, but also think about when to use lists. This list is a bulleted list. You can also use a numbered list.

- **Use left-aligned text with a ragged-right margin.** Fully justified text aligns the right margin, which gives a more formal look but can also leave unsightly rivers of extra white space running through the middle of your text. Ragged-right text is easier to read.

■ **Be conscious of white space.** White space can make your text more readable and set off more important elements. Headings stand out more with white space surrounding them. Leave room around graphics. Don't crowd words too close to graphics because both the words and the visuals will become hard to read.

■ **Be aware of MLA and APA design specifications.** MLA and APA styles have specifications for margins, indentions, reference lists, and other aspects of paper formatting. See the sample paper on pages 276–282 for guidelines on designing a paper using MLA style.

Design Multimedia Arguments

Digital technologies now make it possible to create multimedia projects on your home computer that formerly required entire production staffs. You can publish multimedia projects on the Internet (either as Web sites or as downloadable files), as stand-alone media distributed on CDs and DVDs, or in print with posters, brochures, and essays with images.

College viewers and listeners have the expectations of multimedia projects that they do of essays and research papers. They expect

■ your project to be well organized and free of errors,

■ your claims to be supported with evidence,

■ your analysis to be insightful,

■ your sources to be documented, and

■ your work clearly distinguished from the work of others.

Creating multimedia projects

If you decide to create a multimedia project, find out what resources are available for students on your campus. Many colleges and universities have digital media labs, which offer workshops and can provide video and audio studios, technical assistance, equipment, and software. Look for links to digital media services on your college's Web site.

Oral presentation with visuals **(see Chapter 15)**

Essay with images

■ **Example project**: Evaluation argument concerning the poor condition of parks in your city

■ Plan: Visit several parks, make notes, and take photographs.

■ Produce: Write the project. Edit your images with an image editor and insert them in your project with captions.

■ Edit: Revise with the comments of classmates and your instructor.

Web site production

- **Example project:** Web site making a definition argument that censorship of the Internet is a violation of the right to free speech
- Plan: Collect all the materials you will need for your site including text; digital images; graphics; and audio, video, and animation files.
- Produce: If you don't have a Web editor on your computer, find a campus lab that has Dreamweaver or similar software. Upload your site to a server. Many colleges offer server space to host student Web sites.
- Edit: Test your site to ensure that all links are working and all images and other files are showing up correctly. Edit with a Web editor.

Audio production

- **Example project:** Oral history of neighborhood residents making a causal argument about why a neighborhood declined after a freeway was built through the middle of it
- Plan: Arrange and record interviews and write a script.
- Produce: Reserve a campus audio production lab or record on your computer. Create an audio file by combining the interviews with your narration.
- Edit: Edit with an audio editor. Export the video into a format such as WAV or MP3 that you can put on the Web or share as a downloadable file.

Video production

- **Example project:** Proposal to create bike lanes on a busy street near your campus
- Plan: Identify locations, get permission to film if necessary, and write a script.
- Produce: Shoot video of the street with cars and bikes competing. Interview cyclists, drivers, and local business owners about their sense of urgency of the problem and the effects of creating bike lanes.
- Edit: Edit with a video editor. Export the video into a format such as QuickTime that you can put on the Web or share as a downloadable file.

15 | Presenting Arguments

QUICK TAKE

In this chapter, you will learn that

1. Planning an effective presentation requires putting the audience first (see below)
2. Simple slides with visual impact work best (see page 214)
3. Delivering an effective presentation is all about you (see page 216)
4. When converting a written text into a presentation, avoid the temptation to dump sentences and paragraphs onto the slides (see page 217)

Plan a Presentation

If you are assigned to give a presentation, look carefully at the assignment for guidance on finding a topic. The process for finding a topic is similar to a written assignment (see Chapter 3). If your assignment requires research, you will need to document the sources of information just as you do for a research paper (see Chapters 16–19).

Start with your goal in mind

What is the real purpose of your presentation? Are you informing, persuading, or motivating? Take the elevator test. Imagine you are in an elevator with the key people who can approve or reject your ideas. Their schedule is very tight. You have only thirty seconds to convince them. Can you make your case?

This scenario is not far-fetched. One executive demanded that every new idea had to be written in one sentence on the back of a business card. What's your sentence?

It's all about your audience

Who is your audience? In college your audience is often your instructor and fellow students—an audience you know well. Many times you will not have this advantage.

Take a few minutes to answer these questions.

- Will my audience be interested in the topic?
- Why does it matter to them?
- What are they likely to know and believe about the topic?
- What are they likely to not know?
- Where are they likely to disagree?
- What do I want them to do?
- How much time do I have?
- If they remember only one thing, what should it be?

Get organized

Start with pen and paper before you begin creating slides. Post-it notes are another useful planning tool.

- **Make a list of key points.** Think about the best order for your major points.
- **Plan your introduction.** Your success depends on your introduction. You must gain the attention of your audience, introduce your topic, indicate why it's important, and give a sense of where you are headed. It's a tall order, but if you don't engage your audience in the first two minutes, you will lose them.
- **Plan your conclusion.** You want to end on a strong note. Stopping abruptly or rambling on only to tail off leaves your audience with a bad impression. Give your audience something to take away, a compelling example or an idea that captures the gist of your presentation.

Build content

Content alone does not make a presentation successful, but you cannot succeed without solid content. Support your major points with relevant evidence.

- **Facts.** Speakers who know their facts build credibility.
- **Statistics.** Effective use of statistics can give the audience the impression that you have done your homework. Statistics can also indicate that a particular example is representative.
- **Statements by authorities.** Quotations from credible experts can support key points.
- **Narratives.** Narratives are brief stories that illustrate key points. Narratives can hold the attention of the audience—but keep them short or they will become a distraction.

Design Visuals for a Presentation

Less is more with slides. One text-filled slide after another is mind-numbingly dull. Presentations using slides don't have to be this bad.

Keep it simple

Imagine you are making an argument that fewer animals would be euthanized at animal shelters if more people in your city knew that they could save a pet's life by adopting it. You could fill your slides with statistics alone. Or you tell your audience the facts while showing them slides that give emotional impact to your numbers.

Simple design rules! Keep in mind these principles.

- One point per slide
- Very few fonts
- Quality photos, not clipart
- Less text, more images
- Easy on the special effects

Compare the following examples.

Pet Overpopulation in the United States

- **Estimated number of animals that enter shelters each year: 6-8 million**
- **Estimated number of animals euthanized at shelters each year: 3-4 million**
- **Estimated number of animals adopted at shelters each year: 3-4 million**

Source: "HSUS Pet Overpopulation Estimates." *Humane Society of the U.S.* Humane Society of the U.S.,
9 Nov. 2009. 18 Oct. 2010.

Pet Overpopulation in the United States

- Estimated number of animals entering shelters each year: 6-8 million
- Estimated number of animals euthanized at shelters each year: 3-4 million
- Estimated number of animals adopted at shelters: 3-4 million

Source: "HSUS Pet Overpopulation Estimates." *Humane Society of the U.S.* Humane Society of the U.S., 9 Nov. 2009. Web. 18 Oct. 2010.

Save a pet

Which slide makes the point most effectively?

But what if you have a lot of data to show? Make a handout that the audience can study later. They can make notes on your handout, which gives them a personal investment. Keep your slides simple and emphasize the main points in the presentation.

Use audio and video clips strategically

Short audio and video clips can offer concrete examples and add some variety to your presentation. An audience appreciates hearing and even seeing the people you interview. PowerPoint makes it simple to embed the files within a presentation. Be careful, however, in using the built-in sound effects in PowerPoint such as canned applause. Most sound effects are annoying and make you come off as inexperienced.

Deliver an Effective Presentation

If you are not passionate about your subject, you will never get your audience committed to your subject, no matter how good your slides. Believe in what you say; enthusiasm is contagious.

It's all about you

The audience didn't come to see the back of your head in front of slides. Move away from the podium and connect with them. Make strong eye contact with individuals. You will make everyone feel like you were having a conversation instead of giving a speech.

Prepare in advance

Practice your presentation, even if you have to speak to an empty chair. Check out the room and equipment in advance. If you are using your laptop with a projector installed in the room, make sure it connects. If the room has a computer connected to the projector, bring your presentation on a flash drive and download it to the computer. PowerPoint works much the same on a Mac or Windows platform.

Be professional

Pay attention to the little things.

- **Proofread carefully.** A glaring spelling error can destroy your credibility.
- **Be consistent.** If you randomly capitalize words or insert punctuation, your audience will be distracted.

■ **Pay attention to the timing of your slides.** Stay in sync with your slides. Don't leave a slide up when you are talking about something else.

■ **Use the "B" key.** If you get sidetracked, press the "B" key, which makes the screen go blank so the audience can focus on you. When you are ready to resume, press the "B" key again and the slide reappears.

■ **Involve your audience.** Invite response during your presentation where appropriate, and leave time for questions at the end.

■ **Add a bit of humor.** Humor can be tricky, especially if you don't know your audience well. But if you can get your audience to laugh, they will be on your side.

■ **Slow down.** When you are nervous, you tend to go too fast. Stop and breathe. Let your audience take in what's on your slides.

■ **Finish on time or earlier.** Your audience will be grateful.

■ **Be courteous and gracious.** Remember to thank anyone who helped you and the audience for their comments. Eventually you will run into someone who challenges you, sometimes politely, sometimes not. If you remain cool and in control, the audience will remember your behavior long after the words are forgotten.

Convert a Written Text into a Presentation

The temptation when converting a written text into a presentation is to dump sentences and paragraphs onto the slides. Indeed, it's simple enough to cut and paste big chunks of text, but you risk losing your audience.

Make a list of the main points in your written text, and then decide which ones you need to show on slides and which you can tell the audience. Your voice supplies most of the information; your slides help your audience to remember and organize your presentation.

People learn better when your oral presentation is accompanied by engaging images and graphics. Slides can also add emotional involvement.

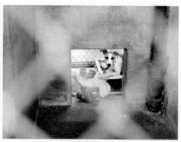

Unwanted dogs

Carlos

a playful mixed-
breed pup who was
recently adopted

Arrange your slides so they tell a story. For example, if you are arguing that fewer dogs would be euthanized if your city were more active in promoting adoption, you can show slides that give statistics, or you can report statistics in your presentation while letting your audience identify with individual dogs.

For support in learning this chapter's content, follow this path in MyCompLab:
> Resources > Writing > Writing Samples: Technical and Workplace Writing
> Writing Samples: Presentation. Review the Instruction and Multimedia resources, then complete the Exercises and click on Gradebook to measure your progress.

Researching Arguments

PART

5

16 | Planning Research

QUICK TAKE

In this chapter, you will learn that

1. Analyzing the assignment is the first step in completing a research project (see below)
2. The next step is finding a topic and asking a research question (see page 221)
3. For local and campus issues, you may need to conduct field research, including interviews, surveys, and observations (see page 222)
4. Your preliminary research should lead to a working thesis, which will guide you through further research and the development of your argument (see page 225)

Analyze the Research Task

Research is a creative process, which is another way of saying it is a messy process. Even though the process is complex, your results will improve if you keep the big picture in mind while you are immersed in research. If you have an assignment that requires research, look closely at what you are being asked to do.

Look for key words

Often the assignment will tell you what is expected.

- An assignment that asks you, for example, how the usual *definition* of intellectual property applies to YouTube invites you to write a definition argument (see Chapter 8).
- An *analysis of causes* requires you to write a causal argument (see Chapter 9).
- An *evaluation* requires you to make critical judgments based on criteria (see Chapter 10).
- A *proposal* requires you to assemble evidence in support of a solution to a problem or a call for the audience to do something (see Chapter 13).

Identify your potential readers

- How familiar are your readers with your subject?
- What background information will you need to supply?
- If your subject is controversial, what opinions or beliefs are your readers likely to hold?
- If some readers are likely to disagree with you, how can you convince them?

Assess the project's length, scope, and requirements

- What kind of research are you being asked to do?
- What is the length of the project?
- What kinds and number of sources or field research are required?
- Which documentation style is required such as MLA (see Chapter 20) or APA (see Chapter 21)?

Set a schedule

- Note the due dates on the assignment for drafts and final versions.
- Set dates for yourself on finding and evaluating sources, drafting your thesis, creating a working bibliography, and writing a first draft.
- Give yourself enough time to do a thorough job.

Find a Subject

One good way to begin is by browsing, which may also show you the breadth of possibilities included in a topic and possibly lead you to new topics (see Chapter 3).

You might begin browsing by doing one or more of the following.

- **Visit "Research by Subject" on your library's Web site.** Clicking on a subject such as "African and African American Studies" will take you to a list of online resources. Often you can find an e-mail link to a reference librarian who can assist you.
- **Look for topics in your courses.** Browse your course notes and readings. Are there any topics you might want to explore in greater depth?
- **Browse a Web subject directory.** Web subject directories, including Yahoo Directory (dir.yahoo.com), are useful when you want to narrow a topic or learn what subcategories a topic might contain. In addition to

the Web subject directories, your library's Web site may have a link to the *Opposing Viewpoints* database.

■ **Look for topics as you read.** When you read actively, you ask questions and respond to ideas in the text. Review what you wrote in the margins or the notes you have made about something you read that interested you. You may find a potential topic.

Ask a Research Question

Often you'll be surprised by the amount of information your initial browsing uncovers. Your next task will be to identify a question for your research project within that mass of information. This **researchable question** will be the focus of the remainder of your research and ultimately of your research project or paper. Browsing on the subject of organic foods, for example, might lead you to one of the following researchable questions.

■ How do farmers benefit from growing organic produce?
■ Why are organic products more expensive than nonorganic products?
■ Are Americans being persuaded to buy more organic products?

Once you have formulated a research question, you should begin thinking about what kind of research you will need to do to address the question.

Gather Information About the Subject

Most researchers rely partly or exclusively on the work of others as sources of information. Research based on the work of others is called **secondary research**. In the past this information was contained almost exclusively in collections of print materials housed in libraries, but today enormous amounts of information are available through library databases and on the Web (see Chapter 17).

Much of the research done at a university creates new information through **primary research**—experiments, examination of historical documents—and **field research**, including data-gathering surveys, interviews, and detailed observations, described below.

Conducting field research

Sometimes you may be researching a question that requires you to gather firsthand information with field research. For example, if you are researching a campus issue such as the impact of a new technology fee on students' budgets, you may need to conduct interviews, make observations, and give a survey.

Interviews

College campuses are a rich source of experts in many areas, including people on the faculty and in the surrounding community. Interviewing experts on your research subject can help build your knowledge base. You can use interviews to discover what the people most affected by a particular issue are thinking, such as why students object to some fees and not others.

Arrange interviews

Before you contact anyone, think carefully about your goals. Knowing what you want to find out through your interviews will help you determine whom you need to interview and what questions you need to ask. Use these guidelines to prepare for an interview.

- Decide what you want or need to know and who best can provide that for you.
- Schedule each interview in advance, and let the person know why you are conducting the interview. Estimate how long your interview will take, and tell your subject how much of her or his time you will need.
- Choose a location that is convenient for your subject but not too chaotic or loud. An office or study room is better than a noisy cafeteria.
- Plan your questions in advance. Write down a few questions and have a few more in mind.
- If you want to record the interview, ask for permission in advance. A recording device sometimes can intimidate the person you are interviewing.

Conduct interviews

- Come prepared with your questions, a notebook, and a pen or pencil.
- If you plan to record the interview (with your subject's permission), make sure whatever recording device you use has an adequate power supply and will not run out of tape, disc space, or memory.
- Listen carefully so you can follow up on key points. Make notes when important questions are raised or answered, but don't attempt to transcribe every word the person is saying.
- When you are finished, thank your subject, and ask his or her permission to get in touch again if you have additional questions.

Surveys

Extensive surveys that can be projected to large populations, like the ones used in political polls, require the effort of many people. Small surveys, however, often can provide insight on local issues, such as what percentage of students might be affected if library hours were reduced.

Plan surveys

What information do you need for your research question? Decide what exactly you want to know and design a survey that will provide that information. Likely you will want both close-ended questions (multiple choice, yes or no, rating scale) and open-ended questions that allow detailed responses. To create a survey, follow these guidelines.

- Write a few specific, unambiguous questions. People will fill out your survey quickly, and if the questions are confusing, the results will be meaningless.
- Include one or two open-ended questions, such as "What do you like about X?" or "What don't you like about X?" Open-ended questions can be difficult to interpret, but sometimes they turn up information you had not anticipated.
- Test the questions on a few people before you conduct the survey.
- Think about how you will interpret your survey. Multiple-choice formats make data easy to tabulate, but often they miss key information. Open-ended questions will require you to figure out a way to sort responses into categories.

Administer surveys

- Decide on who you need to survey and how many respondents your survey will require. For example, if you want to claim that the results of your survey represent the views of residents of your dormitory, your method of selecting respondents should give all residents an equal chance to be selected. Don't select only your friends.
- Decide how you will contact participants in your survey. If you are conducting your survey on private property, you will need permission from the property owner. Likewise, e-mail lists and lists of mailing addresses are usually guarded closely to preserve privacy. You will need to secure permission from the appropriate parties if you want to contact people via an e-mail list.
- If you mail or e-mail your survey, include a statement about what the survey is for.

Observations

Observing can be a valuable source of data. For example, if you are researching why a particular office on your campus does not operate efficiently, observe what happens when students enter and how the staff responds to their presence.

Make observations

- Choose a place where you can observe with the least intrusion. The less people wonder about what you are doing, the better.
- Carry a notebook and write extensive field notes. Record as much information as you can, and worry about analyzing it later.
- Record the date, exactly where you were, exactly when you arrived and left, and important details like the number of people present.
- Write on one side of your notebook so you can use the facing page to note key observations and analyze your data later.

Analyze observations

You must interpret your observations so they make sense in the context of your argument. Ask yourself the following questions.

- What patterns of behavior did you observe?
- How was the situation you observed unique? How might it be similar to other locations?
- What constituted "normal" activity during the time when you were observing? Did anything out of the ordinary happen?
- Why were the people there? What can you determine about the purposes of the activities you observed?

Draft a Working Thesis

Once you have done some preliminary research into your question, you can begin to craft a working thesis. Let's take one topic as an example—the increasing popularity of organic products, including meat, dairy products, and produce. If you research this topic, you will discover that due to this trend, large corporations such as Walmart are beginning to offer organic products in their stores. However, the enormous demand for organic products is endangering smaller organic farmers and producers. As you research the question of why small farmers and producers in the United States are endangered and what small farmers and producers in other countries have done to protect themselves, a working thesis begins to emerge.

Write your subject, research question, and working thesis on a note card or sheet of paper. Keep your working thesis handy. You may need to revise it several times until the wording is precise. As you research, ask yourself, does this information tend to support my thesis? Information that does not support your thesis is still important! It may lead you to adjust your thesis or even to abandon it altogether. You may need to find another source or reason that shows your thesis is still valid.

Example

SUBJECT: Increased demand for organic products endangering smaller farmers and producers

RESEARCH QUESTION: How can smaller organic farms and producers protect themselves from becoming extinct?

WORKING THESIS: In order to meet the increasing demand for organic products that has been created by larger corporations such as Walmart, smaller organic farmers and producers should form regional co-ops. These co-ops will work together to supply regional chains, much as co-ops of small farmers and dairies in Europe work together, thereby cutting transportation and labor costs and ensuring their survival in a much-expanded market.

For support in learning this chapter's content, follow this path in MyCompLab: > Resources > Research > The Research Assignment > Understanding a Research Assignment. Review the Instruction and Multimedia resources, then complete the Exercises and click on Gradebook to measure your progress.

17 | Finding Sources

QUICK TAKE

In this chapter, you will learn that

1. Developing a search strategy at the beginning will get you to quality sources faster (see below)

2. Using your working thesis to generate a list of keywords will enable you to search library databases, the Web, and print sources in your library (see page below)

3. Library sources, including databases, online references, and printed books and journals offer the highest quality because they have been screened by reference librarians (see page 228 and page 236)

4. Valuable sources are also on the Web, but you have to know how and where to find them (see page 231)

Develop Strategies for Finding Sources

The distinction between doing research online and in the library is blurring as more and more libraries make their collections accessible on the Web. Nevertheless, libraries still contain many resources not available on the Web. Even more important, libraries have professional research librarians who can help you locate sources quickly.

Determine where to start looking

Searches using *Google* or *Yahoo!* turn up thousands of items, many of which are often not useful for research. Considering where to start is the first step.

Scholarly books and articles in scholarly journals often are the highest-quality sources, but the lag in publication time makes them less useful for very current topics. Newspapers cover current issues, but often not in the depth of books and scholarly journals. Government Web sites and publications are often the best for finding statistics and are also valuable for researching science and medicine.

Learn the art of effective keyword searches

Keyword searches take you to the sources you need. Start with your working thesis and generate a list of possible keywords for researching your thesis.

First, think of keywords that make your search more specific. For example, a search for sources related to Internet privacy issues might focus more specifically on privacy *and*

Internet
cookies
Web profiling
Flash
spyware

You should also think about more general ways to describe what you are doing—what synonyms can you think of for your existing terms? Other people may have discussed the topic using those terms instead. Instead of relying on "privacy," you can also try keywords like

identity theft
data protection
electronic records

You can even search using terms that refer to related people, events, or movements that you are familiar with.

Facebook
Internet vigilantism
MySpace
phishing

Many databases have a thesaurus that can help you find more keywords.

Find Sources in Databases

Sources found through library **databases** have already been filtered for you by professional librarians. They will include some common sources like popular magazines and newspapers, but the greatest value of database sources are the many journals, abstracts, studies, e-books, and other writing produced by specialists whose work has been scrutinized and commented on by other experts. When you read a source from a library database, chances are you are hearing an informed voice in an important debate.

Locate databases

You can find databases on your library's Web site. Sometimes you will find a list of databases. Sometimes you select a subject, and then you are directed to databases. Sometimes you select the name of a database vendor such as EBSCO or ProQuest. The vendor is the company that provides databases to the library.

Use databases

Your library has a list of databases and indexes by subject. If you can't find this list on your library's Web site, ask a **reference librarian** for help. Follow these steps to find articles.

1. Select a database appropriate to your subject or a comprehensive database like *Academic Search Complete, Academic Search Premier,* or *LexisNexis Academic.*

2. Search the database using your list of keywords.

3. Once you have chosen an article, print or e-mail to yourself the complete citation to the article. Look for the e-mail link after you click on the item you want.

4. Print or e-mail to yourself the full text if it is available. The full text is better than cutting and pasting because you might lose track of which words are yours, leading to unintended plagiarism.

5. If the full text is not available, check the online library catalog to see if your library has the journal.

Your library will probably have printed handouts or information on the Web that tells you which database to use for a particular subject. Ask a librarian who works at the reference or information desk to help you.

If you wish to get only full-text articles, you can check that option. Full-text documents give you the same text you would find in print. Sometimes the images are not reproduced in the HTML versions, but the PDF versions show the actual printed copy. Get the PDF version if it is available. Articles in HTML format usually do not contain the page numbers.

Common Databases

Academic OneFile	Indexes periodicals from the arts, humanities, sciences, social sciences, and general news, with full-text articles and images. (*Formerly Expanded Academic ASAP*)
Academic Search Premier and Complete	Provide full-text articles for thousands of scholarly publications, including social sciences, humanities, education, computer sciences, engineering, language and linguistics, literature, medical sciences, and ethnic-studies journals.

(*Continued*)

Common Databases

ArticleFirst	Indexes journals in business, the humanities, medicine, science, and social sciences.
EBSCOhost Research Databases	Gateway to a large collection of EBSCO databases, including *Academic Search Premier* and *Complete, Business Source Premier* and *Complete, ERIC,* and *Medline.*
Factiva	Provides full-text articles on business topics, including articles from the *Wall Street Journal.*
Google Books	Allows you to search within books and gives you snippets surrounding search terms for copyrighted books. Many books out of copyright have the full text. Available for everyone.
Google Scholar	Searches scholarly literature according to criteria of relevance. Available for everyone.
General OneFile	Contains millions of full-text articles about a wide range of academic and general-interest topics.
LexisNexis Academic	Provides full text of a wide range of newspapers, magazines, government and legal documents, and company profiles from around the world.
Opposing Viewpoints Resource Center	Provides full-text articles representing differing points of view on current issues.
ProQuest Databases	Like EBSCOhost, ProQuest is a gateway to a large collection of databases with over 100 billion pages, including the best archives of doctoral dissertations and historical newspapers.

Find Sources on the Web

Because anyone can publish on the Web, there is no overall quality control and there is no system of organization—two strengths we take for granted in libraries. Nevertheless, the Web offers you some resources for current topics that would be difficult or impossible to find in a library. The key to success is knowing where you are most likely to find current and accurate information about the particular question you are researching, and knowing how to access that information.

Use search engines wisely

Search engines designed for the Web work in ways similar to library databases and your library's online catalog but with one major difference. Databases typically do some screening of the items they list, but search engines potentially take you to everything on the Web—millions of pages in all. Consequently, you have to work harder to limit searches on the Web or you can be deluged with tens of thousands of items.

Kinds of search engines

A search engine is a set of programs that sort through millions of items at incredible speed. There are four basic kinds of search engines.

1. **Keyword search engines** (e.g., *Bing, Google, Yahoo!*). Keyword search engines give different results because they assign different weights to the information they find.
2. **Meta-search engines** (e.g., *Dogpile, MetaCrawler, Surfwax*). Meta-search engines allow you to use several search engines simultaneously. While the concept is sound, metasearch agents are limited because many do not access *Google* or *Yahoo!*
3. **Web directories** (e.g., *Britannica.com, Yahoo! Directory*). Web directories classify Web sites into categories and are the closest equivalent to the cataloging system used by libraries. On most directories professional editors decide how to index a particular Web site. Web directories also allow keyword searches.
4. **Specialized search engines** are designed for specific purposes:

   - regional search engines (e.g., *Baidu* for China)
   - medical search engines (e.g., *WebMD*)
   - legal search engines (e.g., *Lexis*)
   - job search engines (e.g., *Monster.com*)
   - property search engines (e.g., *Zillow*)

Advanced searches

Search engines often produce too many hits and are therefore not always useful. If you look only at the first few items, you may miss what is most valuable. The alternative is to refine your search. Most search engines offer you the option of an advanced search, which gives you the opportunity to limit numbers.

The advanced searches on *Google* and *Yahoo!* give you the options of using a string of words to search for sites that contain (1) all the words, (2) the exact phrase, (3) any of the words, or (4) that do not contain certain words. They also allow you to specify the site, the date range, the file format, and the domain. For example, if you want to limit a search for *identity theft statistics* to reliable government Web sites, you can specify the domain as **.gov.**

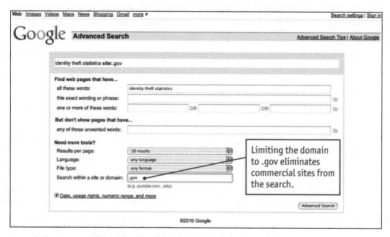

An advanced search on *Google* for government (.gov) sites only.

The **OR** operator is useful if you don't know exactly which term will get the results you want, especially if you are searching within a specific site. For example, you could try this search: "face-to-face OR f2f site:webworkerdaily.com."

You can also exclude terms by putting a minus sign before the term. If you want to search for social network privacy, but not *Facebook*, try "social network privacy–Facebook."

Find online government sources

The federal government has made many of its publications available on the Web. Also, many state governments now publish important documents on the Web. Often the most current and most reliable statistics are government statistics. Among the more important government resources are the following.

- **Bureau of Labor Statistics** (www.bls.gov/). Source for official U.S. government statistics on employment, wages, and consumer prices
- **Census Bureau** (www.census.gov/). Contains a wealth of links to sites for population, social, economic, and political statistics, including the *Statistical Abstract of the United States* (www.census.gov/compendia/statab/)
- **Centers for Disease Control** (www.cdc.gov/). Authoritative and trustworthy source for health statistics
- **CIA World Factbook** (www.cia.gov/library/publications/the-world-factbook/). Resource for geographic, economic, demographic, and political information on the nations of the world
- **Library of Congress** (www.loc.gov/). Many of the resources of the largest library in the world are available on the Web
- **National Institutes of Health** (www.nih.gov/). Extensive health information including MedlinePlus searches
- **NASA** (www.nasa.gov/). A rich site with much information and images concerning space exploration and scientific discovery
- **Thomas** (thomas.loc.gov/). The major source of legislative information, including bills, committee reports, and voting records of individual members of Congress
- **USA.gov** (www.usa.gov/). The place to start when you are not sure where to look for government information

Find online reference sources

Your library's Web site has a link to reference sites, either on the main page or under another heading like "research tools."

Reference sites are usually organized by subject, and you can find resources under the subject heading.

- **Business information** (links to business databases and sites like *Hoover's* that profiles companies)
- **Dictionaries** (including the *Oxford English Dictionary* and various subject dictionaries and language dictionaries)
- **Education** (including *The College Blue Book* and others)
- **Encyclopedias** (including *Britannica Online* and others)
- **Government information** (links to federal, state, and local Web sites)
- **Reference books** (commonly used books like atlases, almanacs, biographies, handbooks, and histories)
- **Statistics and demographics** (links to federal, state, and local government sites; *FedStats* [www.fedstats.gov/] is a good place to start)

Search interactive media

The Internet allows you to access other people's opinions on thousands of topics. Millions of people post messages on discussion lists and groups, *Facebook* groups, blogs, RSS feeds, *Twitter*, and so on. Much of what you read on interactive media sites is undocumented and highly opinionated, but you can still gather important information about people's attitudes and get tips about other sources, which you can verify later.

Several search engines have been developed for interactive media. *Facebook* and *Twitter* also have search engines for their sites.

Discussion list search engines

- **Big Boards** (www.big-boards.com). Tracks over two thousand of the most active discussion forums
- **Google Groups** (groups.google.com). Archives discussion forums dating back to 1981
- **Yahoo Groups** (groups.yahoo.com). A directory of groups by subject

Blog search engines

- **Bloglines** (www.bloglines.com). Web-based aggregator that delivers RSS feeds
- **Google Blog Search** (blogsearch.google.com). Searches blogs in several languages besides English
- **IceRocket** (blogs.icerocket.com). Searches blogs, *MySpace*, and *Twitter*
- **Technorati** (www.technorati.com). Searches blogs and other user-generated content

---

Know the limitations of Wikipedia

Wikipedia is a valuable resource for current information and for popular culture topics that are not covered in traditional encyclopedias. You can find out, for example, that SpongeBob SquarePants's original name was "SpongeBoy," but it had already been copyrighted.

Nevertheless, many instructors and the scholarly community in general do not consider *Wikipedia* a reliable source of information for a research paper. The fundamental problem with *Wikipedia* is stability, not whether the information is correct or incorrect. *Wikipedia* and other wikis constantly change. The underlying idea of documenting sources is that readers can consult the same sources that you consulted. Consult other sources to confirm what you find on Wikipedia and cite those sources.

Find Multimedia Sources

Massive collections of images; audio files including music, speeches, and podcasts; videos; maps, charts, and graphs; and other resources are now available on the Web.

Find images

The major search engines for images include the following.

- **Bing Images** (www.bing.com/images/)
- **Google Image Search** (images.google.com/)
- **Picsearch** (www.picsearch.com/)
- **Yahoo! Image Search** (images.search.yahoo.com)

Libraries and museums also offer large collections. For example, the American Memory collection in the Library of Congress offers an important visual record of the history of the United States (memory.loc.gov/ammem/).

Find videos

- **Bing Videos** (www.bing.com/videos/)
- **blinkx** (www.blinkx.com/)
- **Google Videos** (video.google.com/)
- **Yahoo! Video Search** (video.search.yahoo.com)
- **YouTube** (www.youtube.com)

Find podcasts

- **iTunes Podcast Resources** (www.apple.com/itunes/podcasts/)
- **PodcastDirectory.com** (http://www.podcastdirectory.com/)

Find charts, graphs, and maps

You can find statistical data represented in charts and graphs on many government Web sites.

- **Statistical Abstract of the United States** (www.census.gov/compendia/statab/)
- **Google Earth** (earth.google.com/)

- National Geographic Map Machine
  (mapmachine.nationalgeographic.com/)
- Perry Casteñada Map Collection, University of Texas (www.lib.utexas.
  edu/maps/map_sites/map_sites.html)

Respect copyright

Just because images, videos, and other multimedia files are easy to download from the Web does not mean that everything is available for you to use. Look for the creator's copyright notice and suggested credit line. This notice will tell you if you can reproduce the multimedia file.

Find Print Sources

Print sources may seem "old fashioned" if you grew up with the Internet. You might even feel a little bit intimidated by them. But they are the starting point for much of the research done by experts. In college and beyond, they are indispensable. No matter how current the topic you are researching, you will likely find information in print sources that is simply not available online.

Print sources have other advantages as well.

- Books are shelved according to subject, allowing easy browsing.
- Books often have bibliographies, directing you to other research on the subject.
- You can search for books in multiple ways: author, title, subject, or call letter.
- The majority of print sources have been evaluated by scholars, editors, and publishers, who decided whether they merited publication.

Find books

Nearly all libraries now shelve books according to the Library of Congress Classification System, which uses a combination of letters and numbers to give you the book's unique location in the library. The Library of Congress call number begins with a letter or letters that represent the broad subject area into which the book is classified.

Locating books in your library

The floors of your library where books are shelved are referred to as the stacks. The call number will enable you to find the item in the stacks. You will need to consult the locations guide for your library, which gives the level and section where an item is shelved.

Locating e-books

Use your library's online catalog to find e-books the same way you find printed books. You'll see on the record "e-book" or "electronic resource." Click on the link and you can read the book and often download a few pages.

Find journal articles

Like books, **scholarly journals** provide in-depth examinations of subjects. The articles in scholarly journals are written by experts, and they usually contain lists of references that can guide you to other research on a subject.

Popular journals are useful for gaining general information. Articles in popular magazines are usually short with few, if any, source references and are typically written by journalists. Some instructors frown on using popular magazines, but these journals can be valuable for researching current opinion on a particular topic.

Many scholarly journals and popular magazines are available on your library's Web site. Find them the same way you look for books, using your library's online catalog. Databases increasingly contain the full text of articles, allowing you to read and copy the contents onto your computer. If the article you are looking for isn't available online, the paper copy will be shelved with the books in your library.

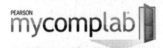

For support in learning this chapter's content, follow this path in MyCompLab:
> Resources > Research > The Research Assignment > Finding Sources.
Review the Instruction and Multimedia resources, then complete the Exercises and click on Gradebook to measure your progress.

18 | Evaluating and Recording Sources

QUICK TAKE

In this chapter, you will learn that

1. Your working thesis will help you to determine the relevance of sources (see below)
2. Librarians have developed methods for evaluating the quality of library database and print sources (see page 241)
3. Evaluating the quality of Web sources presents special challenges (see page 243)
4. Recording all the information you need to cite a source is critical to the research process (see page 244)

Determine the Relevance of Sources

Whether you use print or online sources, a successful search will turn up many more items than you can expect to use in your final product. You have to make a series of decisions as you evaluate your material. Use your research question and working thesis to create guidelines for yourself about importance and relevance.

If you ask a research question about contemporary events such as the NCAA's policy on compensating student athletes (see pages 108–112), you will need to find both background information and current information. You will need to know, for example, the most recent statistics on how many scholarship athletes actually graduate because the NCAA's main defense of not paying scholarship athletes is that they get a free education.

Use these guidelines to determine the importance and relevance of your sources to your research question.

- Does your research question require you to consult primary or secondary sources?
- Does a source you have found address your question?
- Does a source support or disagree with your working thesis? (You should not throw out work that challenges your views. Representing opposing views accurately enhances your credibility.)
- Does a source add significant information?

- Is the source current? (For most topics try to find the most up-to-date information.)
- What indications of possible bias do you note in the source?

Determine the Quality of Sources

In the Internet era, we don't lack for information, but we do lack filters for finding quality information. Two criteria will help you to make a beginning assessment of quality: individual vs. edited sources and popular vs. scholarly sources.

Distinguish individual and anonymous sources from edited sources

Anyone with a computer and access to the Internet can put up a Web site. Furthermore, they can put up sites anonymously or under an assumed name. It's no wonder that so many Web sites contain misinformation or are intentionally deceptive.

In general, sources that have been edited and published in scholarly journals, scholarly books, major newspapers, major online and print magazines, and government Web sites are considered of higher quality than what an individual might put on a personal Web site, a Facebook page, a user review, or in a blog.

Edited sources can have biases, and indeed some are quite open about their perspectives. *National Review* offers a conservative perspective, the *Wall Street Journal* is pro-business, and *The Nation* is a liberal voice. The difference from individual and anonymous sites is that we know the editorial perspectives of these journals, and we expect the editors to check the facts. On self-published Web sites and in self-published books, anything goes.

Distinguish popular sources from scholarly sources

Scholarly books and **scholarly journals** are published by and for experts. Scholarly books and articles published in scholarly journals undergo a **peer review** process in which a group of experts in a field reviews them for their scholarly soundness and academic value. Scholarly books and articles in scholarly journals include

- author's name and academic credentials and
- a list of works cited.

Newspapers, **popular books**, and **popular magazines** vary widely in quality. Newspapers and popular magazines range from highly respected publications such as the *Los Angeles Times, Scientific American,* and the *Atlantic Monthly* to the sensational tabloids at grocery-store checkouts. Popular sources are not peer reviewed and require more work on your part to determine their quality. EBSCO-host databases allow you to limit searches to scholarly journals.

Distinguish primary sources from secondary sources

Another key distinction for researchers is primary versus secondary sources. In the humanities and fine arts, **primary sources** are original, creative works and original accounts of events written close to the time they occurred. **Secondary sources** interpret creative works and primary sources of events.

In the sciences, **primary sources** are the factual results of experiments, observations, clinical trials, and other factual data. **Secondary sources** analyze and interpret those results.

Read sources critically

Evaluating sources requires you to read critically, which includes the following.

- Identifying the source, which is not always easy on the Web
- Identifying the author and assessing the author's credentials
- Understanding the content—what the text says
- Recognizing the author's purpose—whether the author is attempting to reflect, inform, or persuade
- Recognizing biases in the choices of words, examples, and structure
- Recognizing what the author does not include or address
- Developing an overall evaluation that takes into account all of the above

Evaluate the quality of visual sources

Evaluating the quality of visual sources involves skills similar to critical reading. Similar to critical reading, you should

- identify and assess the source,
- identify the creator,
- identify the date of creation,
- describe the content,
- assess the purpose, and
- recognize how the purpose influences the image, graphic, or video.

For graphics including charts and graphs, pay attention to the source of any data presented and see that the data are presented fairly.

Evaluate Database and Print Sources

Books are expensive to print and distribute, so book publishers generally protect their investment by providing some level of editorial oversight. Printed and on-line materials in your library undergo another review by professional librarians who select them to include in their collections.

This initial screening doesn't free you, however, from the responsibility of evaluating the quality of the sources. Many printed and database sources contain their share of inaccurate, misleading, and biased information. Also, all sources carry the risk of becoming outdated if you are looking for current information.

Checklist for evaluating database and print sources

Over the years librarians have developed a set of criteria for evaluating sources, and you should apply them in your research.

1. **Source.** Who published the book or article? Enter the publisher's name on Google or another search engine to learn about the publisher. Scholarly books and articles in scholarly journals are generally more reliable than popular magazines and books, which tend to emphasize what is sensational or entertaining at the expense of accuracy and comprehensiveness.

2. **Author.** Who wrote the book or article? What are the author's qualifications? Enter the author's name on Google or another search engine to learn more about him or her. Does the author represent an organization?

3. **Timeliness.** How current is the source? If you are researching a fast-developing subject such as treating ADHD, then currency is very important, but even historical topics are subject to controversy or revision.

4. **Evidence.** Where does the evidence come from—facts, interviews, observations, surveys, or experiments? Is the evidence adequate to support the author's claims?

5. **Biases.** Can you detect particular biases of the author? How do the author's biases affect the interpretation offered?

6. **Advertising.** For print sources, is advertising a prominent part of the journal or newspaper? How might the ads affect the credibility or the biases of the information that gets printed?

Evaluate Web Sources

Researching on the Web has been compared to drinking from a fire hose. The key to success is not only getting the torrent down to the size of a glass, but also making sure the water in the glass is pure enough to drink.

Pay attention to domain names

Domain names can give you clues about the quality of a Web site.

- **.com** Commercial site. The information on a .com site is generally about a product or company. While the information may be accurate, keep in mind that the purpose of the site is to sell a product or service.
- **.edu** Educational institution. The suffix tells you the site is on a school server, ranging from kindergarten to higher education. If the information is from a department or research center, it is generally credible, but if the site is an individual's, treat it as you would other kinds of self-published information.
- **.gov** Government. If you see this suffix, you're viewing a federal government site. Most government sites are considered credible sources.
- **.org** Nonprofit organization. Initially, nonpartisan organizations like the Red Cross used this domain, but increasingly partisan political groups and commercial interests have taken the .org suffix. Treat this domain with scrutiny.
- **.mil** Military. This domain suffix is owned by the various branches of the armed forces.
- **.net** Network. Anyone can use this domain.

Be alert for biased Web sites

Nearly every large company and political and advocacy organization has a Web site. We expect these sites to represent the company or the point of view of the organization. Many sites on the Web, however, are not so clearly labeled.

For example, if you do a search for "Sudden Infant Death Syndrome (SIDS)" and "vaccines," you'll find near the top of the list an article titled "Vaccines and Sudden Infant Death Syndrome (SIDS): A Link?" (www.thinktwice.com/sids.htm). The article concludes that vaccines cause SIDS. If you look at the home page—www.thinktwice.com—you'll find that the site's sponsor, Global Vaccine Institute, opposes all vaccinations of children.

Always look for other objective sources for verification of your information. The U.S. Centers for Disease Control publishes fact sheets with the latest information about diseases and their prevention (www.cdc.gov/vaccinesafety/

Concerns/sids_faq.html). The fact sheet on SIDS and vaccines reports that people associate sudden infant death syndrome with vaccinations because babies begin vaccinations between 2 and 4 months, the same age babies die of SIDS. There is no scientific evidence that vaccines cause SIDS.

Checklist for evaluating Web sources

Web sources present special challenges for evaluation. When you find a Web page by using a search engine, you will often go deep into a complex site without having any sense of the context for that page. To evaluate the credibility of the site, you would need to examine the home page, not just the specific page you get to first.

Use these criteria for evaluating Web sites.

1. **Source.** What organization sponsors the Web site? Look for the site's owner at the top or bottom of the home page or in the Web address. Enter the owner's name on *Google* or another search engine to learn about the organization. If a Web site doesn't indicate ownership, then you have to make judgments about who put it up and why.

2. **Author.** Is the author identified? Look for an "About Us" link if you see no author listed. Enter the author's name on *Google* or another search engine to learn more about the author. Often Web sites give no information about their authors other than an e-mail address, if that. In such cases it is difficult or impossible to determine the author's qualifications. Be cautious about information on an anonymous site.

3. **Purpose.** Is the Web site trying to sell you something? Many Web sites are infomercials that might contain useful information, but they are no more trustworthy than other forms of advertising. Is the purpose to entertain? to inform? to persuade?

4. **Timeliness.** When was the Web site last updated? Look for a date on the home page. Many Web pages do not list when they were last updated; thus you cannot determine their currency.

5. **Evidence.** Are sources of information listed? Any factual information should be supported by indicating where the information came from. Reliable Web sites that offer information will list their sources.

6. **Biases.** Does the Web site offer a balanced point of view? Many Web sites conceal their attitude with a reasonable tone and seemingly factual evidence such as statistics. Citations and bibliographies do not ensure that a site is reliable. Look carefully at the links and sources cited, and peruse the "About Us" link if one is available.

Keep Track of Sources

As you begin to collect your sources, make sure you get full bibliographic information for everything you might want to use in your project. Decide which documentation style you will use. (Two major documentation styles—MLA and APA—are explained in detail in Chapters 20 and 21.)

Locate elements of a citation in database sources

For any sources you find on databases, MLA style requires you to provide the full print information, the name of the database in italics, the medium of publication (*Web*), and the date you accessed the database. If page numbers are not included, use *n. page.* Do not include the URL of the database.

See pages 262-263 for detailed coverage.

Author's name	Shaughnessy, Dan
Title of article	"They've Had Some Chief Concerns"
Publication information	
Name of periodical	*Boston Globe*
Date of publication	12 Oct. 2007
Section and page number	C5
Database information	
Name of database	*LexisNexis Academic*
Medium of publication	Web
Date you accessed the site	19 Apr. 2010

Citation in MLA-style list of works cited

Shaughnessy, Dan. "They've Had Some Chief Concerns." *Boston Globe* 12 Oct. 2007: C5. *LexisNexis Academic*. Web. 19 Apr. 2010.

Locate elements of a citation in Web sources

As you conduct your online research, make sure you collect the necessary bibliographic information for everything you might want to use as a source. Because of the potential volatility of Web sources (they can and do disappear overnight), their citations require extra information. Depending on the citation format you use, you'll arrange this information in different ways.

See pages 263 for detailed coverage.

Author's name	Zaiger, Alan Scher
Title of work	"Study: NCAA Graduation Rate Comparisons Flawed"
Title of the overall Web site	*ABC News*
Publication information	
Publisher or sponsor	ABC News
Date of publication	20 Apr. 2010
Medium of publication	Web
Date you accessed the site	1 Nov. 2010

Citation in MLA-style list of works cited

> Zaiger, Alan Scher. "Study: NCAA Graduation Rate Comparisons Flawed." *ABC News*. ABC News, 20 Apr. 2010. Web. 1 Nov. 2010.

Locate elements of a citation in print sources

For books you will need, at minimum, the following information, which can typically be found on the front and back of the title page.

See page 263 for detailed coverage.

Author's name	Fleitz, David L.
Title of the book	Louis Sockalexis: The First Cleveland Indian
Publication information	
Place of publication	Jefferson
Name of publisher	McFarland
Date of publication	2002
Medium of publication	Print

Citation in MLA-style list of works cited

Fleitz, David L. *Louis Sockalexis: The First Cleveland Indian*. Jefferson:
McFarland, 2002. Print.

See pages 261–262 for detailed coverage.

> For support in learning this chapter's content, follow this path in MyCompLab:
> > Resources > Research > The Research Assignment > Evaluating Sources.
> Review the Instruction and Multimedia resources, then complete the Exercises and
> click on Gradebook to measure your progress.

19 | Writing the Research Project

QUICK TAKE

In this chapter, you will learn that

1. Before you begin writing, you need to take time to review your thesis and determine your contribution and your main points (see below)
2. Plagiarism means claiming credit for someone else's intellectual work (see page 248)
3. The best way to avoid unintentional plagiarism is to take care to distinguish source words from your own words (see page 250)
4. All quotations should be well integrated into your text (see page 255)

Review Your Goals and Plan Your Organization

If you have chosen a subject you're interested in, asked questions about it, and researched it thoroughly, you have a wealth of ideas and information to communicate to your audience.

Review your assignment and thesis

Before you begin writing a research project, review the assignment to remind you of the purpose of your argument, your potential readers, and the requested length.

By now you should have formulated a **working thesis**, which will be the focus of your project. You also should have located, read, evaluated, and taken notes on enough source material to write your project, and perhaps have conducted field research. At this stage in the writing process, your working thesis may be rough and may change as you write your draft, but having a working thesis will help keep your project focused.

Determine your contribution

A convincing and compelling source-based argument does not make claims based solely on the word of you, the writer. To be persuasive, it must draw on the expertise and reputations of others as well. However, you must also demonstrate that you have thought about and synthesized the evidence you have gathered from your sources, and you must show your readers which elements of your project represent your original thinking.

Determine exactly what you are adding to the larger conversation about your subject by answering these questions.

- Whom do you agree with?
- Whom do you disagree with?
- Which positions do you agree with but can add an additional point or example to?
- What original analysis or theorizing do you have to offer?

See pages 31–34 for examples of how to identify your contribution in relation to your sources.

Determine your main points

Look back over your notes on your sources and determine how to group the ideas you researched. Decide what your major points will be and how those points support your thesis. Group your research findings so that they match up with your major points.

Now it is time to create a working outline. Always include your thesis at the top of your outline as a guiding light. Some writers create formal outlines with roman numerals and the like; others compose the headings for the paragraphs of their project and use them to guide their draft; still others may start writing and then determine how they will organize their draft when they have a few paragraphs written. Experiment and decide which method works best for you.

Avoid Plagiarism

Plagiarism means claiming credit for someone else's intellectual work no matter whether it's to make money or get a better grade. Intentional or not, plagiarism has dire consequences. Reputable authors have gotten into trouble through carelessness by copying passages from published sources without acknowledging those sources. A number of famous people have had their reputations tarnished by accusations of plagiarism, and several prominent journalists have lost their jobs and careers for copying the work of other writers and passing it off as their own.

Deliberate plagiarism

If you buy a paper on the Web, copy someone else's paper word for word, or take an article off the Web and turn it in as yours, it's plain stealing, and people who take that risk should know that the punishment can be severe—usually failure for the course and sometimes expulsion. Deliberate plagiarism is easy for your instructors to spot because they recognize shifts in style, and it is easy for them to use search engines to find the sources of work stolen from the Web.

Patch plagiarism

The use of the Web has increased instances of plagiarism in college. Some students view the Internet as a big free buffet where they can grab anything, paste it in a file, and submit it as their own work. Other students intend to submit work that is their own, but they commit patch plagiarism because they aren't careful in taking notes to distinguish the words of others from their own words.

What you are not required to acknowledge

Fortunately, common sense governs issues of academic plagiarism. The standards of documentation are not so strict that the source of every fact you cite must be acknowledged. You do not have to document the following.

- **Facts available from many sources.** For example, many reference sources report that the death toll of the sinking of the *Titanic* on April 15, 1912, was around 1,500.
- **Results of your own field research.** If you take a survey and report the results, you don't have to cite yourself. You do need to cite individual interviews.

What you are required to acknowledge

The following sources should be acknowledged with an in-text citation and an entry in the list of works cited (MLA style) or the list of references (APA style).

- **Quotations.** Short quotations should be enclosed within quotation marks, and long quotations should be indented as a block. See page 256 for how to integrate quotations with signal phrases.
- **Summaries and paraphrases.** Summaries represent the author's argument in miniature as accurately as possible. Paraphrases restate the author's argument in your own words.
- **Facts that are not common knowledge.** For facts that are not easily found in general reference works, cite the source.
- **Ideas that are not common knowledge.** The sources of theories, analyses, statements of opinion, and arguable claims should be cited.
- **Statistics, research findings, examples, graphs, charts, and illustrations.** As a reader you should be skeptical about statistics and research findings when the source is not mentioned. When a writer does not cite the sources of statistics and research findings, there is no way of knowing how reliable the sources are or whether the writer is making them up.

Plagiarism in college writing

If you find any of the following problems in your academic writing, you may be guilty of plagiarizing someone else's work. Because plagiarism is usually inadvertent, it is especially important that you understand what constitutes using sources responsibly. Avoid these pitfalls.

- **Missing attribution.** Make sure the author of a quotation has been identified. Include a lead-in or signal phrase that provides attribution to the source, and identify the author in the citation.

- **Missing quotation marks.** You must put quotation marks around material quoted directly from a source.

- **Inadequate citation.** Give a page number to show where in the source the quotation appears or where a paraphrase or summary is drawn from.

- **Paraphrase relies too heavily on the source.** Be careful that the wording or sentence structure of a paraphrase does not follow the source too closely.

- **Distortion of meaning.** Don't allow your paraphrase or summary to distort the meaning of the source, and don't take a quotation out of context, resulting in a change of meaning.

- **Missing works-cited entry.** The Works Cited page must include all the works cited in the project.

- **Inadequate citation of images.** A figure or photo must appear with a caption and a citation to indicate the source of the image. If material includes a summary of data from a visual source, an attribution or citation must be given for the graphic being summarized.

Avoid plagiarism when taking notes

The best way to avoid unintentional plagiarism is to take care to distinguish source words from your own words. Don't mix words from the source with your own words.

- ■ **Create a working bibliography and make separate files for content notes.** Create a file for each source and label it clearly with the author's name. If you work on paper, use a separate page for each source. At the top of each page, write down all the information you need for a list of works cited or a list of references in your working bibliography.

- ■ **If you copy anything from a source when taking notes, place those words in quotation marks and note the page number(s) where those words appear.** If you copy words from an online source, take special care to note the source. You could easily copy online material and later not be able to find where it came from.

■ **Print out the entire source so you can refer to it later.** Having photocopies or complete printed files allows you to double-check later that you haven't used words from the source by mistake and that any words you quote are accurate.

Avoid Plagiarism When Quoting Sources

Effective research writing builds on the work of others. You can summarize or paraphrase the work of others, but often it is best to let the authors speak in your text by quoting their exact words. Indicate the words of others by placing them inside quotation marks.

Most people who get into plagiarism trouble lift words from a source and use them without quotation marks. Look carefully at this example to see where the line is drawn. In the following passage, Steven Johnson takes sharp issue with the metaphor of surfing applied to the Web:

> The concept of "surfing" does a terrible injustice to what it means to navigate around the Web. . . .What makes the idea of cybersurf so infuriating is the implicit connection drawn to television. Web surfing, after all, is a derivation of channel surfing—the term thrust upon the world by the rise of remote controls and cable panoply in the mid-eighties. . . . Applied to the boob tube, of course, the term was not altogether inappropriate. Surfing at least implied that channel-hopping was more dynamic, more involved, than the old routine of passive consumption. Just as a real-world surfer's enjoyment depended on the waves delivered up by the ocean, the channel surfer was at the mercy of the programmers and network executives. The analogy took off because it worked well in the one-to-many system of cable TV, where your navigational options were limited to the available channels.
>
> But when the term crossed over to the bustling new world of the Web, it lost a great deal of precision. . . . Web surfing and channel surfing are genuinely different pursuits; to imagine them as equivalents is to ignore the defining characteristics of each medium. Or at least that's what happens in theory. In practice, the Web takes on the greater burden. The television imagery casts the online surfer in the random, anesthetic shadow of TV programming, roaming from site to site like a CD player set on shuffle play. But what makes the online world so revolutionary is the fact that there *are* connections between each stop on a Web itinerant's journey. The links that join those various destinations are links of association, not randomness. A channel surfer hops back and forth between different channels because she's bored. A Web surfer clicks on a link because she's interested.
>
> —Steven Johnson. *Interface Culture: How New Technology Transforms the Way We Create and Communicate.* New York: Harper, 1997. 107–09.

If you were writing a paper or creating a Web site that concerns Web surfing, you might want to mention the distinction that Johnson makes between channel surfing and surfing on the Web.

Quoting directly

If you quote directly, you must place quotation marks around all words you take from the original:

> One observer marks this contrast: "A channel surfer hops back and forth between different channels because she's bored. A Web surfer clicks on a link because she's interested" (Johnson 109).

Notice that the quotation is introduced and not just dropped in. This example follows MLA style, where the citation—(Johnson 109)—goes outside the quotation marks but before the final period. In MLA style, source references are made according to the author's last name, which refers you to the full citation in the list of works cited at the end. Following the author's name is the page number where the quotation can be located. (Notice that there is no comma after the name.)

Attributing every quotation

If the author's name appears in the sentence, cite only the page number, in parentheses:

> According to Steven Johnson, "A channel surfer hops back and forth between different channels because she's bored. A Web surfer clicks on a link because she's interested" (109).

Quoting words that are quoted in your source

Use single quotation marks to quote material that is already quoted in your source:

> Steven Johnson uses the metaphor of a Gothic cathedral to describe a computer interface: "'The principle of the Gothic architecture,' Coleridge once said, 'is infinity made imaginable.' The same could be said for the modern interface" (42).

Avoid Plagiarism When Summarizing and Paraphrasing

Summarizing

When you summarize, you state the major ideas of an entire source or part of a source in a paragraph or perhaps even a sentence. The key is to put the summary in your own words. If you use words from the source, you must put those words within quotation marks.

Plagiarized

> Steven Johnson argues in *Interface Culture* that the concept of "surfing" is misapplied to the Internet because channel surfers hop back and forth between different channels because they're bored, but Web surfers click on links because they're interested. [Most of the words are lifted directly from the original; see page 251.]

Acceptable summary

> Steven Johnson argues in *Interface Culture* that the concept of "surfing" is misapplied to the Internet because users of the Web consciously choose to link to other sites while television viewers mindlessly flip through the channels until something catches their attention.

Paraphrasing

When you paraphrase, you represent the idea of the source in your own words at about the same length as the original. You still need to include the reference to the source of the idea. The following example illustrates an unacceptable paraphrase.

Plagiarized

> Steven Johnson argues that the concept of "surfing" does a terrible injustice to what it means to navigate around the Web. What makes the idea of Web surfing infuriating is the association with television. Surfing is not a bad metaphor for channel hopping, but it doesn't fit what people do on the Web. Web surfing and channel surfing are truly different activities; to imagine them as the same is to ignore their defining characteristics. A channel surfer skips around because she's bored while a Web surfer clicks on a link because she's interested (107–09).

Even though the source is listed, this paraphrase is unacceptable. Too many of the words in the original are used directly here, including much or all of entire sentences. When a string of words is lifted from a source and inserted without quotation marks, the passage is plagiarized. Changing a few words in a sentence is not a paraphrase. Compare these two sentences.

Source

> Web surfing and channel surfing are genuinely different pursuits; to imagine them as equivalents is to ignore the defining characteristics of each medium.

Unacceptable paraphrase

> Web surfing and channel surfing are truly different activities; to imagine them as the same is to ignore their defining characteristics.

The paraphrase takes the structure of the original sentence and substitutes a few words. It is much too similar to the original.

> **A true paraphrase represents an entire rewriting of the idea from the source.**

Acceptable paraphrase

> Steven Johnson argues that "surfing" is a misleading term for describing how people navigate on the Web. He allows that "surfing" is appropriate for clicking across television channels because the viewer has to interact with what the networks and cable companies provide, just as the surfer has to interact with what the ocean provides. Web surfing, according to Johnson, operates at much greater depth and with much more consciousness of purpose. Web surfers actively follow links to make connections (107-09).

Even though this paraphrase contains a few words from the original, such as *navigate* and *connections*, these sentences are original in structure and wording while accurately conveying the meaning of the source.

Decide When to Quote and When to Paraphrase

The general rule in deciding when to include direct quotations and when to paraphrase lies in the importance of the original wording.

- ■ If you want to refer to an idea or fact and the original wording is not critical, make the point in your own words.
- ■ Save direct quotations for language that is memorable or conveys the character of the source.

Use quotations effectively

Quotations are a frequent problem area in research projects. Review every quotation to ensure that each is used effectively and correctly.

- ■ **Limit the use of long quotations.** If you have more than one block quotation on a page, look closely to see if one or more can be paraphrased or summarized. Use direct quotations only if the original wording is important.
- ■ **Check that each quotation is supporting your major points rather than making major points for you.** If the ideas rather than the original wording are what's important, paraphrase the quotation and cite the source.
- ■ **Check that each quotation is introduced and attributed.** Each quotation should be introduced and the author or title named. Check for signal phrases that signal a quotation: Smith *claims*, Jones *argues*, Brown *states*.
- ■ **Check that each quotation is properly formatted and punctuated.** Prose quotations longer than four lines (MLA) or forty words (APA) should be indented one inch in MLA style or one-half inch in APA style. Shorter quotations should be enclosed within quotation marks.
- ■ **Check that you cite the source for each quotation.** You are required to cite the sources of all direct quotations, paraphrases, and summaries.
- ■ **Check the accuracy of each quotation.** It's easy to leave out words or mistype a quotation. Compare what is in your project to the original source. If you need to add words to make the quotation grammatical, make sure the added words are in brackets. Use ellipses to indicate omitted words.
- ■ **Read your project aloud to a classmate or a friend.** Each quotation should flow smoothly when you read your project aloud. Put a check beside rough spots as you read aloud so you can revise later.

Use signal phrases

Signal verbs often indicate your stance toward a quotation. Introducing a quotation with "X says" or "X believes" tells your readers nothing. Find a livelier verb that suggests how you are using the source. For example, if you write "X contends," your reader is alerted that you likely will disagree with the source. Be as precise as possible.

Signal phrases that report information or a claim

> X argues that . . .
> X asserts that . . .
> X claims that . . .
> X observes that . . .
> As X puts it, . . .
> X reports that . . .
> As X sums it up, . . .

Signal phrases when you agree with the source

> X affirms that . . .
> X has the insight that . . .
> X points out insightfully that . . .
> X theorizes that . . .
> X verifies that . . .

Signal phrases when you disagree with the source

> X complains that . . .
> X contends that . . .
> X denies that . . .
> X disputes that . . .
> X overlooks that . . .
> X rejects that . . .
> X repudiates that . . .

Signal phrases in the sciences

Signal phrases in the sciences often use the past tense, especially for interpretations and commentary.

> X described . . .
> X found . . .
> X has suggested . . .

Introduce block quotations

Long direct quotations, called **block quotations**, are indented from the margin instead of being placed in quotation marks. In MLA style, a quotation longer than four lines should be indented 1 inch. A quotation of forty words or longer is indented 1/2 inch in APA style. In both MLA and APA styles, long quotations are double-spaced. You still need to integrate a block quotation into the text of your project by mentioning who wrote or said it.

- No quotation marks appear around the block quotation.
- Words quoted in the original retain the double quotation marks.
- The page number appears in parentheses after the period at the end of the block quotation.

It is a good idea to include at least one or two sentences following the quotation to describe its significance to your thesis.

Double-check quotations

Whether they are long or short, you should double-check all quotations you use to be sure they are accurate and that all words belonging to the original are set off with quotation marks or placed in a block quotation. If you wish to leave out words from a quotation, indicate the omitted words with ellipses (. . .), but make sure you do not alter the meaning of the original quotation. If you need to add words of your own to a quotation to make the meaning clear, place your words in square brackets.

Write a Draft

Some writers begin by writing the title, first paragraph, and concluding paragraph.

Write a specific title

A bland, generic title says to readers that you are likely to be boring.

Generic

> Good and Bad Fats

Specific titles are like tasty appetizers; if you like the appetizer, you'll probably like the main course.

Specific

> The Secret Killer: Hydrogenated Fats

Write an engaging introduction

Get off to a fast start. If, for example, you want to alert readers to the dangers of partially hydrogenated oils in the food we eat, you could begin by explaining the difference in molecular structure between natural unsaturated fatty acids and trans fatty acids. And you would probably lose your readers by the end of the first paragraph.

Instead, let readers know what is at stake along with giving some background and context. State your thesis early on. Then go into the details in the body of your project.

Write a strong conclusion

The challenge in writing ending paragraphs is to leave the reader with something provocative, something beyond pure summary of the previous paragraphs. Connect back to your thesis, and use a strong concluding image, example, question, or call to action to leave your readers with something to remember and think about.

Review and Revise

After you've gone through the peer editing process or assessed your own draft, sit down with your project and consider the changes you need to make. Start from the highest level, reorganizing paragraphs and possibly even cutting large parts of your project and adding new sections. If you make significant revisions, likely you will want to repeat the overall evaluation of your revised draft when you finish (see Chapter 4).

When you feel your draft is complete, begin the editing phase. Use the guidelines on pages 51–52 to revise style and grammatical errors. Finally, proofread your project, word by word, checking for mistakes.

> For support in learning this chapter's content, follow this path in MyCompLab:
> > Resources > Research > The Research Assignment > Integrating Sources.
> Review the Instruction and Multimedia resources, then complete the Exercises and click on Gradebook to measure your progress.

20 | Documenting Sources in MLA Style

QUICK TAKE

In this chapter, you will learn that

1. Citing sources in MLA style is a two-part process, including in-text references and a Works Cited page at the end of your paper (see below)
2. Works cited entries for different kinds of sources follow a basic pattern (see page 261)
3. Research papers using MLA style are formatted according to a few basic conventions (see page 276)

The two styles of documentation used most frequently are APA style and MLA style. APA stands for American Psychological Association, which publishes a style manual used widely in the social sciences and education (see Chapter 21). MLA stands for the Modern Language Association, and its style is the norm for the humanities and fine arts, including English and rhetoric and composition. If you have questions that this chapter does not address, consult the *MLA Handbook for Writers of Research Papers*, Seventh Edition (2009), and the *MLA Style Manual and Guide to Scholarly Publishing*, Third Edition (2008).

Elements of MLA Documentation

Citing a source in your paper

Citing sources is a two-part process. When readers find a reference to a source (called an in-text or parenthetical citation) in the body of your paper, they can turn to the works-cited list at the end and find the full publication information. Place the author's last name and the page number inside parentheses at the end of the sentence.

Anticipating the impact of Google's project of digitally scanning books in major research libraries, one observer predicts that "the real magic will come in the second act, as each word in each book is cross-linked, clustered, cited, extracted, indexed, analyzed, annotated, remixed, re-assembled and woven deeper into the culture than ever before" (Kelly 43).

Author not mentioned in text

If you mention the author's name in the sentence, you do not have to put the name in the parenthetical reference at the end. Just cite the page number.

> Anticipating the impact of Google's project of digitally scanning books in major research libraries, Kevin Kelly predicts that "the real magic will come in the second act, as each word in each book is cross-linked, clustered, cited, extracted, indexed, analyzed, annotated, remixed, re-assembled and woven deeper into the culture than ever before" (43).

Author mentioned in text

The corresponding entry in the work-cited list at the end of your paper would be as follows.

Works Cited

> Kelly, Kevin. "Scan This Book!" *New York Times* 14 May 2006, late ed., sec 6: 43+. Print.

Entry in the works-cited list

Citing an entire work, a Web site, or another electronic source

If you wish to cite an entire work (a book, a film, a performance, and so on), a Web site, or an electronic source that has no page numbers or paragraph numbers, MLA style instructs that you mention the name of the person (for example, the author or director) in the text with a corresponding entry in the works-cited list. You do not need to include the author's name in parentheses. If you cannot identify the author, mention the title in your text.

> Joel Waldfogel discusses the implications of a study of alumni donations to colleges and universities, observing that parents give generously to top-rated colleges in the hope that their children's chances for admission will improve.

Author mentioned in text

Works Cited

> Waldfogel, Joel. "The Old College Try." *Slate*. Washington Post Newsweek Interactive, 6 July 2007. Web. 27 Jan. 2010.

MLA style now requires the medium of publication (print, Web, performance, etc.) to be included in each citation.

Creating an MLA-style works-cited list

To create your works-cited list, go through your paper and find every reference to the sources you consulted during your research. Each in-text reference must have an entry in your works-cited list.

Organize your works-cited list alphabetically by authors' last names or, if no author is listed, the first word in the title other than *a*, *an*, or *the*. (See pages 281–282 for a sample works-cited list.) MLA style uses four basic forms for entries in the works-cited list: books, periodicals (scholarly journals, newspapers, magazines), online library database sources, and other online sources (Web sites, discussion forums, blogs, online newspapers, online magazines, online government documents, and e-mail messages).

Works-cited entries for books

Entries for books have three main elements.

Pollan, Michael. *In Defense of Food: An Eater's Manifesto*. New York: Penguin, 2008. Print.

1. Author's name.
- List the author's name with the last name first, followed by a period.

2. *Title of book.*
- Find the exact title on the title page, not the cover.
- Separate the title and subtitle with a colon.
- Italicize the title and put a period at the end.

3. Publication information.
- Give the city of publication and a colon.
- Give the name of the publisher, using accepted abbreviations, and a comma.
- Give the date of publication, followed by a period.
- Give the medium of publication (Print), followed by a period.

Works-cited entries for periodicals

Entries for periodicals (scholarly journals, newspapers, magazines) have three main elements.

Pilgrim, Sarah, David Smith, and Jules Pretty. "A Cross-Regional Assessment of the Factors Affecting Ecoliteracy: Implications for Policy and Practice." *Ecological Applications* 17.6 (2007): 1742-51. Print.

1. Author's name.
- List the author's name with the last name first, followed by a period.

2. "Title of article."
- Place the title of the article inside quotation marks.
- Insert a period before the closing quotation mark.

3. Publication information.
- Italicize the title of the journal.
- Give the volume number.
- List the date of publication, in parentheses, followed by a colon.
- List the page numbers, followed by a period.
- Give the medium of publication (Print), followed by a period.

Works-cited entries for library database sources

Basic entries for library database sources have four main elements.

Damiano, Jessica. "Growing Vegetables in Small Spaces: Train Them up Trellises and Plant Crops in Succession." *Newsday* 2 May 2010: G107. *LexisNexis Academic*. Web. 8 Apr. 2010.

1. Author's name.
- List the author's name with the last name first, followed by a period.

2. "Title of article."
- Place the title of the article inside quotation marks.
- Insert a period before the closing quotation mark.

3. Print publication information
- Give the print publication information in standard format, in this case for a periodical (see pages 270–272).

4. Database information
- Italicize the name of the database, followed by a period.
- List the medium of publication, followed by a period. For all database sources, the medium of publication is *Web*.
- List the date you accessed the source (day, month, and year), followed by a period.

Works-cited entries for other online sources

Basic entries for online sources (Web sites, discussion forums, blogs, online newspapers, online magazines, online government documents, and e-mail messages) have three main elements. Sometimes information such as the author's name or the date of publication is missing from the online source. Include the information you are able to locate.

There are many formats for the different kinds of electronic publications. Here is the format of an entry for an online article.

Jacobs, Ruth. "Organic Garden Gives Back." Colby Magazine 99:1 (2010): n.pag. Web. 2 Apr. 2010.

1. Author's name.
- List the author's name with the last name first, followed by a period.

2. "Title of work"; Title of the overall Web site
- Place the title of the work inside quotation marks if it is part of a larger Web site.
- Italicize the name of the overall site if it is different from the title of the work.
- Some Web sites are updated periodically, so list the version if you find it (e.g., 2010 edition).

3. Publication information.
- List the publisher or sponsor of the site, followed by a comma. If not available, use *N.p.* (for *no publisher*).
- List the date of publication if available; if not, use *n.d.*
- List the medium of publication (*Web*).
- List the date you accessed the source (day, month, and year).

MLA In-Text Citations

1. Author named in your text
Put the author's name in a signal phrase in your sentence.

> Sociologist Daniel Bell called this emerging U.S. economy the "postindustrial society" (3).

2. Author not named in your text
Put the author's last name and the page number inside parentheses at the end of the sentence.

> In 1997, the Gallup poll reported that 55% of adults in the United States think secondhand smoke is "very harmful," compared to only 36% in 1994 (Saad 4).

3. Work by a single author
The author's last name comes first, followed by the page number. There is no comma.

> (Bell 3)

4. Work by two or three authors
The authors' last names follow the order of the title page. If there are two authors, join the names with *and*. If there are three authors, use a comma between the first two names and a comma with *and* before the last name.

> (Francisco, Vaughn, and Lynn 7)

5. Work by four or more authors
You may use the phrase *et al.* (meaning "and others") for all names but the first, or you may write out all the names. Make sure you use the same method for both the in-text citations and the works-cited list.

> (Abrams et al. 1653)

6. Work by an unnamed author
Use a shortened version of the title that includes at least the first important word. Your reader will use the shortened title to find the full title in the works-cited list.

> A review in the *New Yorker* of Ryan Adams's new album focuses on the artist's age ("Pure" 25).

Notice that "Pure" is in quotation marks because it is the shortened title of an article. If it were a book, the short title would be in italics.

7. Work by a group or organization

Treat the group or organization as the author, but try to identify the group author in the text and place only the page number in parentheses. Shorten terms that are commonly abbreviated.

> According to the *Irish Free State Handbook*, published by the Ministry for Industry and Finance, the population of Ireland in 1929 was approximately 4,192,000 (23).

8. Quotations longer than four lines

When using indented (block) quotations of more than four lines, place the period *before* the parentheses enclosing the page number.

> In her article "Art for Everybody," Susan Orlean attempts to explain the popularity of painter Thomas Kinkade:
>> People like to own things they think are valuable. . . .
>> The high price of limited editions is part of their appeal:
>> it implies that they are choice and exclusive, and that
>> only a certain class of people will be able to
>> afford them. (128)
> This same statement could possibly also explain the popularity of phenomena like PBS's *Antiques Road Show*.

If the source is longer than one page, provide the page number for each quotation, paraphrase, and summary.

9. Web sources including Web pages, blogs, podcasts, wikis, videos, and other multimedia sources

Give the author in the text instead of putting the author's name in parentheses.

> Andrew Keen ironically used his own blog to claim that "blogs are boring to write (yawn), boring to read (yawn) and boring to discuss (yawn)."

If you cannot identify the author, mention the title in your text.

> The podcast "Catalina's Cubs" describes the excitement on Catalina Island when the Chicago Cubs went there for spring training in the 1940s.

10. Work in an anthology

Cite the name of the author of the work within an anthology, not the name of the editor of the collection. Alphabetize the entry in the list of works cited by the author, not the editor.

> In "Beard," Melissa Jane Hardie explores the role assumed by Elizabeth Taylor as the celebrity companion of gay actors including Rock Hudson and Montgomery Cliff (278–79).

11. Two or more works by the same author

When an author has two or more items in the works-cited list, distinguish which work you are citing by using the author's last name and then a shortened version of the title of each source.

> The majority of books written about coauthorship focus on partners of the same sex (Laird, *Women* 351).

Note that *Women* is italicized because it is the name of a book; if an article were named, quotation marks would be used.

12. Different authors with the same last name

If your list of works cited contains items by two or more different authors with the same last name, include the initial of the first name in the parenthetical reference.

> Web surfing requires more mental involvement than channel surfing (S. Johnson 107).

Note that a period follows the initial.

13. Two or more sources within the same sentence

Place each citation directly after the statement it supports.

> In the 1990s, many sweeping pronouncements were made that the Internet is the best opportunity to improve education since the printing press (Ellsworth xxii) or even in the history of the world (Dyrli and Kinnaman 79).

14. Two or more sources within the same citation

If two sources support a single point, separate them with a semicolon.

> (McKibbin 39; Gore 92)

15. Work quoted in another source

When you do not have access to the original source of the material you wish to use, put the abbreviation *qtd. in* (quoted in) before the information about the indirect source.

> National governments have become increasingly what Ulrich Beck, in a 1999 interview, calls "zombie institutions"—institutions that are "dead and still alive" (qtd. in Bauman 6).

16. Literary works

To supply a reference to a literary work, you sometimes need more than a page number from a specific edition. Readers should be able to locate a quotation in any edition of the book. Give the page number from the edition that you are using, then a semicolon and other identifying information.

> "Marriage is a house" is one of the most memorable lines in *Don Quixote* (546; pt. 2, bk. 3, ch. 19).

MLA Works-Cited List: Books

One author

17. Book by one author

The author's last name comes first, followed by a comma, the first name, and a period.

> Doctorow, E. L. *The March*. New York: Random, 2005. Print.

18. Two or more books by the same author

In the entry for the first book, include the author's name. In the second entry, substitute three hyphens and a period for the author's name. List the titles of books by the same author in alphabetical order.

> Grimsley, Jim. *Boulevard*. Chapel Hill: Algonquin, 2002. Print.
> ---. *Dream Boy*. New York: Simon, 1995. Print.

Multiple authors

19. Book by two or three authors

Second and subsequent authors' names appear first name first. A comma separates the authors' names.

> Chapkis, Wendy, and Richard J. Webb. *Dying to Get High: Marijuana as Medicine*. New York: New York UP, 2008. Print.

20. Book by four or more authors

You may use the phrase *et al.* (meaning "and others") for all authors but the first, or you may write out all the names. Use the same method in the in-text citation as you do in the works-cited list.

> Zukin, Cliff, et al. *A New Engagement? Political Participation, Civic Life, and the Changing American Citizen*. New York: Oxford UP, 2006. Print.

Anonymous and group authors

21. Book by an unknown author

Begin the entry with the title.

> *Encyclopedia of Americana*. New York: Somerset, 2001. Print.

22. Book by a group or organization

Treat the group as the author of the work.

> United Nations. *The Charter of the United Nations: A Commentary*. New York: Oxford UP, 2000. Print.

23. Religious texts

Do not italicize the title of a sacred text, including the Bible, unless you are citing a specific edition.

> Holy Bible. King James Text: Modern Phrased Version. New York: Oxford UP, 1980. Print.

Imprints, reprints, and undated books

24. Book with no publication date

If no year of publication is given but can be approximated, put a *c.* ("circa") and the approximate date in brackets: [c. 2009]. Otherwise, put *n.d.* ("no date"). For works before 1900, you do not need to list the publisher.

> O'Sullivan, Colin. *Traditions and Novelties of the Irish Country Folk*. Dublin, [c. 1793]. Print.

> James, Franklin. *In the Valley of the King*. Cambridge: Harvard UP, n.d. Print.

25. Reprinted works

For works of fiction that have been printed in many different editions or reprints, give the original publication date after the title.

> Wilde, Oscar. *The Picture of Dorian Gray*. 1890. New York: Norton, 2001. Print.

Parts of books

26. Introduction, foreword, preface, or afterword

Give the author and then the name of the specific part being cited. Next, name the book. Then, if the author for the whole work is different, put that author's name after the word *By*. Place inclusive page numbers at the end.

> Benstock, Sheri. Introduction. *The House of Mirth*. By Edith Wharton. Boston: Bedford-St. Martin's, 2002. 3–24. Print.

27. Single chapter written by same author as the book

> Ardis, Ann L. "Mapping the Middlebrow in Edwardian England." *Modernism and Cultural Conflict: 1880-1922*. Cambridge: Cambridge UP, 2002. 114–42. Print.

28. Selection from an anthology or edited collection

> Sedaris, David. "Full House." *The Best American Nonrequired Reading 2004*. Ed. Dave Eggers. Boston: Houghton, 2004. 350–58. Print.

29. Article in a reference work

You can omit the names of editors and most publishing information for an article from a familiar reference work. Identify the edition by date. There is no need to give the page numbers when a work is arranged alphabetically. Give the author's name, if known.

> "Utilitarianism." *The Columbia Encyclopedia*. 6th ed. 2001. Print.

Editions and translations

30. Book with an editor

List an edited book under the editor's name if your focus is on the editor. Otherwise, cite an edited book under the author's name as shown in the second example below.

> Lewis, Gifford, ed. *The Big House of Inver*. By Edith Somerville and Martin Ross. Dublin: Farmar, 2000. Print.

> Somerville, Edith, and Martin Ross. *The Big House of Inver*. Ed. Gifford Lewis. Dublin: Farmar, 2000. Print.

31. Book with a translator

> Benjamin, Walter. *The Arcades Project*. Trans. Howard Eiland and Kevin McLaughlin. Cambridge: Harvard UP, 1999. Print.

32. Second or subsequent edition of a book

> Hawthorn, Jeremy, ed. *A Concise Glossary of Contemporary Literary Theory*. 3rd ed. London: Arnold, 2001. Print.

Multivolume works

33. Multivolume work

Identify both the volume you have used and the total number of volumes in the set.

> Samuel, Raphael. *Theatres of Memory*. Vol. 1. London: Verso, 1999. 2 vols. Print.

If you refer to more than one volume, identify the specific volume in your in-text citations, and list the total number of volumes in your list of works cited.

> Samuel, Raphael. *Theatres of Memory*. 2 vols. London: Verso, 1999. Print.

MLA Works-Cited List: Periodicals

Journal articles

34. Article by one author

> Mallory, Anne. "Burke, Boredom, and the Theater of Counterrevolution." *PMLA* 118.2 (2003): 329–43. Print.

35. Article by two or three authors

> Miller, Thomas P., and Brian Jackson. "What Are English Majors For?" *College Composition and Communication* 58.4 (2007): 825–31. Print.

36. Article by four or more authors

You may use the phrase *et al.* (meaning "and others") for all authors but the first, or you may write out all the names.

> Breece, Katherine E., et al. "Patterns of mtDNA Diversity in Northwestern North America." *Human Biology* 76.1 (2004): 33–54. Print.

Pagination in journals

37. Article in a scholarly journal

List the volume and issue number after the name of the journal.

> Duncan, Mike. "Whatever Happened to the Paragraph?" *College English* 69.5 (2007): 470–95. Print.

38. Article in a scholarly journal that uses only issue numbers

List the issue number after the name of the journal.

> McCall, Sophie. "Double Vision Reading." *Canadian Literature* 194 (2007): 95–97. Print.

Magazines

39. Monthly or seasonal magazines

Use the month (or season) and year in place of the volume. There is no comma before the date. Abbreviate the names of all months except May, June, and July.

> Barlow, John Perry. "Africa Rising: Everything You Know about Africa Is Wrong." *Wired* Jan. 1998: 142–58. Print.

40. Weekly or biweekly magazines

Give both the day and the month of publication, as listed on the issue.

> Brody, Richard. "A Clash of Symbols." *New Yorker* 25 June 2007: 16. Print.

Newspapers

41. Newspaper article by one author

The author's last name comes first, followed by a comma and the first name.

> Marriott, Michel. "Arts and Crafts for the Digital Age." *New York Times* 8 June 2006, late ed.: C13. Print.

42. Article by two or three authors

The second and subsequent authors' names are printed in regular order, first name first:

> Schwirtz, Michael, and Joshua Yaffa. "A Clash of Cultures at a Square in Moscow." *New York Times* 11 July 2007, late ed.: A9. Print.

43. Newspaper article by an unknown author

Begin the entry with the title.

> "The Dotted Line." *Washington Post* 8 June 2006, final ed.: E2. Print.

Reviews, editorials, letters to the editor

44. Review

If there is no title, just name the work reviewed.

> Mendelsohn, Daniel. "The Two Oscar Wildes." Rev. of *The Importance of Being Earnest*, dir. Oliver Parker. *The New York Review of Books* 10 Oct. 2002: 23–24. Print.

45. Editorial

> "Hush-hush, Sweet Liberty." Editorial. *Los Angeles Times* 7 July 2007: A18. Print.

46. Letter to the editor

> Doyle, Joe. Letter. *Direct* 1 July 2007: 48. Print.

MLA Works-Cited List: Library Database Sources

47. Work from a library database

Begin with the print publication information, then the name of the database (italicized), the medium of publication (*Web*), and the date of access.

> Snider, Michael. "Wired to Another World." *Maclean's* 3 Mar. 2003: 23–24. *Academic Search Premier*. Web. 14 Jan. 2010.

MLA Works-Cited List: Online Sources

Web publications

When do you list a URL? MLA style no longer requires including URLs of Web sources. URLs are of limited value because they change frequently and they can be specific to an individual search. Include the URL as supplementary information only when your readers probably cannot locate the source without the URL.

48. Publication by a known author

> Boerner, Steve. "Leopold Mozart." *The Mozart Project: Biography*. The Mozart
>   Project, 21 Mar. 1998. Web. 30 Oct. 2010.

49. Publication by a group or organization

If a work has no author's or editor's name listed, begin the entry with the title.

> "State of the Birds." *Audubon*. National Audubon Society, 2008. Web.
>   19 Aug. 2010.

50. Article in a scholarly journal on the Web

Some scholarly journals are published on the Web only. List articles by author, title, name of journal in italics, volume and issue number, and year of publication. If the journal does not have page numbers, use *n. pag.* in place of page numbers. Then list the medium of publication (*Web*) and the date of access (day, month, and year).

> Fleckenstein, Kristie. "Who's Writing? Aristotelian Ethos and the Author Position
>   in Digital Poetics." *Kairos* 11.3 (2007): n. pag. Web. 6 Apr. 2010.

51. Article in a newspaper on the Web

The first date is the date of publication; the second is the date of access.

> Brown, Patricia Leigh. "Australia in Sonoma." *New York Times*. New York
>   Times, 5 July 2008. Web. 3 Aug. 2010.

52. Article in a magazine on the Web

> Brown, Patricia Leigh. "The Wild Horse Is Us." *Newsweek*. Newsweek,
>   1 July 2008. Web. 12 Dec. 2010.

53. Book on the Web

> Prebish, Charles S., and Kenneth K. Tanaka. *The Faces of Buddhism in America*. Berkeley: U of California P, 2003. *eScholarship Editions*. Web. 2 May 2010.

Other online sources

54. Blog entry

If there is no sponsor or publisher for the blog, use *N.p.*

> Arrington, Michael. "Think Before You Voicemail." *TechCrunch*. N.p., 5 July 2008. Web. 10 Sept. 2010.

55. E-mail

Give the name of the writer, the subject line, a description of the message, the date, and the medium of delivery (*E-mail*).

> Ballmer, Steve. "A New Era of Business Productivity and Innovation." Message to Microsoft Executive E-mail. 30 Nov. 2010. E-mail.

56. Video on the Web

Video on the Web often lacks a creator and a date. Begin the entry with a title if you cannot find a creator. Use *n.d.* if you cannot find a date.

> Wesch, Michael. *A Vision of Students Today*. *YouTube*. YouTube, 2007. Web. 28 May 2010.

57. Personal home page

List *Home page* without quotation marks in place of the title. If no date is listed, use *n.d.*

> Graff, Harvey J. Home page. Dept. of English, Ohio State U, n.d. Web. 15 Nov. 2010.

58. Wiki entry

A wiki is a collaborative writing and editing tool. Although some topic-specific wikis are written and carefully edited by recognized scholars, the more popular wiki sites—such as *Wikipedia*—are often considered unreliable sources for academic papers.

> "Snowboard." *Wikipedia*. Wikimedia Foundation, 2009. Web. 30 Jan. 2010.

59. Podcast

> Sussingham, Robin. "All Things Autumn." No. 2. *HighLifeUtah*. N.p.,
> 20 Nov. 2006. Web. 28 Feb. 2010.

60. PDFs and digital files

PDFs and other digital files can often be downloaded through links. Determine the kind of work you are citing, include the appropriate information for the particular kind of work, and list the type of file.

> Glaser, Edward L., and Albert Saiz. "The Rise of the Skilled City." Discussion
> Paper No. 2025. Harvard Institute of Economic Research. Cambridge:
> Harvard U, 2003. PDF file.

MLA Works-Cited List: Other Sources

61. Sound recording

> McCoury, Del, perf. "1952 Vincent Black Lightning." By Richard Thompson.
> *Del and the Boys*. Ceili, 2001. CD.

62. Film

Begin with the title in italics. List the director, the distributor, the date, and the medium. Other data, such as the names of the screenwriters and performers, is optional.

> *Wanted*. Dir. Timur Bekmambetov. Perf. James McAvoy, Angelina Jolie, and
> Morgan Freeman. Universal, 2008. Film.

63. DVD

> *No Country for Old Men*. Dir. Joel Coen and Ethan Coen. Perf. Tommy Lee
> Jones, Javier Bardem, and Josh Brolin. Paramount, 2007. DVD.

64. Television or radio program

> "Kaisha." *The Sopranos*. Perf. James Gandolfini, Lorraine Bracco, and Edie
> Falco. HBO. 4 June 2006. Television.

Sample MLA paper

Brian Witkowski

Professor Mendelsohn

RHE 309K

3 May 2010

Need a Cure for Tribe Fever?

How About a Dip in the Lake?

Everyone is familiar with the Cleveland Indians' Chief Wahoo logo—and I do mean everyone, not just Clevelanders. Across America people wear the smiling mascot on Cleveland Indians caps and jerseys, and recent trends in sports merchandise have popularized new groovy multicolored Indians sportswear. Because of lucrative contracts between major league baseball and Little League, youth teams all over the country don Cleveland's famous (or infamous) smiling Indian each season as fresh-faced kids scamper onto the diamonds looking like mini major leaguers (Liu). Various incarnations of the famous Chief Wahoo—described by writer Ryan Zimmerman as "a grotesque caricature grinning idiotically through enormous bucked teeth"—have been around since the 1940s. Now redder and even more cartoonish than the original hook-nosed, beige Indian with a devilish grin, Wahoo often passes as a cheerful baseball buddy like the San Diego Chicken or the St. Louis Cardinals' Fredbird.

Though defined by its distinctive logo, Cleveland baseball far preceded its famous mascot. The team changed from the Forest Citys to the Spiders to the Bluebirds/Blues to the Broncos to the Naps and finally to the Indians. Dubbed the Naps in 1903 in honor of its star player and manager Napoleon Lajoie, the team gained their current appellation in 1915. After Lajoie was traded, the team's president challenged sportswriters to devise a suitable "temporary" label for the floundering club. Publicity material claims that the writers decided on the Indians to celebrate Louis Sockalexis, a Penobscot Indian who played for the team from 1897 to 1899. With a high batting average and the notability of being the first Native American in professional baseball, Sockalexis was immortalized by the new Cleveland label (Schneider 10-23). (Contrary to popular lore, some cite alternative—and less reverent—motivations behind the team's

---

Annotations:

MLA style does not require a title page. Ask your instructor whether you need one.

Include your last name and page number as page header, beginning with the first page, 1/2" from the top.

Center your title. Do not put the title in quotation marks or type it in all capital letters.

Use 1" margins all around. Double-space everything.

Cite publications by the name of the author (or authors).

Indent each paragraph 1/2" on the ruler in your word processing program.

naming and point to a lack of Sockalexis publicity in period newspaper articles discussing the team's naming process [Staurowsky 95-97].) Almost ninety years later, the "temporary" name continues to raise eyebrows, in both its marketability and its ideological questionability.

Today the logo is more than a little embarrassing. Since the high-profile actions of the American Indian Movement (AIM) in the 1970s, sports teams around the country—including the Indians—have been criticized for their racially insensitive mascots. Native American groups question these caricatured icons—not just because of grossly stereotyped mascots, but also because of what visual displays of team support say about Native American culture. Across the country, professional sporting teams, as well as high schools and colleges, perform faux rituals in the name of team spirit. As Tim Giago, publisher of *The Lakota Times*, a weekly South Dakotan Native American newspaper, has noted,

> The sham rituals, such as the wearing of feathers, smoking of so-called peace pipes, beating of tomtoms, fake dances, horrendous attempts at singing Indian songs, the so-called war whoops, and the painted faces, address more than the issues of racism. They are direct attacks upon the spirituality of the Indian people. (qtd. in Wulf).

Controversy over such performances still fuels the fire between activists and alumni at schools such as the University of Illinois at Champaign-Urbana, where during many decades of football halftimes fans cheered the performance of a student (often white) dressed as Chief Illiniwek. In March of 2007, the University of Illinois board of trustees voted in a nearly unanimous decision to retire the mascot's name, regalia and image ("Illinois").

Since 1969, when Oklahoma disavowed its "Little Red" mascot, more than 600 school and minor league teams have followed a more ethnically sensitive trend and ditched their "tribal" mascots (Price). High-profile teams such as Stanford, St. Johns University, and Miami (Ohio) University have changed their team names from the Indians to the Cardinal (1972), the Redmen to the Red Storm (1993), and the Redskins to the Redhawks (1996), respectively. In 2005, the NCAA officially ruled that "colleges whose nicknames or mascots refer to American Indians will not be permitted to hold National Collegiate Athletic Association tournament events" (Wolverton). By September 2005, only seventeen schools remained in violation (Wolverton). While many people see such controversies as mere bowing to the pressures of the late twentieth and early twenty-first centuries, others see the mascot issue as a topic well worthy of debate.

Cleveland's own Chief Wahoo has far from avoided controversy. Multiple conflicts between Wahoo devotees and dissenters occur annually during the baseball season. At the opening game of 1995, fifty Native Americans and supporters took stations around Jacobs Field to demonstrate against the use of the cartoonish smiling crimson mascot (Kropk). Arrests were made in 1998 when demonstrators from the United Church of Christ burned a three-foot Chief Wahoo doll in effigy ("Judge"). Opinions on the mascot remain mixed. Jacoby Ellsbury, outfielder for the Boston Red Sox and a member of the Colorado River Indian Tribes, said in 2007, "I'm not offended [by the mascot]. You can look at it two different ways. You can look at it that it's offensive or you can look at it that they are representing Native Americans. Usually I'll try to take the positive out of it" (Shaughnessy). Nonetheless, Ellsbury still acknowledges that he "can see both sides of [the controversy]" (Shaughnessy). Wedded to their memorabilia, fans proudly stand behind their Indian as others lobby vociferously for its removal, splitting government officials, fans, and social and religious groups.

In 2000 Cleveland mayor Michael White came out publicly against the team mascot, joining an already established group of religious leaders, laypersons, and civil rights activists who had demanded Wahoo's retirement. African American religious and civic leaders such as Rev. Gregory A. Jacobs pointed to the absurdity of minority groups who embrace the Wahoo symbol. "Each of us has had to fight its [sic] own battle, quite frankly," Jacobs stated. "We cannot continue to live in this kind of hypocrisy that says, Yes, we are in solidarity with my [sic] brothers and sisters, yet we continue to exploit them" (qtd. in Briggs).

This controversy also swirls outside of the greater Cleveland area. In 2009 the image of Wahoo was removed from the team's training complex in Goodyear, Arizona ("Cleveland"), while the *Seattle Times* went so far as to digitally remove the Wahoo symbol from images of the Cleveland baseball cap ("Newspaper"). As other teams make ethnically sensitive and image-conscious choices to change their mascots, Cleveland stands firm in its resolve to retain Chief Wahoo. Despite internal division and public ridicule fueled by the team icon, the city refuses to budge.

Cleveland's stubbornness on the issue of Wahoo runs contrary to the city's recently improved image and downtown revitalization. As a native of Cleveland, I understand the power of "Tribe Fever" and the unabashed pride one feels when wearing Wahoo garb during a winning (or losing) season. Often it is not until we leave northeastern Ohio that we realize the negative image that Wahoo projects. What then can Cleveland do to simultaneously save face and bolster its burgeoning positive city image? I propose that the team finally change the "temporary" Indians label. In a city so proud of its diverse ethnic heritage—African American, Italian American, and Eastern European American to name a few examples—why stand as a bearer of retrograde ethnic politics? Cleveland should take this opportunity to link its positive Midwestern image to the team of which it is so proud. I propose changing the team's name to the Cleveland Lakers.

The city's revival in the last twenty years has embraced the geographic and aesthetic grandeur of Lake Erie. Disavowing its "mistake on the lake" moniker of the late 1970s, Cleveland has traded aquatic pollution fires for a booming lakeside business district. Attractions such as the Great Lakes Science Center, the Rock and Roll Hall of Fame, and the new Cleveland Browns Stadium take advantage of the beauty of the landscape and take back the lake. Why not continue this trend through one of the city's biggest and highest-profile moneymakers: professional baseball? By changing the team's name to the Lakers, the city would gain national advertisement for one of its major selling points, while simultaneously announcing a new ethnically inclusive image that is appropriate to our wonderfully diverse city. It would be a public relations triumph for the city.

Of course this call will be met with many objections. Why do we have to buckle to pressure? Do we not live in a free country? What fans and citizens alike need to keep in mind is that ideological pressures would not be the sole motivation for this move. Yes, retiring Chief Wahoo would take Cleveland off AIM's hit list. Yes, such a move would promote a kinder and gentler Cleveland. At the same time, however, such a gesture would work toward uniting the community. So much civic division exists over this issue that a renaming could help start to heal these old wounds.

Additionally, this type of change could bring added economic prosperity to the city. First, a change in name will bring a new wave of team merchandise. Licensed sports apparel generates more than a 10-billion-dollar annual retail business in the United States, and teams have proven repeatedly that new uniforms and logos can provide new capital. After all, a new logo for the Seattle Mariners bolstered severely slumping merchandise sales (Lefton). Wahoo devotees need not panic; the booming vintage uniform business will keep him alive, as is demonstrated by the current ability to purchase replica 1940s jerseys with the old Indians logo. Also, good press created by this change will hopefully help increase tourism in Cleveland. If the goodwill created by the Cleveland Lakers can prove half as profitable as the Rock and Roll Hall of Fame, then local businesses will be humming a happy tune. Finally, if history repeats itself, a change to a more culturally inclusive logo could, in and of itself, prove to be a cash cow. When Miami University changed from the Redskins to the Redhawks, it saw alumni donations skyrocket (Price). A less divisive mascot would prove lucrative to the ball club, the city, and the players themselves. (Sluggers with inoffensive logos make excellent spokesmen.)

Perhaps this proposal sounds far-fetched: Los Angeles may seem to have cornered the market on Lakers. But where is their lake? (The Lakers were formerly the Minneapolis Lakers, where the name makes sense in the "Land of 10,000 Lakes.") Various professional and collegiate sports teams—such as baseball's San Francisco Giants and football's New York Giants—share a team name, so licensing should not be an issue. If Los Angeles has qualms about sharing the name, perhaps Cleveland could persuade Los Angeles to become the Surfers or the Stars; after all, Los Angeles players seem to spend as much time on the big and small screens as on the court.

Witkowski 6

Now is the perfect time for Cleveland to make this jump. Perhaps a
new look will help usher in a new era of Cleveland baseball and a World
Series ring to boot. Through various dry spells, the Cleveland Indians institution has symbolically turned to the descendants of Sockalexis, asking
for goodwill or a latter-generation Penobscot slugger (Fleitz 3). Perhaps
the best way to win goodwill, fortunes, and the team's first World Series
title since 1948 would be to eschew a grinning life-size Chief Wahoo for
the new Cleveland Laker, an oversized furry monster sporting water
wings, cleats, and a catcher's mask. His seventh-inning-stretch show
could include an air-guitar solo with a baseball bat as he quietly reminds
everyone that the Rock Hall is just down the street.

Witkowski 7

Works Cited

> Center "Works Cited" on a new page.

Briggs, David. "Churches Go to Bat Against Chief Wahoo." *Cleveland
Plain Dealer* 25 Aug. 2000: 1A. *LexisNexis Academic*. Web. 19 Apr.
2010.

"Cleveland Indians' Chief Wahoo Logo Left Off Team's Ballpark, Training
Complex in Goodyear, Arizona." *Cleveland.com*. Cleveland Plain
Dealer, 12 Apr. 2009. Web. 23 Apr. 2010.

Fleitz, David L. *Louis Sockalexis: The First Cleveland Indian*. Jefferson:
McFarland, 2002. Print.

"Illinois Trustees Vote to Retire Chief Illiniwek." *ESPN*. ESPN Internet
Ventures, 13 Mar. 2007. Web. 26 Apr. 2010.

"Judge Dismisses Charges Against City in Wahoo Protest." *Associated
Press* 6 Aug. 2001. *LexisNexis Academic*. Web. 19 Apr. 2010.

Kropk, M. R. "Chief Wahoo Protestors Largely Ignored by Fans." *Austin
American Statesman* 6 May 1995: D4. Print.

Lefton, Terry. "Looks Are Everything: For New Franchises, Licensing Bat-
tles Must Be Won Long Before the Team Even Takes the Field."
Sport 89 (May 1998): 32. Print.

> Double-space all entries. Indent all but the first line in each entry one-half inch.

> Alphabetize entries by the last names of the authors or by the first important word in the title if no author is listed.

Witkowski 8

Liu, Caitlin. "Bawl Game." *Portfolio.com*. Condé Nast, 21 Oct. 2008.
 Web. 28 Apr. 2009.

"Newspaper Edits Cleveland Indian Logo from Cap Photo." *Associated
 Press* 31 Mar. 1997. *LexisNexis Academic*. Web. 27 Apr. 2010.

Price, S. L. "The Indian Wars." *Sports Illustrated* 4 Mar. 2002: 66+.
 Academic OneFile. Web. 20 Apr. 2010.

Schneider, Russell. *The Cleveland Indians Encyclopedia*. Philadelphia:
 Temple UP, 1996. Print.

Shaughnessy, Dan. "They've Had Some Chief Concerns." *Boston Globe* 12
 October 2007: C5. *LexisNexis Academic*. Web. 19 Apr. 2010.

Staurowsky, Ellen J. "Sockalexis and the Making of the Myth at the Core of
 the Cleveland's 'Indian' Image." *Team Spirits: The Native American
 Mascots Controversy*. Eds. C. Richard King and Charles Fruehling
 Springwood. Lincoln: U of Nebraska P, 2001. 82-106. Print.

Wolverton, Brad. "NCAA Restricts Colleges With Indian Nicknames and
 Mascots." *Chronicle of Higher Education* 2 Sept. 2005: A65.
 ProQuest. Web. 25 Apr. 2010.

Wulf, Steve. "A Brave Move." *Sports Illustrated* 24 Feb. 1992: 7. Print.

Zimmerman, Ryan. "The Cleveland Indians' Mascot Must Go." *Christian
 Science Monitor* 15 Oct. 2007: 5. *LexisNexis Academic*. Web. 19
 Apr. 2010.

Italicize the titles of books and periodicals.

Check to make sure all the sources you have cited in your text are in the list of works cited.

PEARSON

For support in learning this chapter's content, follow this path in MyCompLab:
> Resources > Research > Citing Sources > MLA (2009 updates).
Review the Instruction and Multimedia resources, then complete the Exercises and
click on Gradebook to measure your progress.

21 | Documenting Sources in APA Style

QUICK **TAKE**

In this chapter, you will learn that

1. APA documentation style uses a name + date system to cite sources in the body of a paper (see below)

2. Every source used in a paper needs to be included in a References list at the end of the paper (see page 284)

3. Reference list entries for different kinds of source follow a basic pattern (see page 284)

Papers written for the social sciences, including government, linguistics, psychology, sociology, and education, frequently use the APA documentation style. For a detailed treatment of APA style, consult the *Publication Manual of the American Psychological Association*, sixth edition (2010).

Elements of APA Documentation

Citing a source in your paper

APA style emphasizes the date of publication. When you cite an author's name in the body of your paper, always include the date of publication. Notice too that APA style includes the abbreviation for page "(p.)" in front of the page number. A comma separates each element of the citation.

> Zukin (2004) observes that teens today begin to shop for themselves at age 13 or 14, "the same age when lower-class children, in the past, became apprentices or went to work in factories" (p. 50).

If the author's name is not mentioned in the sentence, cite the author, date, and page number inside parentheses.

> One sociologist notes that teens today begin to shop for themselves at age 13 or 14, "the same age when lower-class children, in the past, became apprentices or went to work in factories" (Zukin, 2004, p. 50).

The corresponding entry in the references list would be as follows.

> Zukin, S. (2004). *Point of purchase: How shopping changed American culture.*
> New York, NY: Routledge.

Creating an APA-style references list

To create your references list, go through your paper and find every reference to the sources you consulted during your research. Each in-text citation must have an entry in your references list.

Organize your references list alphabetically by authors' last names or, if no author is listed, the first word in the title other than *a, an,* or *the.* APA style uses three basic forms for entries in the references list: books, periodicals (scholarly journals, newspapers, magazines), and online sources (online library database sources, Web sites, blogs, online newspapers, online magazines, and online government documents).

References entries for books

> Orum, A. M., & Chen, X. (2003). *The world of cities: Places in comparative and historical perspective.* Malden, MA: Blackwell.

1. Author's or editor's name.
- List the author's name with the last name first, followed by a comma and the author's initials.
- Join two authors' names with an ampersand.
- If an editor, put "(Ed.)" after the name: Kavanaugh, P. (Ed.).

2. (Year of publication).
- Give the year of publication in parentheses. If no year of publication is given, write *(n.d.)* ("no date") : Smith, S. (n.d.).
- If it is a multivolume edited work, published over a period of more than one year, put the time span in parentheses: Smith, S. (1999–2001).

3. Title of book.
- Italicize the title.
- Capitalize only the first word, proper nouns, and the first word after a colon.
- If the title is in a foreign language, copy it exactly as it appears on the title page.

4. Publication information.

- For all books list the city with a two-letter state abbreviation (or full country name) after the city name. If more than one city is given on the title page, list only the first.
- Do not shorten or abbreviate words like *University* or *Press*. Omit words such as *Co., Inc.,* and *Publishers*.

References entries for periodicals

Lee, E. (2007). Wired for gender: Experientiality and gender-stereotyping in computer-mediated communication. *Media Psychology, 10,* 182–210.

1. Author's name.

- List the author's name, last name first, followed by the author's initials.
- Join two authors' names with a comma and an ampersand.

2. (Year of publication).

- Give the year the work was published in parentheses.

3. Title of article.

- Do not use quotation marks. If there is a book title in the article title, italicize it.
- Capitalize only the first word of the title, the first word of the subtitle, and any proper nouns in the title.

4. Publication information.

- Italicize the journal name.
- Capitalize all nouns, verbs, and pronouns, and the first word of the journal name. Do not capitalize any article, preposition, or coordinating conjunction unless it is the first word of the title or subtitle.
- Put a comma after the journal name.
- Italicize the volume number and follow it with a comma.
- If each issue of the journal begins on page 1, give the issue number in parentheses, followed by comma.
- Give page numbers of the article (see sample references 19 and 20 for more on pagination).

References entries for online sources

Department of Justice. Federal Bureau of Investigation. (2004). Hate crime statistics 2004: Report summary. Retrieved from http://www.fbi.gov /ucr/hc2004/openpage.htm

1. Author's name, associated institution, or organization.
- List the author's name, if given, with the last name first, followed by the author's initials.
- If the only authority you find is a group or organization (as in this example), list its name as the author.
- If the author or organization is not identified, begin the reference with the title of the document.

2. (Date of publication).
- List the date the site was produced, last revised, or copyrighted.

3. Title of page or article.
- If you are citing a page or article that has a title, treat the title like an article in a periodical. If you are citing an entire Web site, treat the name like a book.
- If the Web site has no title, list it by author or creator.

4. Retrieval information
- If your source has been assigned a DOI (Digital Object Identifier), list it after the title. Do not add a period at the end of a DOI.
- If the source does not have a DOI, list the URL of the journal's home page.

APA In-Text Citations

1. **Author named in your text**

Influential sociologist Daniel Bell (1973) noted a shift in the United States to the "postindustrial society" (p. 3).

2. **Author not named in your text**

In 1997, the Gallup poll reported that 55% of adults in the United States think secondhand smoke is "very harmful," compared to only 36% in 1994 (Saad, 1997, p. 4).

3. Work by a single author

(Bell, 1973, p. 3)

4. Work by two authors
Notice that APA uses an ampersand (&) with multiple authors' names rather than *and*.

(Suzuki & Irabu, 2002, p. 404)

5. Work by three to five authors
The authors' last names follow the order of the title page.

(Francisco, Vaughn, & Romano, 2001, p. 7)

Subsequent references can use the first name and *et al.*

(Francisco et al., 2001, p. 17)

6. Work by six or more authors
Use the first author's last name and *et al.* for all in-text references.

(Swallit et al., 2004, p. 49)

7. Work by a group or organization
Identify the group author in the text and place only the page number in parentheses.

The National Organization for Women (2001) observed that this "generational shift in attitudes towards marriage and childrearing" will have profound consequences (p. 325).

8. Work by an unknown author
Use a shortened version of the title (or the full title if it is short) in place of the author's name. Capitalize all key words in the title. If it is an article title, place it in quotation marks.

("Derailing the Peace Process," 2003, p. 44)

9. Quotations of 40 words or longer

Indent long quotations 1/2 inch and omit quotation marks. Note that the period appears before the parentheses in an indented block quote.

> Orlean (2001) has attempted to explain the popularity of the painter Thomas Kinkade:
>
> > People like to own things they think are valuable. . . . The high price of limited editions is part of their appeal; it implies that they are choice and exclusive, and that only a certain class of people will be able to afford them. (p. 128)

APA References List: Books

10. Book by one author

The author's last name comes first, followed by a comma and the author's initials.

> Ball, E. (2000). *Slaves in the family.* New York, NY: Ballantine Books.

If an editor, put "(Ed.)" in parentheses after the name.

> Kavanagh, P. (Ed.). (1969). *Lapped furrows.* New York, NY: Hand Press.

11. Book by two authors

Join two authors' names with a comma and ampersand.

> Hardt, M., & Negri, A. (2000). *Empire.* Cambridge, MA: Harvard University Press.

If editors, use "(Eds.)" after the names.

> McClelland, D., & Eismann, K. (Eds).

12. Book by three or more authors

List last names and initials for up to seven authors, with an ampersand between the last two names. For works with eight or more authors, list the first six names, then an ellipsis, then the last author's name.

> Anders, K., Child, H., Davis, K., Logan, O., Petersen, J., Tymes, J., . . . Johnson, S.

13. Chapter in an edited collection

Add "In" after the selection title and before the names of the editor(s).

> Howard, A. (1997). Labor, history, and sweatshops in the new global economy. In A. Ross (Ed.), *No sweat: Fashion, free trade, and the rights of garment workers* (pp. 151–172). New York, NY: Verso.

14. Published dissertation or thesis

If the dissertation you are citing is published by University Microfilms International (UMI), provide the order number as the last item in the entry.

> Price, J. J. (1998). Flight maps: Encounters with nature in modern American culture. *Dissertation Abstracts International, 59*(5), 1635. (UMI No. 9835237)

15. Government document

When the author and publisher are identical, use "Author" as the name of the publisher.

> U.S. Environmental Protection Agency. (2002). *Respiratory health effects of passive smoking: Lung cancer and other disorders.* (EPA Publication No. 600/6-90/006 F). Washington, DC: Author.

APA References List: Periodicals

16. Article by one author

> Kellogg, R. T. (2001). Competition for working memory among writing processes. *American Journal of Psychology, 114*, 175–192.

17. Article by multiple authors

Write out all of the authors' names, up to seven authors. For works with eight or more authors, list the first six names, then an ellipsis, then the last author's name.

> Blades, J., & Rowe-Finkbeiner, K. (2006). The motherhood manifesto. *The Nation, 282*(20) 11–16.

18. Article by a group or organization

National Organization for Women (2002). Where to find feminists in Austin. *The NOW guide for Austin women.* Austin, TX: Chapter Press.

19. Article in a journal with continuous pagination
Include the volume number and the year, but not the issue number.

Engen, R., & Steen, S. (2000). The power to punish: Discretion and sentencing reform in the war on drugs. *American Journal of Sociology, 105,* 1357–1395.

20. Article in a journal paginated by issue
List the issue number in parentheses (not italicized) after the volume number. For a popular magazine that does not commonly use volume numbers, use the season or date of publication.

McGinn, D. (2006, June 5). Marriage by the numbers. *Newsweek,* 40–48.

21. Monthly publication

Barlow, J. P. (1998, January). Africa rising: Everything you know about Africa is wrong. *Wired,* 142–158.

22. Newspaper article

Hagenbaugh, B. (2005, April 25). Grads welcome an uptick in hiring. *USA Today,* p. A1.

APA References List: Library Database Sources

23. Document from a library database
Increasingly, articles are accessed online. Because URLs frequently change, many scholarly publishers have begun to use a Digital Object Identifier (DOI), a unique alphanumeric string that is permanent. If a DOI is available, use the DOI.

APA no longer requires listing the names of well-known databases. The article below was retrieved from the PsychARTICLES database, but there is no need to list the database, the retrieval date, or the URL if the DOI is listed.

Erdfelder, E. (2008). Experimental psychology: Good news. *Experimental Psychology, 55*(1), 1–2. doi: 0.1027/1618-3169.55.1.1

APA References List: Online Sources

24. Online publication by a known author

Authorship is sometimes hard to discern for online sources. If you do have an author or creator to cite, follow the rules for periodicals and books.

> Carr, A. (2003. May 22). AAUW applauds senate support of title IX resolution. Retrieved from http://www.aauw.org/about/newsroom/press_releases /030522.cfm

25. Online publication by a group or organization

If the only authority you find is a group or organization, list its name as the author.

> Girls Incorporated. (2003). Girls' bill of rights. Retrieved from http://www.girlsinc.org/gc/page.php?id=9

26. Article in an online scholarly journal

> Brown, B. (2004). The order of service: the practical management of customer interaction. *Sociological Research Online, 9*(4). Retrieved from http://www.socresonline.org.uk/9/4/brown.html

27. Article in an online newspaper

> Slevin, C. (2005, April 25). Lawmakers want to put limits on private toll roads. *Boulder Daily Camera*. Retrieved from http://www.dailycamera.com

28. Article in an online magazine

> Pein, C. (2005, April 20). Is Al-Jazeera ready for prime time? *Salon*. Retrieved from http://www.salon.com

APA References List: Other Sources

29. Television program

> Burgess, M., & Green, M. (Writers). (2004). Irregular around the margins. [Television series episode]. In D. Chase (Producer), *The sopranos*. New York: HBO.

30. Film, Video, or DVD

> Kaurismäki, A. (Director). (1999). *Leningrad cowboys go America* [DVD].
> United States: MGM.

31. Musical recording

List both the title of the song and the title of the album or CD. In the in-text citation, include side or track numbers.

> Lowe, N. (2001). Lately I've let things slide. On *The convincer* [CD]. Chapel
> Hill, NC: Yep Roc Records.

> For support in learning this chapter's content, follow this path in MyCompLab:
> > Resources > Research > Citing Sources > APA (2010 Updates).
>
> Review the Instruction and Multimedia resources, then complete the Exercises and
> click on Gradebook to measure your progress.

Glossary

abstract A summary of an article or book

aesthetic criteria Evaluative criteria based on perceptions of beauty and good taste

analogy An extended comparison of one situation or item to another

APA American Psychological Association

APA documentation Documentation style commonly used in social-science and education disciplines

argument A claim supported by at least one reason

assumption An unstated belief or knowledge that connects a claim with evidence

audience Real or assumed individuals or groups to whom a verbal or written communication is directed

B

bandwagon appeal A fallacy of argument based on the assumption that something is true or correct because "everyone" believes it to be so

bar chart Visual depiction of data created by the use of horizontal or vertical bars that comparatively represent rates or frequencies

because clause A statement that begins with the word *because* and provides a supporting reason for a claim

begging the question A fallacy of argument that uses the claim as evidence for its own validity

bias A personal belief that may skew one's perspective or presentation of information

bibliography List of books and articles about a specific subject

blog A Web-based journal or diary featuring regular entries about a particular subject or daily experiences (also known as a Web log)

brainstorming A method of finding ideas by writing a list of questions or statements about a subject

C

causal argument An argument that seeks to identify the reasons behind a certain event or phenomenon

claim A declaration or assertion made about any given topic

claim of comparison A claim that argues something is like or not like something else

common factor method A method used by scientists to identify a recurring factor present in a given cause–effect relationship

consequence The cause–effect result of a given action

context The combination of author, subject, and audience and the broader social, cultural, and economic influences surrounding a text

contextual analysis A type of rhetorical analysis that focuses on the author, the audience, the time, and the circumstances of an argument

counterargument An argument offering an opposing point of view with the goal of demonstrating that it is the stronger of two or more arguments

criteria Standards used to establish a definition or an evaluation

critical reading A process of reading that surpasses an initial understanding or impression of basic content and proceeds with the goal of answering specific questions or examining particular elements

cropping In photography, the process of deleting unwanted parts of an image

cultural assumptions Widely held beliefs that are considered common sense in a particular culture

D

database Large collection of digital information organized for efficient search and retrieval

debate A contest or game in which two or more individuals attempt to use arguments to persuade others to support their opinion

definition argument An argument made by specifying that something does or does not possess certain criteria

diction The choice and use of words in writing and speech

E

either–or A fallacy of argument that presents only two choices in a complex situation

emotional appeal An argumentation strategy that attempts to persuade by stirring the emotions of the audience

empirical research Research that collects data from observation or experiment

ethos An appeal to the audience based on the character and trustworthiness of the speaker or writer

evaluation argument An argument that judges something based on ethical, aesthetic, and/or practical criteria

evaluation of sources The assessment of the relevance and reliability of sources used in supporting claims

evidence Data, examples, or statistics used to support a claim

experimental research Research based on obtaining data under controlled conditions, usually by isolating one variable while holding other variables constant

F

fallacy of argument Failure to provide adequate evidence to support a claim. See *bandwagon appeal, begging the question, false analogy, hasty generalization, name calling, non sequitur, oversimplification, polarization, post hoc fallacy, rationalization, slippery slope, straw man*

false analogy A fallacy of argument that compares two unlike things as if they were similar

feasibility The ability of a proposed solution to be implemented

figurative language The symbolic transference of meaning from one word or phrase to another, such as with the use of metaphor, synecdoche, and metonymy

firsthand evidence Evidence such as interviews, observations, and surveys collected by the writer

font The specific size and weight of a typeface

freewriting A method of finding ideas by writing as fast as possible about a subject for a set length of time

G

generalization A conclusion drawn from knowledge based on past occurrences of the phenomenon in question

good reason A reason that an audience accepts as valid

H

hasty generalization A fallacy of argument resulting from making broad claims based on a few occurrences

I

idea map A brainstorming tool that visually depicts connections among different aspects of an issue

image editor Software that allows you to create and manipulate images

intellectual property Any property produced by the intellect, including copyrights for literary, musical, photographic, and cinematic works; patents for inventions and industrial processes; and trademarks

J

journal A general category of publications that includes popular, trade, and scholarly periodicals

K

keyword search A Web-based search that uses a robot and indexer to produce results based on a chosen word or words

L

line graph A visual presentation of data represented by a continuous line or lines plotted at specific intervals

logos An appeal to the audience based on reasoning and evidence

M

metaphor A figure of speech using a word or phrase that commonly designates one thing to represent another, thus making a comparison

metonymy A type of figurative language that uses one object to represent another that embodies its defining quality

MLA Modern Language Association

MLA documentation Documentation style commonly used in humanities and fine-arts disciplines

multimedia The use of multiple content forms including text, voice and music audio, video, still images, animation, and interactivity

N

name calling A fallacy of argument resulting from the use of undefined, and therefore meaningless, names

narrative arguments A form of argument based on telling stories that suggest the writer's position rather than explicitly making claims

non sequitur A fallacy of argument resulting from connecting two or more unrelated ideas

O

oversimplification A fallacy in argument caused by neglecting to account for the complexity of a subject

P

pathos An appeal based on the audience's emotions or deeply held values

periodical A journal, magazine, or newspaper published at standard intervals, usually daily, weekly, monthly, or quarterly

periodical index Paper or electronic resource that catalogs the contents of journals, magazines, and newspapers

pie chart A circular chart resembling a pie that illustrates percentages of the whole through the use of delineated wedge shapes

plagiarism The improper use of the unauthorized and unattributed words or ideas of another author

podcast Digital media files available on the Internet for playback on a portable media player, such as an iPod

polarization A fallacy of argument based on exaggerating the characteristics of opposing groups to highlight division and extremism

popular journal A magazine aimed at the general public; usually includes illustrations, short articles, and advertisements

position argument A general kind of argument in which a claim is made for an idea or way of thinking about a subject

post hoc fallacy A fallacy of argument based on the assumption that events that follow each other have a causal relationship

practical criteria Evaluative criteria based on usefulness or likely results

primary research Information collected directly by the writer through observations, interviews, surveys, and experiments

process of elimination method A means of finding a cause by systematically ruling out all other possible causes

proposal argument An argument that either advocates or opposes a specific course of action

R

rationalization A fallacy of argument based on using weak explanations to avoid dealing with the actual causes

reason In an argument, the justification for a claim

rebuttal argument An argument that challenges or rejects the claims of another argument

reference librarian Library staff member who is familiar with information resources and who can show you how to use them (you can find a reference librarian at the reference desk in your library)

refutation A rebuttal argument that points out the flaws in an opposing argument

rhetorical analysis Careful study of a written argument or other types of persuasion aimed at understanding how the components work or fail to work

rhetorical situation Factors present at the time of writing or speaking, including the writer or speaker, the audience, the purpose of communicating, and the context

S

sans serif type A style of type recognized by blunt ends and a consistency in thickness

scholarly journals Journals containing articles written by experts in a particular field; also called peer-reviewed or academic journals

secondary research Information obtained from existing knowledge, such as research in the library

secondhand evidence Evidence from the work of others found in the library, on the Web, and elsewhere

serif type A style of type developed to resemble the strokes of an ink pen and recognized by wedge-shaped ends on letter forms

single difference method A method of finding a cause for differing phenomena in very similar situations by identifying the one element that varies

slippery slope A fallacy of argument based on the assumption that if a first step is taken, additional steps will inevitably follow

straw man A fallacy of argument based on the use of the diversionary tactic of setting up the opposing position in such a manner that it can be easily rejected

sufficiency The adequacy of evidence supporting a claim

synecdoche A type of figurative language in which a part is used to represent the whole

T

textual analysis A type of rhetorical analysis that focuses exclusively on the text itself

thesis One or more sentences that state the main idea of an argument

typeface A style of type, such as serif, sans serif, or decorative

U

URL (Universal Resource Locator) An address on the Web

V

visual argument A type of persuasion using images, graphics, or objects

voice In writing, the distinctive style of a writer that provides a sense of the writer as a person

W

Web directory A subject guide to Web pages grouped by topic and subtopic

Web editors Programs that allow you to compose Web pages

wiki A Web-based application designed to let multiple authors write, edit, and review content, such as Wikipedia

working thesis A preliminary statement of the main claim of an argument, subject to revision

Credits

Photo Credits

Page 2: © MadV; 15: © Rebecca Roth; 22, 27: © Frank O'Connell/The New York Times/Redux; 76: © BP p.l.c.; 78 (both): © Dr. Michael Wesch; 83: © Courtesy Hofstra University; 96: © Popperfoto/Getty Images; 99: © jacksfilms; 113: © Sylvain Sonnet/Getty Images; 122: © Ruby Washington/The New York Times/Redux; 139 © Car Culture/Corbis; 143: © Transtock Images; 157 © Amanda Byrd/Alaska Stock; 167: © Phil Crawford/Greenpeace/Reuters/Landov; 173: FOXTROT © 2010 Bill Amend. Reprinted with permission of Universal Press Syndicate. All rights reserved.; 190: © David Bebber, Pool/AP Images. All other photos provided by the author.

Text Credits

Glenn Loury, "A Nation of Jailers," from CATO Unbound, 3/11/09. www.catounbound.org/2009/03/11/glennloury/anationofjailers. Copyright © 2009 CATO. Used with permission.

Michael Pollan, excerpt from "Eat Food: Food Defined" from In Defense of Food by Michael Pollan. Copyright © 2008 by Michael Pollan. Used by permission of The Penguin Press, a division of Penguin Group (USA) Inc.

Emily Raine, "Why Should I Be Nice to You? Coffee Shops and the Politics of Good Service," from Bad Subjects, issue 74, 12/05. Copyright © 2005 Emily Raine. Reprinted with permission.

Gregory Rodriguez, "Illegal Immigrants — They're Money," © Gregory Rodriguez, "Illegal Immigrants They're Money" Los Angeles Times, Reprinted with permission.

San Francisco Bicycle Coalition, Copyright © San Francisco Bicycle Coalition. www.sfbike.org.

Leslie Marmon Silko, "The Border Patrol State," The Nation, October 17, 1994. Copyright © 1994. Reprinted by permission of The Wylie Agency.

Yahoo! Screen shot, Reproduced with permission of Yahoo! Inc. © 2010 Yahoo! Inc. *Yahoo!* and the *Yahoo!* logo are registered trademarks of Yahoo! Inc.

Index